KU-617-263

By the
Pen Green
Team

Working
with Families

in Children's Centres and Early Years Settings

Wiltshire College

90417

Working with Families

By the Pen Green Team

in Children's Centres and Early Years Settings

Edited by:

Margy Whalley
Cath Arnold
Robert Orr

HODDER
EDUCATION
AN HACHETTE UK COMPANY

Every effort has been made to trace and acknowledge the ownership of copyright material. The publishers apologise if any inadvertently remain unacknowledged and will be glad to make suitable arrangements to rectify this at the earliest opportunity.

Contains public sector information licensed under the Open Government Licence v1.0.

Although every effort has been made to ensure that website addresses are correct at time of going to press, Hodder Education cannot be held responsible for the content of any website mentioned in this book. It is sometimes possible to find a relocated web page by typing in the address of the home page for a website in the URL window of your browser.

Hachette UK's policy is to use papers that are natural, renewable and recyclable products and made from wood grown in sustainable forests. The logging and manufacturing processes are expected to conform to the environmental regulations of the country of origin.

Orders: please contact Bookpoint Ltd, 130 Milton Park, Abingdon, Oxon OX14 4SB. Telephone: +44 (0)1235 827827. Fax: +44 (0)1235 400401. Lines are open from 9 a.m. to 5 p.m., Monday to Saturday, with a 24-hour message-answering service. Visit our website at www.hoddereducation.co.uk

© 2013 Margy Whalley, Cath Arnold, Robert Orr and the Pen Green Centre team

Hodder Education
An Hachette UK Company
338 Euston Road
London NW1 3BH

Impression number   10 9 8 7 6 5 4 3 2 1

Year   2018 2017 2016 2015 2014 2013

All rights reserved. Apart from any use permitted under UK copyright law, no part of this publication may be reproduced or transmitted in any form or by any means, electronic or mechanical, including photocopying and recording, or held within any information storage and retrieval system, without permission in writing from the publisher or under licence from the Copyright Licensing Agency Limited. Further details of such licences (for reprographic reproduction) may be obtained from the Copyright Licensing Agency Limited, Saffron House, 6–10 Kirby Street, London EC1N 8TS.

Cover photo & photographs © the Pen Green Centre team

Typeset in 10/12 Bembo Std by Datapage (India) Pvt. Ltd.

Printed in Italy for Hodder Education, an Hachette UK Company.

A catalogue record for this title is available from the British Library

ISBN: 978 1 4441 7882 1

Contents

Acknowledgements

We would like to thank the following parents, who contributed to this book:

Eilidh McLeod

Hannah Howe

Lesley Fazackarley

Tracy Dyson

Rachael Kearney

Mairi McLeod

Ashley Williamson

Alan Williamson

Kristen McGilvray

Christine Hardie

Scott Litster

Sian Owens

Jamie Townsend

Phil Hall

Giles Owen

and many other families, whose case studies are too sensitive for them to be named. We would also like to thank all the families and volunteers of Corby who give Home-Start Corby its unique identity.

Contributors

Editors:

Margy Whalley has managed multi-disciplinary early years services in Brazil, Papua New Guinea and England. She was the founding Head of the Pen Green Centre for Under 5's and their families, and has worked there since 1983.

Margy is currently Head of Pen Green Children's Centre and Director of the Research, Development and Training Base at the Pen Green Centre and is involved in research, training and consultancy work in this country and in relation to policy transfer and integrated services internationally.

On a personal note, she has a wonderful 30-year-old daughter and is grandmother to gorgeous four-year-old Molly and more recently to two-year-old Tom. She is very committed to local politics, loves eating out with friends, visiting new places, meeting new people and is addicted to reading and study.

Cath Arnold has worked in the field of early childhood for 36 years. She is a proud parent of three children and grandparent of four, two of which she has written books about. Her enduring interest has been in how young children learn and how adults can work together to support their development and learning.

Robert Orr worked in special education from 1969 to 1998, latterly with visually impaired children about whom he wrote *My Right to Play* in 2003 while working at Pen Green in the after-school club. Since his retirement in 2004, he has continued to teach classes there and work on the MA team. His M.Ed. is in Human Relations and he has trained as a TA psychotherapist. He and Meryal, his wife since 1966, are busy with three offspring and five grandchildren.

The Pen Green Team:

Joanne Armstrong first visited Pen Green seven years ago to use the Breast Feeding Support Group. Since then, all three of her daughters have attended the nursery. She has been a parent-governor then a community governor, and now she is Vice Chair of the Governing Body. She has been party to a few research projects and has presented at conferences. She has co-run a group for parents of children with special rights.

Jo Benford has worked at the centre for nearly 13 years. During this time, she has held responsibility for the crèche provision. Over the years, her interest in the training and development of staff has increased, and she has recently become part of the centre leadership team with responsibility for adult learning and education. Jo is a lead tutor on the Foundation Degree in Early Years, and is leading the work with practitioners who are working towards the Early Years Professional Status.

Katherine Clark is a mother of four beautiful children who have inspired her to work with young children and families. She began using the centre as a parent with her first son 15 years ago. During this time, she has had various roles within the centre. Her current position as Nurture Group Family Worker has been wonderfully challenging.

Following her degree and PGCE, **Cessie Cole** taught for several years, after which she did a five-year course in Psychodynamic Counselling and Group Work. As she built up varied clinical experience, trained with Relate and started teaching on a Counselling Course, she did two post graduate trainings at the Tavistock Centre: the Initial and Advanced Diploma in Systemic Therapy. Cessie has had a private practice in Cambridge as an Individual, Couple and Family Psychotherapist since 1990. During that time, she has worked in varied settings of Local Health Authority, a Charity for children of drug- and substance-abusing families, as well as receiving referrals from schools and legal firms. Cessie is a Senior Accredited Member of BACP and is also accredited with UKCP, and started to work in the Growing Together groups at Pen Green in 2006.

Jackie Cole lives in Corby with her partner and her two children. She has worked at Pen Green for the last 13 years. In the past she provided different groups in various community venues and provided support in family homes. Presently, she is a Family Worker in the nursery and a co-leader of the Dads and Kids Group at the weekend. There are not many people that can say they enjoy their job as much as she does. She loves what she does and is very passionate about her home town and providing the best for the families that live there.

Tracey Coull has worked at the Centre for 13 years and most recently works in the post of Crèche Manager as a job-share. She is married to Chris and has three children: Jessica, Darrison and Lois. This is the first time she has contributed to the writing of a book. Tracey has enjoyed many learning experiences. Her most recent achievement is gaining her BA Hons Degree.

Ann Crichton works as a lecturer and consultant at Pen Green. Ann has a background in children's centre leadership in the North West and has served as Chair of the Children's Centre Leaders Reference Group, an advisory group for the DfE. Ann lives in Lancashire, has two grown-up daughters and was awarded an OBE for services to children and families.

Annette Cummings came to Pen Green as a parent in 1990 with her children, Alexandria and Olivia, and has never left. Alexandria has just graduated with a 1st in English and Education and Olivia is currently studying Politics.

Annette has had an amazing learning journey at Pen Green as a parent, parent volunteer, parent-governor and paid worker. In 1997 she joined the staff team as a Senior Family Worker in the nursery, and completed her Masters in Early Education with Care in 2004. In 2011 she joined the Centre Leadership Team and still firmly believes that Pen Green has an embedded philosophical and principled approach of working for the benefit of children and families.

Heather Donoyou has always been involved with early years education as a teacher, head teacher, and head of Pen Green Centre for Children and Families. She recognises the importance of working together with parents and involving them in their children's learning if the best outcomes are to be achieved for children, and has striven to make this involvement a reality for as many of the families that she has worked with as possible.

Rebecca Elliott has been working at the Pen Green Research Base for over six years as an administrator. Following the birth of her son three years ago, she became very interested in the work of the children's centre and decided that it was a career route she wanted to take. She is currently studying towards the Foundation Degree in Early Years and has been very fortunate to undertake placements within different areas of the children's centre. Her current placement is within the Growing Together group, which she is enjoying immensely and finding it to be a very rewarding role.

Susan Fleming is married to Colin and has four children: Matthew, Mark, Connor and Nicole. She has worked at the centre for 12 years within the crèche provision. Within this time, she has been able to undertake many learning opportunities. These include the Crèche Workers Course, NVQ Level 3 and Foundation Degree. Most recently, she completed her BA (Hons). She is now in the position of job-sharing the Crèche Manager post and also co-leads the Introduction to Childcare Course and a Growing Together group out in the local community.

Tracy Gallagher has worked with children and families since 1986. She has a particular interest in hearing the voice of the youngest children and ensuring that the provision for them is of the highest quality. Tracy is also interested in supporting the professional development of staff in the organisation.

Jo Ghani has worked as a Health Visitor in Corby since 1986 and has witnessed its growth, demographic changes and more recent regeneration.

Jo was Team Leader for the Corby Health Visiting Team for six years: her links with Pen Green Children's Centre are longstanding and she has been involved with running a variety of Health Promotion Groups over the years.

After becoming involved with running her children's play group and later helping in their school, **Anne Gladstone** returned to university to train as an infant teacher, and subsequently worked in primary education, further education and Sure Start Children's Centres. Anne is particularly interested in the links between early experiences of learning and subsequent achievement, both in school and in adult life. Anne is currently an independent consultant and a proud grandparent.

Caroline Griffiths is a proud mother of three amazing children and has fostered six young children over four years for the local authority. She has undertaken different aspects of volunteering within the community and at Pen Green whilst raising the children and now works within the Family Room as a Family Worker.

Sheena Griffiths-Baker has been a teacher and Family Worker at Pen Green since 2000. She has a particular interest in early mathematics. She is married with one child.

Laura Kiff has worked at the centre for over 12 years and during that time she has worked in various positions, including family work, group work and a secondment to the health service. She has one daughter who is her world, inspiring and challenging her every day. She currently works as a Nurture Group Worker, working with vulnerable families, which is something she is very passionate about.

Carol McFarlane is a proud parent of three children: Nicola, Liam and Poppy. She is honoured and privileged that over the years, families have allowed her into their lives and homes.

Maggie McKay's career began as a volunteer with Northants Probation Service where she found volunteering to be enjoyable and rewarding. Prior to joining Home-Start in 2004, her professional experience involved working alongside children and their families within Northants County Council and at Pen Green. She has a daughter and son and values family life.

During her working life within Pen Green, **Lorna McLeod** has been a Family Worker in the nursery and currently she is the 0–3 year Groupwork Co-coordinator. She has come to value the importance of groupwork as a significant route into the centre, and regard it as an integral part of our services for families.

Sandra Mole had four children in as many years and loved being a full-time mother during their formative years. She used Pen Green as a parent, moving into volunteering then employment. She is currently finishing her masters degree. She is staunchly egalitarian and her passions include encouraging parental voice and political participation.

Margaret Myles was warmly welcomed into the Pen Green community when she first walked through the door with her 11-month-old son. That was 29 years ago, and in that time she has been on the most amazing learning journey; from being a parent deeply involved and excited about her own children's learning to where she is now – a Senior Family Worker in the nursery. She is every bit as interested in and excited by the learning journeys of the children and families she is privileged to work with.

Felicity Norton is a mum of two with one on the way. She has always worked in the field of Early Years. She has been working at the Children Centre for six years. During this time, Fliss has held responsibility for the undergraduate degree programmes. She has a particular interest in psychoanalysis, group dynamics, as well as working with families. She is passionate about the mental health of infants and adults, and the importance of good, robust supervision.

After **Judy Potts** had her three children, she became a community mental health worker in rural Northamptonshire before training as a social worker. She then went to Pen Green as a group work co-ordinator. She subsequently became Principal Social Worker and then Deputy Head with responsibility for Family Support. While at Pen Green, she was privileged to continue her professional development studying for an MA at the Tavistock Centre, which deepened her interest and understanding in infant-parent relationships. Her grandchildren now bring delight, and new opportunities to learn about early years development and parenting.

Angela Prodger has worked with children and families since 1984. A steep learning curve, as well as a very rewarding experience, has been having a daughter of her own. She is passionate about children's rights and engaging parents in their children's learning.

Flávia Ribeiro is originally from Portugal. She completed her teaching degree in Early Years at Universidade do Minho. She moved to England eight years ago for a five-month placement at Pen Green. Since then, Flávia has had the opportunity to become a practitioner at the Centre. She works as a Family Worker/Teacher in the nursery. Flávia has a passion for parental involvement, and has been co-leading a PICL (Parents Involvement in their Children's Learning) study group for quite some time.

Colette Tait was a parent, volunteer and member of staff at the Pen Green Centre for many years. Currently, she manages a small and vibrant, phase two children's centre in Northamptonshire.

Judith Woodhead is a Jungian analyst working in private practice in Bedford. She also works as consultant parent–infant psychotherapist at the Anna Freud Centre, London. She very much enjoyed working with parents, babies and staff at Pen Green to help develop the Growing Together groups.

Elaine Young has worked with children and their families for over 28 years. During this time, she has developed an understanding of relationships within families which continues to grow with each new encounter. She is a parent herself to two children.

Introduction

Margy Whalley

The 1997 edition of *Working with Parents* began with this quotation and it is as true today as it was then, and remains as challenging to those who want to deliver services as a pre-prepared package.

> **The sheer diversity of family life now means that 'one size fits all' approaches are unlikely to be successful and that instead, giving families access to information, advice and support of various kinds that they can make use of as and when they think best, is much more likely to be effective.**
>
> (DCSF, *Support for All*, 2010: 25)

This new edition updates Pen Green's considered response to this challenge and includes the work of practitioners, our researchers, past and present staff and, of course, parents. It is a great tribute to everybody involved that this work has been accomplished within the hectic working lives that all of the contributors lead – and every word confirms their commitment to families and how children best learn and develop. Carving time out from demanding jobs and hectic personal lives to write is just one way in which staff and parents express their social solidarity and commitment to the Pen Green Learning Community.

The Pen Green Centre for under-fives and their families stands on the shoulders of early childhood services that have developed nationally and internationally over the last 100 years. The centre now blazes trails of its own.

Each chapter reflects the views and value base, the training and experience, and the deep personal interest of each individual contributor, many of whose names appear in print here for the first time.

Our shared beliefs are:

- in parents' commitment to their children
- that shared power counters oppression
- that our services must be accessible to all carers and parents, and must respond to the challenges accessibility poses
- that families need to choose the services that are useful to them
- that we get nowhere by blaming the parents, who all want the best for their children
- that families with various cultures and languages derive no benefit from being stereotyped
- that we do not have to struggle alone; our networks are our strength
- that our duty is to respond flexibly rather than to expect families to adapt to our ways
- that of all our teachers, parents are often the smartest.

1

From community development to co-production of services

Margy Whalley

In this chapter, we are going to:

■ reflect on why it is fundamentally important for early years practitioners to work closely with the families as well as their young children
■ look at the nature of families and the different ways that we can engage with them
■ describe how we can develop an equal and active partnership with families, however they are constituted
■ examine how ways of working with parents have changed over the last 40 or 50 years, from models of 'community development' in the 1960s and 1970s, to 'partnership working' in the 1980s and 1990s, and 'co-production' in the 21st century.

Introduction

Children's centres matter. They matter to all the children and families who use them, to the staff who work in them and to the local authorities who are accountable for them and have a duty to develop them. At Pen Green we have over 30 years' worth of evidence on the impact of our successful work with children and their families, including some of the most disadvantaged families in the country. We work with a cross-section of children in our community. All have parents who profoundly want their children to have a better deal than they had themselves. We work with families who are on the edge of social services intervention, families who have profoundly disabled children, and families whose children would enter the care system without our help.

As a fully integrated centre for children and families, Pen Green has been the inspiration for the model of children's centres adopted by government, and we continue to pioneer innovative and cost-effective ways of working with the most disadvantaged. We have a local, regional and national reputation as one of the most successful centres in the UK. When we first wrote about our work with parents and families in 1997, children's centres had not yet been invented. Today, we stand on the threshold of the demolition of all the amazing work that centres have achieved between 1997 and 2012.

> It is inconceivable that we can make the foundation years effective if Sure Start children's centres all over the place are being slaughtered. Local authorities must seek to employ innovative methods to ensure families – especially the poorest families – do not lose the vital support they need.
>
> (Field, 2011)

The issue today is, will we hold on to the amazing children's centres and integrated services that have developed during this period? With only a few years to go until the next election, it's hard to tell which way things will go.

Pen Green has been a vital agent for social change in Corby, a small town in the East Midlands, and we have developed a raft of services for children and families from the poorest areas of the town. Pen Green has played an important role in one small town's regeneration. We have become a centre for the whole community. Three generations of families have used the services and volunteered in the centre, and each year we work with more than 1,500 families with children under five. We offer a comprehensive range of services for parents with babies, toddlers and nursery-age children, while children from four to eleven years use our after-school clubs and play schemes. We have learnt to 'sweat the assets' at Pen Green so that the centre is open seven days a week, a minimum of 48 weeks a year. On Saturdays and Sundays, we have dads' groups and contact visits, and on weekday evenings the centre is used for adult learning and recreational purposes.

When Pen Green opened in 1983, the staff were well aware that the quality of the whole learning environment is the greatest single determinant of children's attainment. All families are regularly home-visited and parents and staff work together as co-educators. Over 30 years, we've managed to engage roughly 89 per cent of families every year in our Parents' Involvement with their Children's Learning programme. You will hear more about this in later chapters.

Pen Green: a summary

Pen Green provides a wide range of adult community education opportunities for parents. Our experience and expertise in training is significant and we have developed a 'University of the Workplace' (what some people call a training hospital or Early Years Training Centre), offering local families everything from basic literacy and numeracy classes, family learning, CACHE Diplomas, foundation degrees, Early Years Professional Status qualifications, masters degrees and PhDs. Some of our masters level graduates first came to the centre as parents. We have built capacity in our local community, and today 56 per cent of our 130 full-time and part-time staff started their learning journeys at Pen Green as parents, then trained here and became paid workers.

Pen Green also makes a major contribution to the safeguarding of children under five in Corby. Several hundred families each year receive intensive family support services from highly experienced and highly qualified family support workers. Families are supported where mental health impacts on mother and child relationships, where drug and alcohol misuse impinge on children's growth and development, where domestic violence and family breakdown shatter young lives.

Our comprehensive groupwork programme for families means that we can engage with many families each week. Despite waiting lists, our policy has always been to 'find a way' to engage with a troubled family. Families who need immediate support are engaged in building up their social network so we can safeguard children from the first referral. Parents can then re-engage with their relationship building and take up education and training on our campus. Over the last decade we have worked intensively in our Nurture Group with many children at immediate risk of placement in care. Very few of these children have entered the care system.

Pen Green is both a maintained nursery school and a well-established integrated centre for children and families. We have extensive early education and childcare services, a social work team and a large repertoire of family support. Pen Green's scale, reach and additional responses make it fundamentally different from a traditional nursery school. We employ a large staff group, have grounds and premises and a budget equivalent to a very large primary school. Pen Green's development over 30 years has been concerted, planned and deliberate, and today we offer the following range of services:

- Pen Green nursery school provision for children from two to five years that goes well beyond the free entitlement, with three nursery classes, a den, snug and Baby Nest, running 48 weeks a year
- Baby Nest and 'Couthie' provision for children from nine months to three years with sponsored places for the poorest and most vulnerable children
- a Nurture Group for children requiring child protection plans or looked after children
- respite crèche provision for more than 100 children a week from birth to five years
- after-school club services and holiday play schemes for local children from four to eleven years – includes Easter and summer holidays and half-terms
- parent and infant support groups, including Growing Together, infant and toddler massage sessions, groups for parents with adult mental health issues and for parents who have alcohol and other addictions, extensive drop-in community groups, weekend groups for fathers, adult learning groups, groups for parents and children with disabilities
- extended hours and extended all-year provision to support families where respite is needed
- adult community education
- training and support for all local early years practitioners
- family support services in the centre and in the community
- a focus for voluntary work and community regeneration.

User engagement

Why have we *built* services *with* families rather than *delivered* services *to* families? Pen Green staff have been heard to comment that you can 'deliver pizzas but not public services'. Public services that are funded through taxpayers' money need to be designed and developed by the people who might want to use them. Over 30 years Pen Green has consistently targeted those families who needed services most. We know that this is good policy, good practice and good economics. We also know that if targeted services are to be accessible and acceptable to the most disadvantaged families, there needs to be a universal gateway. Families in our community have always voted with their feet and do not readily engage with services that carry a stigma or that are delivered as a pre-prepared package or 'one size fits all'. In 1982 when the centre opened, the only voluntary group in a community with 43 per cent unemployment was a local action group against the centre. Families in the Pen Green estate were incensed that Northamptonshire County Council had decided to impose a centre on the community without any local consultation. They were deeply concerned that the proposed new centre might be a 'problem family' centre, and they wanted something very different. Our experience is that families have a powerful understanding of what might be useful to them. Newly appointed Pen Green staff worked in the local community, in local schools and neighbourhood centres to conceptualise the new service alongside families. Parents described the service in this way:

> In every small community there should be a service for children and their families. This service should honour the needs of young children and celebrate their existence. It should also support families however they are constituted within the community.
>
> (Pen Green, 1983)

Parents involved in this consultation process went on to support staff and work as volunteers during the period 1983–85. Subsequently, during 1985–87, they trained alongside staff and became service providers in the Pen Green Centre, often engaged in their own learning and development. Many parents went on to train at the centre and become employees at Pen Green or in other children's centres in Corby. In 1987–90, when unemployment was still high, volunteering was key to the delivery of services for increasingly large numbers of users. Local parents trained alongside staff and became group leaders, indeed some of them gained MA credits in group work, accredited through our research base.

When the centre was threatened with cuts in 1999, parents once again became community activists, defending the services they had co-produced. In the 1990s, there was a huge expansion of our Parents-as-Co-educators programme, and in the first three years 84 per cent of mothers and 60 per cent of fathers got involved. Parents who had been involved with the Pen Green steering groups and advisory groups welcomed the chance to become governors, and elections were always competitive. All four local schools had former Pen Green parents on their governing bodies. Once we became a school (in 2006), parents ran vigorous campaigns to be among the ten elected parents and community governors at Pen Green. Parents currently demonstrate enormously high levels of collaboration with staff: they are policy makers, troubleshooters, researchers and continue to become paid workers, both in nursery and in the family visiting team. Parents interview for all staff appointments and have done since 1983. They take up Home-Start training and volunteer to visit other families. Parents train as crèche workers and often see this as a first step in a career as an early childhood education worker or family support worker.

1981–82	Campaign against the local borough council to re-roof local housing stock
1982–83	LAG (Local Advisory Group) against the Pen Green Centre
1983–85	Parents conceptualising services
	Parents appointing staff
	Parents as volunteers
	Parents sharing power
1985–87	Parents as service providers
	Parents engaged in their own learning
1987–90	Parents as group leaders
	Parents as community activists
1990–97	Parents as co-educators involved in their children's learning
	Parents as paid workers
1997–07	Parents as troubleshooters
	Parents as policy makers
	Parents as co-researchers and evaluators
	Parents as governors
2007–12	Parents developing innovative projects, such as Total Place Corby, one Corby parent coalition
	Parents developing websites and Facebook and Twitter pages
	Parents running national campaigns

Table 1.1 Community development at Pen Green

How do we know we make a difference?

Children's centres and all early childhood settings need to show they are making a difference if they are going to continue to get funding to engage in working with parents. Pen Green's core funding rests on its capacity to have a greater impact on children, families and their communities than other, separate, existing services. This impact must extend to many levels and must be shown to have the greatest effect on the poorest and most vulnerable children and families.

As a well-established centre, Pen Green has the capacity to impact on children and families in the following ways:

- on children's learning and development
- on parents' involvement in their children's learning and development/parental advocacy
- on capacity building – training and development of parents to become part of the future workforce
- on better supported and stronger families
- on community engagement – stronger citizenship and more cohesive communities.

Impacts 1 and 2: children's learning and development; Parents' involvement in children's learning and development/parental advocacy

The evidence is unequivocal that working in partnership with families to build on the learning that goes on in the home is the best way to have an effective impact on the development of children. This is dealt with in Chapter 3 in some depth. Pen Green has pioneered a shift away from a conventional model of teaching and learning to a new model where parents and staff work together as co-educators. For example in 2011–12, Pen Green engaged 89 per cent of nursery and Baby Nest parents in the following ways:

- by sharing sessions on key child development concepts – developing a shared language for thinking about children's learning
- daily dialogues achieved via flexible starts and finishes to the day
- diaries
- weekly study groups: a.m., p.m. and evening
- portfolios of children's learning
- sharing DVD vignettes of children's learning in the home and in the nursery
- annual trips to the Science Museum with parents, staff and children
- open evenings focusing on key learning issues
- Pen Green staff publishing their work alongside parents, for example *Involving Parents in Their Children's Learning* (Whalley *et al.*, 2007).

Impact 3: capacity building – training and development of parents to become part of the future workforce

At Pen Green, we provide parents with the opportunity to return to education and training. Corby has a very low percentage of adults who have gained further qualifications post-school and has the lowest percentage in England of adults who have gained a level 6 qualification (degree level). Our community education programme gives parents a chance to embark on a range of courses and we have a climbing frame of opportunity for Pen Green and for parents at Pen Green, where families want to participate in this learning route.

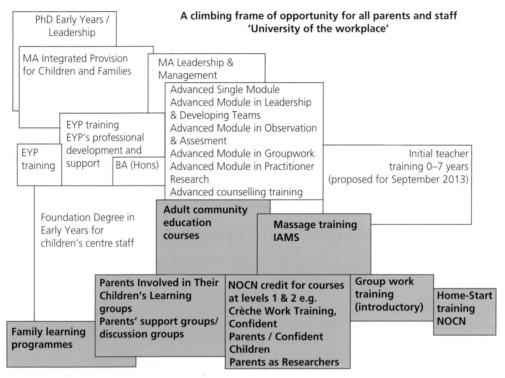

Figure 1.1 Pen Green as a learning organisation

Impact 4: better supported and stronger families

Pen Green has adopted a systemic approach to engaging with children and their families. We acknowledge the critical importance of developing relations with all the important adults in the child's life and work in a deep and respectful way in order to develop sustained engagement with families over time. Our principles for engaging with families are:

- *Successful and sustained engagement with families is maintained when practitioners work alongside families in a valued working relationship.*
- *Successful and sustained engagement with families involves practitioners and parents being willing to listen to and learn from each other.*
- *Successful and sustained engagement with families happens when practitioners respect what families know and already do.*
- *Successful and sustained engagement with families needs practitioners to find ways to actively engage those who do not traditionally access services.*

- Successful and sustained engagement with families happens when parents are decision-makers in organisations and services.
- Successful and sustained engagement with families happens when families' views, opinions and expectations of services are raised and their confidence as service users increases.
- Successful and sustained engagement with families happens where there is support for the whole family.
- Successful and sustained engagement with families is through universal services but with opportunities for more intensive support where it is needed most.
- Successful and sustained engagement with families requires effective support and supervision for staff, encouraging evaluation and self-reflection.
- Successful and sustained engagement with families requires an understanding and honest sharing of issues around safeguarding.

(ELPPEG, 2010: 3)

At Pen Green we recognise the fact that disadvantaged families benefit from a comprehensible and accessible system, not a series of individual services. For example, a young parent who has had continuous and regular contact with one consistent midwife who attended the birth, visits the home and co-ordinates a weekly group for teenage mothers has experienced a seamless system, and one in which she has exercised control and influence. We recognise that services need to be both locally relevant and personalised. Different activities, for example, will appeal to different groups of people. Single mothers, fathers and families where parents are divorcing or divorced, families where English is not their first language, survivors of domestic violence or abuse in childhood or refugees, all have different priorities for engagement. The quality of the social networks forged at Pen Green and in community groups, or through parent support groups, is critical to sustaining family life and enabling all children to thrive. *In highly effective centres for children and families where a real sense of community is developed most families will experience services and activities as one seamless system.*

Impact 5: community engagement – stronger citizenship and more cohesive communities

There are good reasons for putting relationships at the core of effective public provision. Relationships are at the heart of what makes for a good life. Living as a solitary individual for most people is a recipe for unhappiness. Much of what we most value – love, friendship, trust, recognition, care – comes from relationships with families, friends and social networks. People grow up well and age well if they have supported relationships.

(Leadbetter, 2009)

Over 30 years local people have been supported by Pen Green to do more for themselves and have become discerning consumers of public services over which they have a lot of control. Our aim was to develop more mutual self-help. Currently, there are two parents at Pen Green who have children with special rights, and who run support groups for other parents with disabled children. Both of them are powerful advocates for services for families across Corby. One has decided to become a paid worker and is also undertaking a masters degree at Pen Green, and is a powerful advocate for other parents. The other has become an extremely active parent-governor, taking on a position of senior responsibility as deputy chair of governors.

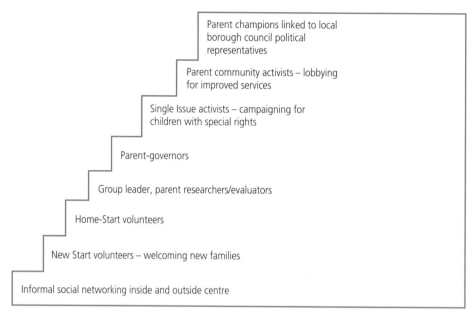

Figure 1.2 Volunteer engagement in co-production 2012 – the steps imply a rigid hierarchy but the reality is that the sequence is more fluid and individual.

Total Place Corby

Developing social capital has always been central to Pen Green's core purpose: Pen Green is a place where community is being built. Our highly qualified staff work alongside volunteers all of the time and are aware that there is a need to offer minoritised groups in the community distinctive and finely tuned services. We recently conducted a series of parent-to-parent interviews with non-users of children's centre services (Total Place Corby study, July 2010). We wanted to deepen our understanding of the barriers that some families experience when engaging with the public sector. Subsequently, we have worked tirelessly with other colleagues in our community and with the Innovation Unit in London to shift our professional practice and establish new ways of working in order to improve the experience of families with a long-held distrust of schools and social workers and the public sector in general. Pen Green has used the data from this project to good effect, making sure that the pilot funding nursery provision for two-year-olds from the most disadvantaged families is made available to traditional non-users of services, such as travellers and families with significant drug and alcohol problems. One of the things that emerged from the study was the great untapped energies of these minoritised parents and their commitment to their children's learning and development.

Emerging themes of this Total Place Corby study for 'disillusioned and disengaged' families were that parents:
- look primarily within the family for emotional, practical and financial support
- have poor experiences with public services
- look to support others in the community, especially the elderly, in practical ways, e.g. gardening, putting out rubbish bins, keeping streets clean and safe
- have a high incidence of illness and disability across the generations
- have relatively narrow horizons, e.g. home-school-shops-home-school-home

Working with Families in Children's Centres and Early Years Settings

- have relatively low material aspirations – articulating a sense of relative poverty they identify a desire for secure, well-paid jobs so that they can afford a 'house with a garden', 'days out', 'an annual holiday' – things that most people take for granted
- want their children to achieve at school and have adult learning opportunities for themselves
- would like more time to spend with their children and extended family
- really appreciate (but want more) well-resourced parks, playgrounds, open spaces, leisure and sports facilities
- are very unhappy about anti-social behaviour, especially when alcohol- or drug-related, particularly when it involves teenagers
- appreciate and want more accessible early education and childcare and family support to combat isolation, loneliness, stress and depression.

As an organisation, we are absolutely committed to engaging with all of the parents in our reach area and we systematically home-visit families that we have not yet engaged. From October 2010 to February 2011, for example, we home-visited 396 families that we had not engaged – 60 households per fortnight (we used interpreters where necessary). Through those interviews we explored:
- how families connected and interacted in their community
- information regarding daily routines/places visited
- what they identified as key issues
- challenges to the community
- what organisations and groups they were using
- what additional services they would welcome.

These families were asked to mark on a Corby map the services they used across an average week. We discovered a significant number of these families were already using Pen Green services but simply did not appear on our database. Families are often reluctant to fill in the appropriate forms. Forms can indeed be a serious barrier to access, alongside signs that put parents off and keypads that keep parents out. We used to talk about 'Rottweiler receptionists' and imaginary 'barbed-wire fences' around early years settings, schools, housing offices and social work offices in the 1980s. Front-of-house staff seemed to have been trained specifically to keep families at bay. Today, the desire to have intense security for children often makes it even more difficult for families to get into public buildings.

In this project families gave us invaluable critical feedback to inform the way we were offering existing services and gave us wonderful ideas about developing new, highly focused interventions for specific families.

Parent champions

Pen Green parents value the services at Pen Green and have demonstrated their ability to become highly effective parent champions. Most recently, they have demonstrated their commitment to the centre through protests and marches and Facebook campaigns. They have hand delivered petitions to 10 Downing Street. They have lobbied MPs to ask questions in the House of Commons, they have visited MPs and borough councillors in their surgeries and have presented their case studies to a cross-party group of MPs at Portcullis House, Westminster. They have spoken at local and national conferences and have launched a website to help other children's centres across the country that are also facing cuts. They have demonstrated citizenship and are powerful advocates for their children and for the services in Corby. All these parents are single-minded in their aspirations for their children: they want more for their children than they had themselves and know that it is through their participation in the education system that their children's life chances can be transformed. Social justice requires that all these families have high-quality, effective services to support them in the challenges that they face in the 21st century.

How to improve your practice

As an early years educator and carer or family support worker in a children's centre or early childhood setting, it is vital that you see your role as being a mediator or broker on behalf of parents. Without a doubt you will at times find yourself making comparisons between parents and assuming that certain family combinations are intrinsically better than others. You will need to talk about your thoughts and feelings with your colleagues. In any staff group, a diverse range of perspectives on family life will be represented. Some staff will have been brought up by single parents, others will have lived in traditional two-parent families. Some may have been brought up in care. You will find that some will have had happy childhoods but others may have been hurt or badly treated by their families. Their positive and negative experience of being parented will have very little to do with the kinds of parents they had – gay, straight, divorced, married, step or biological parents can all build effective and supportive families. Families in the 21st century are increasingly complex and this is what makes our society rich and diverse.

The following two case studies are examples of different kinds of family structures and the different ways that parents sometimes behave towards their children. The highly differentiated parenting styles that parents adopt have a huge impact on their children's self-esteem and sense of self. You might find it useful to discuss these case studies in your workplace.

Examples from practice

Examples from practice

Tom

Three-year-old Tom has a single-parent father. When Tom comes into nursery and says 'My dad's proud of me', he shows he feels both loved and lovable. He also knows that his father believes in his ability to do things. Alan, Tom's dad, takes him to dance once a week with 'the old folk', and on daily cycle rides. He takes Tom for walks through a public park which most nursery parents avoid since it tends to be a hangout for 'winos'. Alan's comment is that Tom knows all the winos by name! Alan is deeply committed to politics and talks of his son as a 'socialist soldier'. He is so concerned about his son's education that he attends a study group every week at the nursery where he can find out more about the early years curriculum and what his son is learning. Alan spends hours talking to Tom, listening to him, telling him stories and supporting his play. Clearly some children don't get such positive messages from their parents' parenting style as Tom does. Some parents may be struggling too hard themselves to be able to support their children appropriately. Perhaps their own experiences of being parented were very negative and damaging.

Christopher

Christopher is three-and-a-half and has been in and out of care three times already. Esther, his mum, was abused as a child and is now an alcoholic. Esther is a single parent, and every Thursday evening after she has received her benefits she goes out and gets drunk and is often incapable of looking after Christopher or his little sister. Christopher is very anxious when he comes into nursery and he needs lots of support from his special key worker. He generally holds his head down and makes little eye contact and is quiet and withdrawn. He often needs to be allowed to play in just one area of the nursery for long periods of time because he is frightened of anything new. Moving out of his safe play space is too daunting. He often wants the same story over and over again. Christopher needs a very predictable environment when he comes to nursery. He needs to be greeted every session by his key worker who makes sure he gets listened to in group times. Christopher's key worker home-visits both Esther and his foster parents and this helps reaffirm the nursery's relationship with all the important adults in Christopher's life.

As an early childhood educator you will be working with children like Tom who have a very positive home experience and you will also work with children like Christopher. Clearly Tom's experience of 'family life' has been much more positive than Christopher's, although both have parents who love them very much. Tom's and Christopher's parents both live on benefits and struggle to give their children the tangible things that more affluent children take for granted; however, both parents care deeply about what happens to their children and both want them to have better experiences of the education system than they themselves had. Tom is getting a lot of nurturing from his dad who loves and accepts him but also has high expectations of him. Tom has high self-esteem and is fairly confident – he is willing to have a go at most things in nursery. Tom's dad, Alan, also provides a reasonable amount of structure in his life. Alan sets clear boundaries for Tom about what is okay and what's not okay.

Christopher, on the other hand, has a very chaotic and unstructured life which means that nursery routines are incredibly important. He doesn't ever know what will happen. For example, at the end of a week, will he end up in care or find himself in the middle of a row between his mum and the neighbours, Kirsty and Mark? Esther does nurture him a lot when she is feeling on top of things and Christopher knows that he is loved, but he has very little confidence in his own abilities.

Instead of making judgements about either parent and finding them wanting, we need to recognise the pressures that work, unemployment, poor health and poverty will bring. As an early childhood educator you may not share the same values as the parents who use your nursery, you may not like some of the things that they are doing; however, it will be critically important for you to build on the strengths within every family.

> When we draw children, parents and families into our early childhood centres I think we should be sure that what we are about is making these people strong, providing them with the means to appreciate their destinies, giving them a measure of control and influence about what goes on, encouraging them to stop accepting their lot and start creating the world they would like to be part of.
>
> (Pascal, 1996)

Co-production

Working in partnership with parents can be painful and difficult for us as early years educators but it can also be enormously rewarding.

production of early childhood services with families and encouraging families to drive the services ward can be very time-consuming but it is much more likely that services will be well used and sustainable over time if families have been active participants.

What we set up in Corby in 1983 was not an entirely new concept – after all there was nothing new about putting a baby clinic next to a community nursery inside a family centre where daycare was on offer. Margaret McMillan worked in this way, in Deptford, at the beginning of the 20th century. What was new was *how* we chose to work with families. We developed a genuine collaboration between parents and workers, 'a radical notion of self-help as personal growth and the development of a sense of community responsibility' (Hevey, 1982).

In the 1980s, in education, social work and health, there were principles of community development evolving, founded upon a belief that the professionals had a responsibility to challenge and influence public policy rather than 'submissively assisting families to live with its consequences' (Goodwin, 1988).

In the 1980s we wanted to make services relevant, responsive and acceptable to local people and we knew that it was important to work *with* people rather than impose things *on* people. We had to be very clear about our values and our power base. We did not want to be part of a service where all the power and control was retained by the workers. We wanted to relocate at least some of it back into the community. Giving back power, or more accurately letting go of it, requires a willingness on the part of the professional worker to give up some control. Staff had to be open and accessible to families. At times staff needed to 'back off' and accept the fact that professionals or paid workers as we call them do not have to be the only providers of services nor are they necessarily the best at group facilitating, engaging new parents or home-visiting. From the beginning, parents made decisions about how rooms were used, which services got priority, how services were delivered and by whom. As a local authority provision there were clearly tensions between what we as a staff group wanted to put up for negotiation with parents and what the funding agencies considered appropriate – and that is still the case. We aimed for a partnership with parents that was equal, active and responsible (Nicoll, 1986). This meant that we needed to be confident and secure professionals (Tomlinson, 1986), well trained in our own profession and able to co-operate and work in an integrated way with other agencies.

Co-production in the 21st century

Co-production means delivering public services in an equal and reciprocal relationship between professionals, people using services, their families and their neighbours. Where activities are co-produced in this way, both services and neighbourhoods become far more effective agents of change.

(Boyle & Harris, 2009)

In 2012 most public services are coming to recognise the fact that *co-production* is the way forward to ensure the most effective use of resources, greater personalisation, community cohesion and satisfaction. Co-production is defined as a strong and equal partnership between the users and providers of public services to achieve a valued outcome (Horne & Shirley, 2009).

In our experience the most successful children's centres and early childhood settings are like community centres. They have demonstrated their effectiveness in reaching families, strengthening networks for families and operating in recognisable and familiar neighbourhoods. They are very local.

Children's centres today are popular, well used and have the potential to be the most successful and effective agents of community development. Not only because of the involvement of parents, the promotion of education, the improvements in health, but also because these children's centres generate better and closer social networks between families. It has become clear to us at Pen Green that children's centres and early childhood settings can move forward into a new way of working where agencies co-conceptualise, co-design and co-produce their services with parents, and have management committees and governance structures with devolved budgets where parents actually have real control and can decide priorities. We believe that it is possible for centres to engage with families effectively and empower them to plan, deliver and evaluate services, and we have been able to make that happen over the last 30 years.

Within a philosophy of co-production:
- everyone has something to contribute
- reciprocity is important
- social relationships matter
- social contributions (rather than financial contributions) are encouraged.

In many children's centres and early childhood settings staff are well on the way to working within this philosophy. Parents and staff are involved jointly in children's learning and development. Parents share the responsibilities with staff and develop their own skills and deepen their understanding about how children learn – this in turn supports them as confident parents. Relationships between staff and parents are always strengthened when parents are encouraged to contribute as volunteers and sit on advisory and management committees. Friendships and active membership of the informal social networks created by children's centres or early childhood settings give parents confidence, pleasure and reassurance. Helping other parents to run activities, undertaking fundraising and serving on committees as governors and managers is becoming common currency in effective centres.

Examples of co-production are:
- when parents co-ordinate groups and activities that help other people
- when parents take responsibility for designing and running services
- when parents become practitioner researchers and evaluators identifying both what is needed and reviewing the quality of what is on offer.

Children's centres can become *communities of interest* – all parents want more for their children than they had themselves and a shared common interest in babies and small children has proved to be, unsurprisingly, a powerful motivating force. Parents want to do what is best for their children and developing opportunities for them to become part of a community of interest reinforces and increases their enthusiasm and ability to do so.

At Pen Green we are proud to have released the great untapped energy within local families and the local community.

Points for discussion

- What successes make your work worthwhile?
- When are families the driving force for change in your organisation?
- How can you make a contribution to the social and cultural capital in your community?

References

Boyle, D. and Harris, M. (2009) 'The Challenge of Co-production: How equal partnerships between professionals and the public are crucial to improving public services', London: NEF.

ELPPEG (Early Learning Partnership Parental Engagement Group) (2010) *Principles for Engaging with Families: A framework for local authorities and national organisations to evaluate and improve engagement with families*, London: NQIN.

Field, F. (2011) Hansard, HC, col. 1076 (20 Jan. 2011), London: HMG.

Goodwin, S. (1988) 'Whither Health Visiting?', keynote speech, *Health Visitor Association Annual Study Conference*, London.

Hevey, D. (1982) 'The Wider Issues of Support and Planning', Parenting Papers No. 3, *Supporting Parents in the Community*, London: National Children's Bureau.

Horne, M. and Shirley, T. (2009) 'Co-production in public services: A new partnership with citizens', London: Cabinet Office.

Leadbeater, C. (2009) 'Seven ways to protect public services', *The Guardian*, 1 July.

Nicoll, A. (1986) 'New approaches to build health care: Is there a role for parents?', in *Developing a Partnership with Parents in the Child Health Services*, Partnership Papers No. 8, ed. De'Ath, E., London: National Children's Bureau.

Pascal, C. (1996), lecture at the Pen Green Centre, Corby, March 1996, unpublished.

Pen Green (1983) Curriculum Document, unpublished, available from Pen Green Centre, Corby.

Tomlinson, J. R. G. (1986) 'The Co-ordination of Services for Under-fives', *Early Years Journal of Tutors of Advanced Courses for Teachers of Young Children*, vol. 71, autumn, pp. 3–13.

Whalley, M. and the Pen Green team (2007) *Including Parents in Their Children's Learning* (2nd edn), London: Paul Chapman.

United Nations (1994) *Families and Disability*, Occasional Papers Series No. 10, Vienna: UN.

2 Sharing knowledge with families using our nursery: the Family Worker role

Angela Prodger

Nobody would doubt the fact that parents play the most significant role in influencing their children's futures and the evidence backs up this instinctive belief.

(Field, 2010: 37)

What parents do is more important than who parents are. Especially in a child's earliest years, the right kind of parenting is a bigger influence on their future than wealth, class, education or any other common social factor.

(Allen, 2011: xiv)

In this chapter we will consider:

- the importance of trying to understand a child's situation or family context
- the benefits that shared knowledge about the child and his or her family can bring to early years workers
- how to plan and create a warm and welcoming environment for parents or carers
- the importance of the key worker role if we are to have positive relationships with parents and carers as well as children.

Introduction

The new Early Years Foundation Stage (DfE, 2012) seeks to provide partnership working between practitioners and parents or carers. If we want to do the best for children we need to involve those parents and carers. Through current research, it is now widely accepted that engaging parents in their child's early education and listening to what they have to tell us about their child will enhance the experience and outcomes for the child. It is worth emphasising that:

Fathers' interest and involvement in their children's learning is statistically associated with better educational outcomes ... There is a strong relationship between different aspects of parenting and parents' health and well-being and their children's outcomes.

(Field, 2010: 44)

It makes sense therefore to engage the most significant adults in a child's life.

The child's home context will include the people who are important influences, for example parents, siblings and extended family, as well as other factors such as the child's cultural background, race, gender and possible special educational needs. We also consider the child's home learning environment. All of these factors will have an impact on the child and their family members.

> *An early growth-promoting environment, with adequate nutrients, free of toxins, and filled with social interactions with an attentive caregiver, prepares the architecture of the developing brain to function optimally in a healthy environment.*
>
> (Allen, 2011: 14)

Getting to know each other

In our nursery cohort, we have children who live in the lowest 10 per cent 'super-output areas' and those who live in 70+ per cent super-output areas. We have a diverse population with 17 different languages spoken. Each child's family context will differ; some will have the support of an extended family, others may have recently arrived in the country and feel quite isolated. Using an illustrative case study, I would like to demonstrate how having a shared knowledge about a child and their home context might influence how we plan for their learning and development opportunities within the nursery.

Example from practice

Example from practice

Tania: a parent who recently used the nursery provision

I was very familiar with the nursery [as] my younger brothers and mum were always here. My oldest daughter went to a different nursery in the town as we lived in that area. The children's dad sadly passed away and we were rehoused in this area. I went to the centre with my mum and just felt so welcomed by everyone. I was able to use the nursery space and beach when other children and families weren't around. Angela [Head of Nursery] helped me to get Chloe into school and offered Abbie a place in the nursery.

Margaret [Family Worker] came to visit us at home. I was excited 'cause I knew Abbie was ready for nursery, although she was only two-and-a-half. Abbie took a shine to Margaret straight away. On the third home visit, Margaret watched the whole of the *Lion King* DVD with her and then went with Abbie to her bedroom to look at her dinosaurs. I was keen to share information about Abbie so you would know about her, what she is like and what she is into.

When Abbie started nursery, I was a bit wary 'cause she is feisty and she wasn't always in control of her temper. But, as the weeks went by, Margaret was able to give me reassurance and share some strategies that she was using in nursery. Although I knew what kind of things Abbie liked to do, I didn't always know how to handle the emotions of both girls. I wanted to make it right and okay for them both.

Margaret has made us lots of DVDs and I've got them in my keepsake cupboard. I went to PICL [Parents' Involvement in Their Children's Learning study group] – I wasn't sure what it was, but I understand a lot more now about schemas. I was able to use my PICL experience to secure a place on the crèche course. I'm now doing voluntary work in the local primary school. I'm hoping to do a diploma in childcare. At home we shared lots of books and stories. We would paint, build blocks – I played with them.

Me and Margaret shared everything. I brought photos, drawings etc. from home. I helped Margaret with Abbie's assessment. Abbie loves dinosaurs and 'Sonic the Hedgehog'. It would be lovely to keep in touch with Margaret 'cause she's helped me through loads. She has supported me with the crèche course.

I regularly took Abbie's file home on a Friday to keep on top of it. The Learning to Be Strong sessions (assertiveness for children) were really important – Abbie regularly told people she hated them. Margaret told Abbie that hate is a strong word and Abbie still remembers that to this day.

Margaret supported Abbie and me to go to the Natural History Museum [rather than the Science Museum] as she knew that Abbie's deep interest was dinosaurs. Margaret knew Abbie loved reading and would give her homework like her sister and put it in a wallet.

This case study illustrates the individualised approach to planning for each child's learning that Pen Green nursery staff aspire to, and is a good, worked example of the 'Pen Green Loop'.

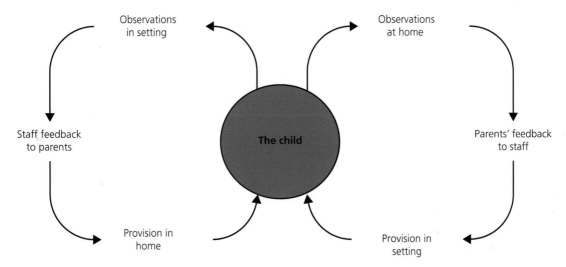

Figure 2.1 The Pen Green Loop

Points for discussion

How can all this sharing of knowledge about Abbie's home context help us to support and extend the rich experiences which Abbie is already enjoying at home? Or to look at it another way - how could you as an early years practitioner begin to plan appropriate and meaningful learning opportunities for Abbie without all of this knowledge about Abbie's context? Once you know something of what is in Abbie's mind you, as an adult, can begin to understand what is of importance to Abbie.

Chris Athey talked of 'a genuine open-ended type of enquiry [where] parents are respected and recognized as experts on their own children in that they had had them full-time from birth and therefore knew them better as individuals than anyone else' (Athey, 1990: 61). With this model of engagement with parents, we are clearly planning an individual curriculum which takes account of the child and their context.

Tina Bruce calls this the 'Three Cs of Early Childhood Curriculum – Child; Context; Content' (Bruce, 1991: 8).

Parents have told us that their involvement in their children's education has not only had a positive impact on their children's learning but has also boosted their own skills and brought them support, friendship, enjoyment and a better understanding of their own child and a sense of achievement. Through this engagement there are immediate benefits to the child, the parent or carer and the practitioner. The child will have enriched opportunities and self-esteem, the carers will feel acknowledged and valued and the practitioner will be better informed to plan more effectively for the children.

A welcoming environment

How does your physical environment appear to parents?

Here are some questions to ask:
- Can parents get into the building with a buggy?
- Do you have access for adults or children who are wheelchair users?
- Are you able to support with childcare when parents want to volunteer in your setting?
- Does your main entrance reflect your philosophy?
- Is the main entrance friendly and welcoming? Does it reflect the diversity of families using your setting?
- Do you have an area where it is safe for carers to have a hot drink?
- Are the toilets and baby change areas clearly signposted for all?
- Is there a parents' notice board in your setting that they can browse, or put up their own notices?
- Do you have a flexible start and end to all sessions to allow practitioners the opportunity to individually greet all children and parents?
- Is there somewhere comfortable for carers to sit and relax? For example, a soft seating area with newspapers and magazines to read or hide behind for those feeling a bit uncomfortable when first accessing the setting?

It is important to remember that some parents who are coming to your setting may have only negative memories and feelings of their time in education. You may be able to do something about these feelings if you make sure your setting is welcoming and friendly to all carers and children. Do not let staffing or resourcing constraints stop you from doing this, as parents and children will be appreciative of a friendly smile and respectful greeting. You may not be in a position to change your setting but you can change your attitude and methods of working, which in turn could influence others.

Home-visiting

One of the best ways of getting to know more about a child's context and home learning environment is by visiting them at home. Home-visiting has often been seen as the job for health visitors, social workers and Home-Start volunteers. However, it has become more common practice for nurseries, children's centres and reception class teachers too. Home-visiting has several key functions. It is a great opportunity for the worker to introduce themselves to the family so that when they come to the setting they will recognise at least one familiar face. It gives carers the chance to ask questions about the setting and to spend some time getting to know the worker. Parents might feel more relaxed and confident in their own home. Ideally the person who is home-visiting should be the person who will be the child's key worker when they start in the setting. The main focus of the initial visit to a child's home is to begin to foster a warm, friendly relationship with both the carers and the child. This visit should not be too overwhelming for parents. Choose carefully what is the most beneficial information that you feel they need to know, for example:

- the settling-in period
- times of sessions
- costs.

All other information can be shared and clarified when the child starts in the setting.

On the initial home visit you will want to encourage the parents to talk about their child to enable you to find out as much as possible about them. Your role is to listen carefully and begin to understand the child's context.

Key information

Some key points to help shape the conversation on the initial home visit are:

- Who are the important adults in the child's life?
- What hobbies or interests does the child or family have?
- What does the child like to eat?
- What health problems or allergies does the child have?
- What might help the child to settle smoothly into the setting?
- How can the setting support the parent and child with the first moments of separation?
- When does the child sleep during the day?

All of this information will be really helpful when thinking about the child managing the transition into the setting. It will also be the foundation for a real conversation with the child in the setting.

The thought of home-visiting may fill you with fear or you may feel that you have not had suitable training to carry out home visits. If you do not feel confident, then it would be advisable to carry out the visit with a more experienced member of staff or make sure you access some training. The benefits of home-visiting by far outweigh the risks. Parents may be anxious about the home visit so it is best that workers make the reasons for visiting clear. A telephone conversation with parents means workers can clarify any concerns and negotiate a date and time that is convenient for the family's routine. When writing to a family, it is important to include the following information:

- Staff visit all families at home to get to know them.
- An explanation about why you want to visit the family at home.
- Staff are sensitive and respectful of the family's cultural, religious and economic backgrounds.

Sometimes it is appropriate to take photographs on the initial visit to use in the setting when the child starts. These could be family members, pets, front doors or favourite things. It is important to negotiate this with the family and to be clear about how these photographs will be used. We have learnt from our colleagues in New Zealand about the importance of children and their families feeling a 'sense of belonging'. We use photographs to help create this 'sense of belonging' in their key group in the setting.

Children and their families experience an environment where:

- *connecting links with family and the wider world are affirmed and extended*
- *they know that they have a place*
- *they feel comfortable with the routines, customs and regular events*
- *they know the limits and boundaries of acceptable behaviour.*

(Ministry of Education, 1996: 54)

Finding time to home-visit will be particular to your individual setting. If you work in a school where there is a non-teaching head, you may be able to negotiate that the head takes your class for a specific period to allow you to home-visit. If you work in a nursery setting you may be able to stagger the intake so that you can get out on home visits. If you believe home-visiting is central to your work, you will want to make it happen but you will need to think creatively to enable this.

Settling in to nursery

A settling-in period is key to a child's transition into your setting. This would involve the child being accompanied for a period of time, usually the first two weeks, by an adult who is important in the child's life. If you have previously home-visited, you may have already met or heard about the important adult. The familiar adults can be parents, other carers, grandparents, childminders, neighbours or other adult members of the family. If you establish the settling-in period as one of your good practice principles and it is discussed fully with parents prior to starting then you are unlikely to have any complaints. You can make this time easier for carers if you encourage them to negotiate annual leave if they are employed and by being flexible about start dates to accommodate the family's needs. Parents will be very keen for their child to settle well, therefore if you explain the long-term benefits to the child of these transitional arrangements, parents will be happy to co-operate. You might both have concerns about this settling-in period.

Parental concerns

- What if my child won't share with others?
- What if my child has a tantrum?
- What if my child hurts another child?
- What if my child won't leave my side and clings to my leg?
- What if I cry when I need to leave?

Early years practitioner concerns

- What will I do if the child doesn't want to engage with me?
- What if the parent doesn't like my style of being with the child?
- What if there is conflict between the parent and child?
- How will I encourage the parent to leave if they are upset?

If we as early years practitioners can be humble enough to ask parents to share their expertise about their child, then we can learn a lot from them about their child's individual needs and interests. For example, the parent can tell us how the child likes to be comforted when they are upset – successful strategies the parent uses to settle their child. If the child is struggling to engage with you, then ask the parent what the child really enjoys doing and plan this for the next time the child attends the setting. Remember that the parent is an expert and can be of great value. These exchanges can be a learning opportunity for you and they will benefit your long-term relationship with the child. If parents can see you as not always having all the answers and at times making mistakes or not quite getting it right, then it may be easier for them to share some of their difficulties around parenting their child or to ask for support when their child is being challenging.

A key person approach

A key person approach is now commonplace in most early years settings and should have 'meaning and significance for those involved in it' (Elfer *et al.*, 2012: 40). A key person is seen as crucial in this relationship to support secure attachments for our youngest children and their families. There is good evidence to support the idea that secure attachments in early years settings are critical to children's healthy emotional and cognitive development.

Elinor Goldschmied reminds us about the importance of 'our internal textbooks'. By this she means 'drawing on our own experience ... and valuing it as a source of knowledge and

Figure 2.2 A worker greeting a parent

understanding'. From here, Goldschmied argued that 'we could be stronger in thinking, with the help of external as well as internal evidence, about the significance of building special relationships with the children for whom we have a professional responsibility'.

(Elfer *et al.*, 2012: 41)

The approach in practice

Figure 2.3 A parent and worker looking at an invitation together

The basis of a key person approach is that each child and their family are assigned or choose an individual practitioner within the setting. This can be problematic when children are using a setting for an extended day as staff will not necessarily be there for the whole day. However, a named practitioner itself would not ensure intimacy; for that it would be important to:

- carry out regular home visits
- greet the child and carer each day on arrival and facilitate a smooth separation and transition into the setting
- observe the child's play, interact with and support the play and plan to extend their learning and development in collaboration with parents where possible
- spend planned time with the child as an individual or in small groups each day.

During the child's time in your setting they will have to share their key person with other children and they will be cared for by other members of staff throughout the day as well, especially if your setting is open for extended days and offers a year-round service to children and families. The key person would be the person to make contact with the parents and share information about the child's time in the setting, building up a trust, respect and intimacy over time.

In some early years settings, the head, managers or supervisors may want to retain some overall responsibilities for children and families. In others, the responsibilities may be devolved and the practitioners take a lead on work with children and families who have been assigned to them. For example, the lead person at a Common Assessment Framework (CAF) meeting or attending case conferences could be the key person. If you are new to the role of key person you might want to assume responsibilities gradually until you feel more confident, or it could be difficult for you to take on this responsibility due to your setting's staffing ratios. If you work in a small setting or work on 1:13 ratio it can be very difficult to be released to attend meetings. If you are unable to attend a meeting it is good practice to send a report, as you might be the person (professionally) who knows the child best or the only advocate for that particular child.

Benefits

The primary benefit to the child is a strong emotional attachment to one key member of staff. However, the key person approach will benefit parents and carers too.

Carers may find it easier to share more intimate information or ask for advice if they are finding some aspects of their parenting difficult.

Each parent will get an individual greeting and be offered the opportunity to pass on any important information about their child, for instance if the child has eaten before coming to nursery or slept well. They may want to share a significant event with you, for example the arrival of a new pet or a family outing. This information can be used by you to further your intimate relationship with the child and to plan for possible future opportunities in the setting.

As an early years practitioner and key person you too can build on your skills and knowledge base through this approach.

Key information

Being a key person

If you have a child in your group with special rights, you might have the possibility to learn about the process for supporting children with additional needs. You may be the family's named person and take on the advocacy role.

You may learn the basics of other languages and cultures when supporting children in your group for whom English is an additional language. You might need to work with interpreters, which can change the way you build up a relationship with families.

You will be able to offer continuity of care as younger siblings come into your setting – you are already a trusted person whom the younger child in the family will know through daily contact and regular home visits.

Potential difficulties

What if a child doesn't want to come into your group?

Talk it through with the child and find out why. Plan opportunities that will excite and encourage the child to come to your group. Talk it through with the parents to see if they are aware of any worries their child may have, perhaps arrange another home visit to reconnect with the child in their domestic context.

You may have to accept that a child likes to spend time in another group as they have a particular friendship with a child or adult in that group.

What about holidays and illness?

If you are going on holiday, then plan in advance to make provision for your key children. Often children will choose a substitute themselves or they can be introduced to any 'supply' member of staff you intend using. If the same adults are available on a regular basis, then cover can be arranged if and when you are ill. Children with communication difficulties may need an object that represents you that they can refer to in your absence.

What if a child does not want to come to nursery?

It is important to talk through any issues with parents as they are likely to have deeper insights into their child's fears and worries. An extra home visit often helps to re-establish your relationship. Also talk about it honestly with the child. Respect their fears and reassure them that their mum or dad will come back each day.

Feedback from parents

It is important to constantly review what we offer families and also how the offer is made. Waiting outside to be admitted at 9 a.m., as a group, whatever the weather, does not seem very respectful of children's and parents' needs to say goodbye and to share information with key workers. Giving parents opportunities through a Parent Forum to provide written evaluations to offer feedback on your service can result in a constantly improving service.

Parents' meetings, whether for all parents or each key group, can be an arena to share what parents value and also where there could be improvements. When deciding on regular parent meetings, think about:
- time of day (to suit the majority)
- a crèche (to accommodate children)
- who will chair (and, therefore, who holds the power)
- who will take the minutes (or at least main points)
- making the minutes available to all participants
- making the meeting friendly and informal
- planning the agenda (and making sure parents' issues take precedence).

If the resources are not available to run meetings, then a flexible start or end to your day can offer the opportunity for parents to give impromptu feedback individually.

As a centre staff, we have devised many ways that parents can give and receive feedback:
- during the two-week settling-in period, when primary carers stay on site with their child
- during three home visits each year
- during daily exchanges with their key person
- on open evenings.

Record keeping

Each child has a Celebration of Achievements folder, which is a shared record of their development and learning over the one to two years that they attend the nursery. This consists of observations, drawings, photographs and assessments of learning. The portfolio is started by Family Workers, and parents and the children themselves contribute. When children leave nursery to start school they take this record with them and many families have reported that they and their children treasure them. Abbie's mum spoke of her sadness that her eldest daughter did not have a file as a keepsake as she had not attended our nursery.

Figure 2.4 Connor involved in writing and the result

In addition, when children have settled at nursery, after the first few weeks, Family Workers make a five-minute DVD of each child engaged in play and this is sent home for their family to enjoy. This gives parents the chance to be a 'fly on the wall' and see their child in action in the nursery. For parents who become involved in study groups, this is the start of a video record of their child's time at nursery, which is then added to regularly over the year or two years of attendance.

Figure 2.5 A dad helping his son use a saw

An enriched curriculum

Learning to Be Strong

Pen Green Nursery opened almost 30 years ago and its development has been shaped to some extent by events and by the people that form this community. It was always our intention to encourage children, parents and staff to feel strong but a tragedy (the murder of a five-year-old child on her way to school in Corby in 1986) prompted us to go much further by way of offering an assertiveness programme to young children preparing to leave nursery to move on to 'big school'. Initially, the parents using the nursery at that time were anxious about their children knowing how to keep themselves safe when they were not around. We worked with Michele Elliott, who conceptualised Kidscape, an anti-bullying programme for older children, to think about making the Learning to Be Strong programme appropriate for nursery-aged children. The programme has evolved over the years. Now we run five sessions in small groups for children who are preparing to leave nursery to go on to school:

- Friendship and conflict
- Bullying
- Play boundaries at home
- Dealing with strangers
- Feelings.

We work closely with parents and use role play, stories and toy figures to enact scenarios that prompt discussions with the children about these very serious issues. We offer and practise strategies, for example saying 'No' and asking for help if you are being bullied. The parents support us by providing information, for example about where their child is allowed to play. Written observations are made of each child's reactions and comments, which we feed back to the parents when they collect their children from nursery that day (Arnold & Prodger, 2006).

Residential trips to a farm

During the early 1990s some of our staff heard about a children's farm at Dodford near Birmingham, which was set up by the Cadbury family to give city children opportunities to experience the countryside and to come into close contact with animals. In 2011 for the 18th year Pen Green staff travelled to Dodford during the Spring Bank Holiday week with a small group of children to stay there for three days and two nights. A great deal of preparation precedes the trip each year: discussions with parents about whether their child is ready to take on the big challenge of sleeping over two nights without their parents; deciding who can go (sometimes we have to pick names out of a hat); discussing children's individual needs, sleep patterns and comforters and generally making preparations for a smooth trip. The children who go benefit greatly, becoming visibly more confident after the trip. The staff return exhausted but elated and the parents are extremely proud of their children and excited to hear about their experiences (Arnold, 2008).

Science Museum

Each year we offer parents and children the opportunity to visit the Science Museum in London, supported by their children's Family Workers. For some families it is the first time that they have visited London, as they have been too afraid to travel alone or unsure about where to go. Children and their parents travel to London on a coach and then spend the day in the Science Museum or Natural History Museum, depending on their child's interests. This outing is particularly popular with fathers, who will often take time off work to go with their family.

Professional development opportunities

Family Workers at Pen Green are highly trained professionals, who come to expect that their training needs will be met. A high proportion hold first degrees and several have studied masters modules. A few have masters degrees. In addition to their degree qualifications, they are given opportunities to learn about the key child development concepts used in the nursery (see Chapter 3), which complement and enhance the Early Years Foundation Stage Curriculum; working with parents; all aspects of safeguarding and first aid. We try to support any special interest and ensure any identified training needs are addressed. In addition, each worker is assigned a supervisor. Each worker and supervisor meet for one hour once a month. Both prepare for their meeting with the following three elements in mind:

- supervision and accountability of work with children and families
- support for personal issues
- professional development.

By keeping professional development on the agenda, it is hoped that together we can plan to meet individual aspirations as well as organisational needs.

Family Workers also have the opportunity to engage in work-based discussions focusing on their emotional responses to families, co-led by me and a consultant from the Tavistock Institute.

During the last two years, we have been working with the Northern School of Psychotherapy, which has been running a course for Pen Green staff called 'The Emotional Roots of Learning' (Miller *et al.*, 1989). The course has two parts: regularly observing a child closely over time and meeting fortnightly to discuss those observations, and taking part in a 'work-based discussion' (Elfer & Dearnley, 2007). Several Family Workers participate in this course and report that it has very great benefits in their work with children and families.

Points for discussion

- Consider what are the most important aspects of your role.
- Are you thinking about children as part of their families?
- How would you gather more information about each child's home learning environment and use the information to enhance what you provide?
- How can you demonstrate that you actively listen to and act on information provided by parents?

References

Arnold, C. (2008) 'Learning and Development – Risk: Away Days', *Nursery World*, 31 July.

Arnold, C. and Prodger, A. (2006) 'From Strength to Strength', *Nursery World,* 31 August.

Athey, C. (1990) *Extending Thought in Young Children: A parent-teacher partnership,* London: Paul Chapman.

Bruce, T. (1991) *Time to Play in Early Childhood Education,* Abingdon: Hodder & Stoughton.

DfE (Department for Education) (2012) *Statutory Framework for the Early Years Foundation Stage: Setting the standards for learning development and care for children from birth to five,* Cheshire: Crown Copyright.

Elfer, P. and Dearnley, K. (2007) 'Nurseries and emotional well-being: Evaluating an emotionally containing model of professional development', *Early Years*, vol. 27, no. 3, pp. 267–79.

Elfer, P., Goldschmied, E. and Selleck, D. (2012) *Key Persons in the Nursery: Building relationships for quality provision,* London: David Fulton.

Miller, L., Rustin, M., Rustin, M. and Shuttleworth, J. (eds) (1989) *Closely Observed Infants,* London: Duckworth.

Ministry of Education (1996) *Te Whãriki: Early childhood curriculum,* Wellington: Learning Media.

3 Engaging in a dialogue with parents about their children's learning

Cath Arnold and Annette Cummings

Everyone should do it! If everyone knew about schemas, there'd be fewer stressed parents!

(A parent who attended a study group)

Parents and professionals can help children separately or they can work together to the greater benefit of children.

(Athey, 2007: 209)

In this chapter, we will be introducing:

- the background and history of working with parents in education settings generally and particularly at the Pen Green Centre
- what we mean by 'dialogue' and why it is important
- the Involving Parents in Their Children's Learning research study and how it has impacted on developing a 'knowledge-sharing approach' across the Pen Green Centre and beyond.

Introduction

Many attempts have been made by professional educators to harness parents' interest in their children's education and learning. Much of this work has been underpinned by the belief and stereotype that schools and teachers know best and that they need to teach parents how to engage with their children at home, so that the children will do better at school. At the Pen Green Centre, we believe that parents have information to offer us about their children's learning at home and that we have a great deal to learn from them about their children's play and explorations.

Background

As long ago as 1967, in the Plowden Report, there was a whole chapter devoted to 'Participation by Parents' in which it was clearly stated that, 'There is certainly an association between parental encouragement and educational performance' (Plowden, 1967: 37). The Plowden Report also stated clearly that, 'At the heart of the educational process lies the child' (p.7). This is a sentiment we, at Pen

Green, agree with. Following this report, during the 1970s, 1980s and 1990s, many studies of home–school partnerships were carried out in the UK and the USA; Hannon and colleagues (1991) worked very successfully in Sheffield on promoting children's literacy with parents; Wolfendale (1989) led the way on studies of working with parents whose children have additional needs; Chrispeels and Rivero (2001) considered social class and ethnicity in relation to parental involvement in the USA with the goal being the realisation of potential; Bastiani was very active as part of the 'Nottingham Group' in thinking about a 'parent-centered' approach to working with parents (Atkin & Bastiani, 1988; Bastiani, 1989). The values of the Nottingham Group were close to the values that staff at Pen Green hold, in that parents' views were listened to and their experiences were valued; parents were seen as knowledgeable and it was recognised that when parents and professionals worked together, children achieved more in school (Atkin & Bastiani, 1988: 12–13). Much more recently, in a longitudinal study of 3,000 families, researchers have shown that the home learning environment (HLE) impacts most significantly on children's achievements in school (Sylva *et al.*, 2004).

Finding out about schemas

Staff at the Pen Green Centre worked with parents right from the setting up of the centre in 1983 – it was always for children *and families*. Gradually, groups were set up for parents (with a health, education or therapeutic focus) and for parents with their children (for example Messy Play, Baby Massage). In the mid-1980s staff first heard about schemas when a teacher from Sheffield joined the Pen Green team. In 1988 Chris Athey came to the Family Room at Pen Green to lead a teatime session on schemas for parents. Staff at Pen Green have never looked back!

During that session, 'one parent described how her son was hanging things from trees in the garden, tying ties and string all over the house, connecting up door handles and banisters' (Mairs *et al.*, 2012: xiii). This parent was quite worried about her son's play until Chris was able to explain and reassure her that he was exploring a schema called 'connecting' and that her son was repeating this action with different materials. Then, '18 years later the same mother talked about the first meeting with Chris Athey and how important it had been in terms of her developing understanding of her own child's learning' (Mairs *et al.*). Athey (2007: 50) defines schemas as:

> **A schema is a pattern of repeatable behaviour into which experiences are assimilated and that are gradually co-ordinated. Co-ordinations lead to higher level and more powerful schemas.**

From then on, staff have run sessions for parents about schemas on an annual basis, shortly after their children start attending nursery. For many years, these were led by Tina Bruce and facilitated by a member of the nursery team. Sessions were run in the morning, afternoon and evening so that the maximum number of nursery parents could attend. Schemas are 'patterns *of* action' and 'patterns *for* action' in the sense that we repeat the same action with different materials in order to find out what will happen (Athey, 2007). Young children seem to give attention to certain patterns for a while although there seems to be no strict hierarchical order that can be applied to all children. Gradually, our actions become co-ordinated and our schemas become complex concepts. Sharing information with parents about schemas is a sheer joy, as most parents immediately recognise any patterns their child is demonstrating.

Discovering 'involvement' as a concept

In early 1994, Pen Green Nursery was one of the pilot settings for the Effective Early Learning Project. This was when Pen Green staff began using 'involvement' as a tool for measuring and understanding how effectively we were meeting children's needs and interests in the nursery (Laevers, 1997; Pascal & Bertram, 1997). At that time, however, nursery staff were still running groups on learning, education and curriculum for parents, where the *staff* decided on the agenda. Staff might focus on maths or literacy or problem solving. The groups were fairly active and experiential but, nevertheless, staff decided on the topics in advance.

Ferre Laevers from the University of Leuven drew on Vygotsky's idea of the 'zone of proximal development' and Csikszentmihalyi's of 'flow' to come up with the concept of 'involvement' to signify 'deep level learning' (Vygotsky, 1978; Csikszentmihalyi, 1996). Vygotsky described the 'zone of proximal development' as the '"buds" or "flowers" of development rather than the "fruits" of development' (1978: 86). We understand this to mean that when children are on the cusp of understanding or mastering something, they are in the zone of proximal development, and, as adults, we can sometimes assist. Csikszentmihalyi described as 'flow' the feeling when we are highly motivated by an activity that sufficiently challenges us to fully engage. Both of these ideas are encapsulated by Laevers' concept of 'involvement', which he describes as 'An exploratory attitude, defined by openness for, and alertness to, the wide variety of stimuli that form our surroundings' (Laevers, 2000: 21). When people are deeply engaged we can recognise their involvement from their actions, body language and vitality. Laevers goes on to say that, 'Involvement goes along with strong motivation, fascination and total implication; there is no distance between person and activity, no calculation of possible benefits' (2000: 24). Parents readily take on and recognise involvement both in themselves and in their children. Laevers has come up with descriptors, signs of involvement and a scale, so that involvement can be measured (see Appendix A). When working with colleagues and parents, we emphasise that what we are measuring is how successfully we are meeting each child's needs and interests, not each child's ability or achievement.

Figure 3.1 A child deeply involved

The concept of well-being

Laevers went on to study the emotional well-being of young children and to describe signs of well-being and a scale to measure them (see Appendix B). As workers, we began sharing this concept with parents during settling-in and on home visits. We found, over time, that parents adopted the language associated with well-being, and were more likely to share with Family Workers any changes occurring at home that might impact on their child's well-being at nursery, partly because they knew of our interest and concern and partly because of our shared language.

At the Pen Green Centre, our second major research study focused on emotional well-being and resilience from 2001–04 (Arnold and the Pen Green Centre team, 2010). Researchers worked alongside a total of 58 families, filming children and discussing their well-being with their carers and workers. We studied 'attachment theory' (Bowlby, 1997 [1969]) and became familiar with the concepts of 'containment' (Bion, 1962) and 'holding' (Winnicott, 2006 [1965]). Studying these concepts helped us to more fully understand and to share with parents the importance of and the rationale for some of our established practices, for example:

- the key person system that has been in place since 1983, so that children make an attachment with a special person at nursery
- the two-week settling-in period at nursery when parents or carers are on site, so that children and families can develop trust and confidence in people in this new environment
- always saying goodbye even if that causes distress, so that gradually children come to understand that their parent/carer leaves and returns in a short time. Some children (and parents) particularly struggle with separation, and need help to talk about how best to handle separations (Charlwood & Steele, 2004).

Figure 3.2 A child separating from carer with the support of a worker

Developing our relationships with parents

The most significant study in relation to developing practice at Pen Green was the Froebel Study, carried out in London in the early 1970s and written up by Chris Athey in *Extending Thought in Young Children: A parent–teacher partnership*, which was published in 1990 and revised in 2007. The project was planned as a direct result of the Plowden Report's desire to 'increase knowledge of cognitive functioning in young children' (Athey, 1990: 218). The Froebel research team worked with 20 families over a period of two years. The plan was to gather examples of young children's learning, alongside their parents. Schematic theory was used very successfully as a framework for understanding each child's development and learning. Athey reports that 'a genuine "open-ended" type of enquiry was encouraged, with everyone working together to find patterns of cognition' (2007: 202). This shared search for meaning resulted in a more equal relationship between professionals and parents than was common at that time.

The importance of dialogue

As authors, we use the word 'dialogue' in our chapter title because dialogue is an important concept when it comes to our work with parents. Traditionally, teachers have told parents about education and about their children's achievements and rarely asked for or listened to the parents' views. Any parent who has attended an open evening at school in this country expects to hear how their child has done in class that year. Sometimes, the report focuses on behaviour and usually on how hard a child has been working and what they have achieved (in the classroom). At Pen Green we want to hear, acknowledge and respect the views and experiences of parents. We hope that we can engage in a two-way conversation with the parents using our services.

Paulo Freire, the Brazilian educator, famously wrote about 'dialogue' and made some important points that we can apply to our work with parents. He said that 'dialogue cannot exist without humility' and asks:

> How can I dialogue if I always project ignorance on to others and never perceive my own? How can I dialogue if I regard myself as a case apart from others – mere 'it's in whom I cannot recognize the other 'I's? ... How can I dialogue if I am closed to – and even offended by – the contribution of others?
>
> (Freire, 1970: 71)

Our understanding is that to engage in dialogue, we have to be humble, to identify with other humans and not to be so defensive about our knowledge that we cannot listen to or hear the views of the parents.

Through studying Freire and other texts, our staff team became more aware of our interactions with parents and of the power we held as professionals in relation to parents. Subsequently, we struggled with the idea of sharing our professional knowledge with parents, yet still having an equal relationship. During the mid-1990s we came across the work of Patrick Easen and colleagues (1992). He describes the kind of relationship that professionals and parents can have as a 'developmental partnership'. Easen articulates the distinct roles each bring to the partnership: the professional brings 'general child development theory', while the parent brings their 'personal theory' about their own child (1992: 285). The information that each brings can be seen as equal but different, and with both sets of information we have a better chance of understanding each child. This was already beginning to happen at Pen Green Nursery when we shared schema theory with parents.

The 'Involving Parents in Their Children's Learning' project

Phase one: developing a framework of effective pedagogic strategies

The research base at Pen Green was set up in March 1996 and the first small grant we secured was from the Teacher Training Agency. Our remit was to study 'Parental Involvement in Education'. By then we were using video quite often in the nursery so that we could reflect on children's actions, as a staff team and alongside parents. In that first study the staff worked with a small group of families. We filmed each child being settled in by their parent at the start of the day and then filmed the same child with their own Family Worker later on that same day. We invited the parents to share a nice lunch, and together we watched the filmed clips and tried to work out what was most helpful to each child in terms of our pedagogical approach. This extended discussion resulted in a list of 'pedagogical strategies' that we could use as a framework for thinking about our pedagogy.

Key information

Effective pedagogical strategies:
1. Subtle intervention.
2. Knowledge of a child's embedded context, and ability to recall the child's previous experience.
3. Affirmation of the child through facial expression and physical closeness.
4. Encouraging children to make choices and decisions.
5. The adult supports the child in taking appropriate risks.
6. The adult encourages the child to go beyond the adult's own knowledge base and accompany them into new experiences.
7. The adult has an awareness of the impact of their own attitudes and beliefs and how these might affect the child's learning.
8. The adult demonstrates learning as a partnership; the adult is committed to their own learning and generates a spirit of enquiry.

(Whalley & Arnold, 1997)

This study has been repeated many times in the centre over the years, and most recently in 2012, by parents and staff in the Baby Nest (due for future publication). It is never easy being filmed, as it can feel as though the person holding the camera also holds the power, so an agreement has to be made beforehand about the ethical approach. In the original study, nursery staff each had a 'buddy' whom they trusted, and they filmed each other and viewed the material first. It can be embarrassing to watch and listen to oneself but it also provides a great opportunity for learning. It turned out that the parents were less embarrassed about being filmed than the staff.

Phase two: bringing together four key child-development concepts to share with all nursery parents

Following the success of this small study, the Esmée Fairbairn Trust funded a three-year study called Involving Parents in Their Children's Learning from 1997 to 2000. This funding gave us the opportunity to extend our work right across the nursery population (60 families each year at that time) and to examine closely all the different ways that parents became involved in their children's learning. Every contact with families was documented over the three years, including which member of the family attended or was visited.

Over the three years we managed to engage in a dialogue with 84 per cent of parents about their children's learning (Whalley, 2007). The information gathered informed our highly differentiated planning for each child. We developed a diagram called the 'Pen Green Loop' to illustrate the process of home learning informing what was planned at nursery, and nursery learning informing what parents provided for their children at home (see Figure 2.1, page 17).

We realised that in order to dialogue with parents about their children's learning, we needed a shared conceptual framework. This gave us the language to discuss each child's development and learning with their parents. We had been developing that language over a number of years by sharing the following frameworks with parents:

Key information

Frameworks shared with parents

- Schemas (Athey, 1990 and 2007)
- Involvement (Laevers, 1997)
- Well-being (Laevers, 1997)
- Pedagogic strategies (Whalley & Arnold, 1997)

As part of the study, we formalised the sharing of all four *key child development concepts* with parents when their children first started attending nursery, by running sessions for parents to attend during the settling-in period. This *shared conceptual framework* has been highly significant in improving our practice in working with families right across the centre, and workers from other authorities and settings have reported similar positive results in how effectively they dialogue with parents and plan for children's learning in a more authentic way.

Our approach to running key concept sessions for parents

The environment

Whenever parents are invited to a group or meeting, we create a comfortable and informal environment, where workers greet parents individually, offer them a hot drink and a comfortable armchair to sit down on, and generally try to help them to feel at home. Whenever possible, we arrange the chairs in a circle, so that it looks more like a living room than a classroom. This informal approach tends to work well with mothers. With fathers, we modify our approach and emphasise the importance of the key concept session to their child's education (Whalley, 2007).

Timing

Nursery staff run a morning, afternoon and evening session when parents are given a 'taster' about all four concepts. They normally do this during the two-week settling-in period so that, at least during the day, parents or carers are on site anyway. As workers, we have experimented with doing this in different ways, for example one session on 'well-being' and 'involvement' and a second session on 'schemas' and 'pedagogic strategies'. However, due to the introduction of single-formula funding and the prospect of a 'headcount day' which forms the basis for our nursery funding, there is a lot more pressure than previously to start children at nursery during the first two weeks. So in 2012 staff introduced the four concepts together during the sessions and the majority of parents attended, including lots of dads.

Invitations

As well as putting up a poster in the nursery, parents are invited individually to attend both by letter and in person, through their Family Worker. This helps as we do not always know at this stage the parents' level of literacy, and there are now many families who speak English as an additional language attending our setting.

Running the key concepts session

Usually, two workers run a session. They plan ahead and agree on their roles. It can help if one keeps the task in mind and the other gives attention to the process, how individuals are in the group, sometimes supporting parents by sitting alongside them and offering information about their child at nursery, which the parent can match with information from home. We use videos of children to illustrate the concepts and this is helpful for all parents but particularly for those working in English as an additional language.

Running study groups for parents

As part of the three-year research study, weekly study groups for parents were developed, during which Family Workers and parents view videos of children at nursery and sometimes at home, and engage in an ongoing dialogue, using the four key concepts as frameworks for understanding each child's development and learning.

Figure 3.3 A study group

The parents call the study groups 'PICL groups' (Parents' Involvement in Their Children's Learning). The group runs from October through to July during a morning, an afternoon and an evening once a week to give each family a chance to attend. Although not every parent attends a weekly study group, the 'developmental partnership' and knowledge-sharing approach is well established and is used by workers across the centre in their interactions with families, whether during the spontaneous daily conversations or on a home visit.

The same principles are used when setting up study groups as when setting up one-off sessions:

- creating a comfortable and welcoming environment
- hot drinks to welcome participants
- running one morning, afternoon and evening each week
- two Family Workers running each group
- a crèche available for younger children
- open to all parents.

When we first began running study groups back in 1997, the workers had to make a shift from *being in charge* of the agenda and leading sessions to *listening to what the parents had to say* about their children. This was quite difficult for some workers at first but we were soon convinced by the rich discussions that ensued.

Figure 3.4 A parent looking at her child's Celebration of Achievements folder during a study group

Example from practice

After moving from Doncaster to Corby I started the PICL group late in the year after my grandson settled into nursery. It took me a while to find my feet but as I started the second year I found it easier to express myself. The discussion after the video was very beneficial, as other mums saw things I didn't see and this helped me to see more in what my grandson was doing. It made me more aware what he was doing and what he was capable of doing. I realised that Nathan was resilient and tough and didn't need me around so much. It was good to see him on the video and what he was doing in nursery. It helped me to understand him better. The PICL group gave me a chance to talk, moan and cry. I think it helped everybody who went, both mums and their children. The group gelled together and we could trust each other. We bounced ideas off each other and helped each other. When Nathan's trajectory schema was driving me mad, his perpetual throwing and kicking a ball in the house and losing the ball over the next door neighbour's wall, one mum suggested that I put a blanket on the washing line to stop the ball going over. Another mum suggested an indoor basket ball and soft balls outdoors. Over time Nathan's trajectory schema became more refined and purposeful; he knew not to throw indoors anymore. I was encouraged to let Nathan throw, but to do it in a more controlled way.

The support and ideas from other parents were what was very helpful to this grandparent, in encouraging her grandson's play. This shows that the knowledge-sharing approach adopted is democratic and not dependent on 'expert' workers imparting knowledge to parents.

How the study groups developed

For the first three years (1997–2000), the Family Workers documented each child's learning in their Celebration of Achievements nursery folder with contributions from parents. We then experimented with putting together portfolios of children's special interests but with the support of the parents this time. Then parents began documenting their children's development and learning during the time they attended the study group and we approached the Open College to gain accreditation for two modules: Theories of Child Development at level 2 and Observing a Child's Development at levels 2 and 3. We were anxious at first that introducing accreditation might change the nature of the group, which was based mainly on discussion and viewing video. However, most parents who attend groups do submit a portfolio for accreditation, and some have found the process transformational in their own confidence and knowledge about their child's development and learning. When parents gain accreditation, they receive a certificate from the Open College and we usually have an event with photos in the local newspaper.

As mentioned, the group runs weekly from October through to July and parents and workers spend up until around Easter discussing the learning, and then from Easter to July putting together the portfolios, which are all completely individual.

Example from practice
Example from practice

A parent portfolio (excerpts from Hannah's portfolio about Mackenzie)

Page 1 Mackenzie with high well-being

Mackenzie shows high well-being when he has been given the freedom to choose his activity. He shows excitement and vitality in his play. He will become much more vocal and want others to acknowledge his achievements but can also become quite coy when he feels he is the centre of attention in a group. Mackenzie will call out to grab others' attention to view his work and use facial expressions to show he is pleased with himself. His eyes will be bright and he will be full of energy.

Page 2 Mackenzie with low well-being

Mackenzie sometimes struggles with separation in the mornings at nursery and will have low well-being. He becomes anxious and clings to me and will not settle at an activity. Once I have left, Mackenzie will seek out reassurance from a familiar adult and his well-being will begin to increase after a cuddle and once he has found something of interest that he would like to do.

Figure 3.5 Mackenzie with high well-being

Page 3 Mackenzie with high involvement

Mackenzie shows a particularly high involvement level when building with the wooden blocks in nursery. He enjoys independently building structures and is fully absorbed for long periods of time and not easily distracted. He shows persistence when building more intricately or, if his construction falls, he will stand back and think of how he can rectify it. Mackenzie shows creativity in his buildings and their symmetry and shows complexity in making structures with purpose. Mackenzie demonstrates a strong trajectory schema when building with blocks. He builds tall, straight and symmetrical constructions repeatedly.

Page 4 Mackenzie with low involvement

Mackenzie can sometimes show a low level of involvement when asked to take part in an activity he is not interested in. He will not interact with other children or participate in the group activity. Mackenzie will walk away from the activity or look around the room. He will be easily distracted by other things and show his lack of interest by his facial expressions and body language.

Page 5 Mackenzie's schemas

Mackenzie demonstrates his 'transformation' schema in a number of 'experiments' that he has made. He shows a sequence of transformation in his kitchen experiments by adding ingredients one at a time and noticing the changes that occur after each addition. Mackenzie has also shown reversible transformation in his experiment with 'Jellybaff' crystals, which turn his bath water into jelly and then back to water.

Figure 3.6 Mackenzie preparing to experiment

Page 6 Mackenzie's schemas

Mackenzie has explored his 'enclosure' schema since he was very young. He enjoys all aspects of dressing up and will role play while dressed up as his favourite superheroes. This also shows symbolic representation.

Figure 3.7 Mackenzie enclosing and enveloping himself

Figure 3.7 (Continued) Mackenzie
enclosing and enveloping himself

Adult teaching strategies

We have supported Mackenzie's interest in volcanoes in several ways. Mackenzie first became interested when his Family Worker, Tracy, made a vinegar and bicarbonate of soda volcano at nursery. When Mackenzie came home, he began asking questions about how volcanoes work and where the closest volcano is. I couldn't answer Mackenzie's questions, so we had a look online at videos of volcanoes and websites with information about them and I ordered a science book for us to read together.

Developing Mackenzie's interest further, we made the volcano experiment at home and took our volcano into nursery to recreate it with Tracy's group at storytime.

Mackenzie visited the Science Museum in London with his dad and nursery and really enjoyed the volcano section there. He spent a long time looking at the pieces of hard lava and watching the big screens with footage from a volcano.

This is one example of many where, through dialogue, learning at home extends to nursery and vice versa. Another benefit is that Hannah has been able to share information with Mackenzie's other special people. She reflects: 'Since I have had Mackenzie's brother, Oliver, their dad, Darren, has been bringing Mackenzie to Dads' Group on a Saturday and the staff have planned making volcanoes in the Beach area. They buried the hosepipe in the sand and turned the water on and watched as the water shot up in the air.'

Figure 3.8 Mackenzie making a volcano in the Beach area at Pen Green

Hannah continues: 'Mackenzie's interest in transformation is now commonplace in my house and my mum's. I have explained to Mum about schemas and PICL and now she understands why Mackenzie does the things he does and is okay with it. Mum now lets Mackenzie experiment in the kitchen; he has a mixing bowl and is allowed to make potions from the contents of the cupboards to see what happens when they are all mixed together.'

The challenges of working in this way

As with all of our practice, there are some challenges to working in this way:

- Having the equipment to film and show video to parents can be expensive.
- Some staff struggle with the technical side, for example copying films on to DVDs so families have their own personal copy, which we are committed to doing.
- Staff being released to run groups can be an issue although the whole remit of children's centres is to engage with families.
- Time is always at a premium but sometimes we have to question our own use of time – what we choose to spend time doing may not be the best use of our time.
- Including all families whatever their first language can be difficult, but we do find that video and photos help the communication.

The whole process takes a long time, so it's not the kind of 'quick fix' programme that the government often recommends, a six-week 'prescription' for being a better parent. However, we are interested in outcomes and in making a real difference to children and families, so we are currently working on creating a self-evaluation tool (with parents) to measure change over time.

Over the years, this knowledge-sharing approach has become widely used beyond Pen Green; while, at Pen Green, it is much more widely used than in study groups for nursery parents. If we can engage parents and carers in discussing their children's development and learning and being knowledgeable about these four child development concepts, then often relationships between parents and children improve and parents become more confident and stronger advocates for their children when they start attending school.

Example from practice

Using a 'knowledge-sharing' approach on home visits

A parent whose worker visits her at home and uses the same approach reports: 'My little girl is a transporter. It was a nightmare and we used to have fights with her all the time because I didn't want her to take her pram because she was a nightmare pushing her pram everywhere, but then I thought, after Carol started talking about transporting, that I might as well stop fighting with her. So now she takes it everywhere with her. She's two and there are bollards near the school and she has to count them every time we go past there. She can count up to 14. I'm like, "You're two! That's brilliant!!"'

There are many similar accounts of parents beginning to understand their young children's motives and, therefore, developing better relationships.

Professional development for staff

The Pen Green Research Base staff regularly run a three-day professional development opportunity based on the research and practice on 'Involving Parents in Their Children's Learning' carried out in the Pen Green Centre. Newly appointed staff can attend and carry out their own study of one child and a piece of work with colleagues that helps them explore their own understanding of work with parents and the related power imbalance issues. There are also opportunities for staff to attend initial groupwork training as well as more extended experiential groupwork training (see Chapter 6 for more details). There are also opportunities to consider schemas in more depth by attending a two-day course on schemas.

Just as we would want to provide opportunities for children to follow their interests, we want staff and parents to identify where their interests lie and, as a Centre Leadership Team, we do our best to provide opportunities to follow those interests, either within our organisation or elsewhere.

Points for discussion

- Think about the last conversation you had with a parent – who was offering information to whom? Where does most of the power lie in your relationship?
- How do you share the child development theories you use with parents using your setting? How might you now approach parents with information about child development?
- How do you gather information from parents about what their children become involved with at home? How are you using that information?
- How does each child make the transition from attachment to parent to relationship with nursery worker?

References

Arnold, C. and the Pen Green Centre team (2010), *Understanding Schemas and Emotion in Early Childhood*, London, Sage.

Athey, C. (1990) *Extending Thought in Young Children: A parent–teacher partnership*, London: Paul Chapman.

Athey, C. (2007) *Extending Thought in Young Children: A parent–teacher partnership* (2nd edn), London: Paul Chapman.

Atkin, J. and Bastiani, J., with Goode, J. (1988) *Listening to Parents: An approach to the improvement of home–school relations*, London: Croom Helm.

Bastiani, J. (1989) *Working with Parents: A whole-school approach*, London: Routledge.

Bion, W. (1962) *Learning Through Experience*, London: Heinemann.

Bowlby, J. (1997) [1969] *Attachment and Loss. Vol. 1: Attachment*, London, Pimlico.

Charlwood, N. and Steele, H. (2004) 'Using attachment theory to inform practice in an integrated centre for children and families', *European Early Childhood Education Research Journal*, vol. 12, no. 2, pp. 59–74.

Chrispeels, J. (1996) 'Effective schools and home-school-community partnership roles: a framework for parent involvement', *School Effectiveness and School Improvement*, vol. 7, no. 4, pp. 297–323.

Chrispeels, J. and Rivero, E. (2001) 'Engaging Latino families for student success: how parent education can reshape parents' sense of place in the education of their children', *Peabody Journal of Education*, vol. 76, no. 2, pp. 119–69.

Csikszentmihalyi, M. (1996) *Creativity: Flow and the Psychology of Discovery and Invention*, New York: Harper Perennial.

Easen, P., Kendall, P. and Shaw, J. (1992) 'Parents and educators: dialogue and development through partnership', *Children and Society*, vol. 6, no. 4, pp. 282–96.

Freire, P. (1970) *Pedagogy of the Oppressed*, London: Penguin.

Hannon, P. and Nutbrown, C. (2001) 'Outcomes for children and parents of an early literacy education parental involvement programme', paper presented at the British Educational Research Association Annual Conference, Sept. 2001, Leeds.

Hannon, P., Weinberger, J., and Nutbrown, C. (1991) 'A study of work with parents to promote early literacy development', *Research Papers in Education*, vol. 6, no. 2, pp. 77–97.

Laevers, F. (1997) *A Process-Oriented Child Follow-Up System for Young Children*, Leuven: Centre for Experiential Education.

Laevers, F. (2000) 'Forward to basics! Deep-level-learning and the experiential approach', *Early Years*, vol. 20, no. 2, pp. 20–9.

Mairs, K. and the Pen Green Centre team (2012) *Young Children Learning Through Schemas: Deepening the dialogue about learning in the home and in the nursery*, London: Routledge.

Pascal, C. and Bertram, A. (1997) *Effective Early Learning*, London: Hodder & Stoughton.

Plowden, B. (1967) *Children and Their Primary Schools: A report of the Central Advisory Council for Education (England)* (Plowden Report), London: HMSO.

Proulx, J. (2006) 'Constructivism: A re-equilibration and clarification of the concepts, and some potential implications for teaching and pedagogy', *Radical Pedagogy*, vol. 8, no. 1.

Siraj-Blatchford, I. and Siraj-Blatchford, J. (2010) *Improving Children's Attainment through a Better Quality of Family-based Support for Early Learning*, London: Centre for Excellence and Outcomes in Children and Young People's Services (C4EO). Available from http://www.c4eo.org.uk/themes/earlyyears/familybasedsupport/files/c4eo_family_based_support_full_knowledge_review.pdf.

Sylva, K., Melhuish, E., Sammons, P., Siraj-Blatchford, I. and Taggart, B. (2004) *The Effective Provision of Pre-school Education (EPPE) Project: Final report*, London: DfES.

Vygotsky, L. S. (1978) *Mind in Society*, London: Harvard University Press.

Whalley, M. (2007) *Involving Parents in Their Children's Learning* (2nd edn), London: Paul Chapman.

Whalley, M. and Arnold, C. (1997), *Parental Involvement in Education: Summary of research findings*, London: Teacher Training Agency.

Winnicott, D. W. (2006) [1965] *The Family and Individual Development*, London: Routledge Classic.

Wolfendale, S. (1989) *Parental Involvement: Developing networks between school, home and community*, London: Cassell.

4

Developing advocacy for children with special rights

Joanne Armstrong and Robert Orr

In this chapter we:
- describe how a group for parents of children with special rights was conceptualised
- give feedback from three parents who used the group
- provide some theory underpinning what typically happens in groups.

Introduction

The Pen Green Centre is a patchwork, a network of inter-related social sets that interlock and jostle for space and energy. From time to time a new fragment emerges that smacks of individuality, yet has the taste and tone of belonging to a recognisable tradition. Pen Green has its share of parents confronting the daily and nightly uproar of tending to children with special rights, for whom so many services just don't seem to be a snug fit. For most of its 30-year life, a group of parents, nearly always mothers, has met every Monday morning and taken stock of what it means to draw on, or drag a service out of, the statutory and voluntary agencies. A new group was recently called into being with a different focus on special rights – to be of practical use in the exhausting process of carving out a pathway through the educational and social jungle.

Joanne on setting up the group

I'm Joanne Armstrong and I wrote a booklet describing my daughter Hope's challenges, which I distributed to the nursery staff when I realised that they had stopped asking me questions about her and her needs. Then they all had the essential basic information about Hope that they were reluctant to ask for. I wrote in very simple terms so that children too could understand it. Then, I thought a group of other parents might enjoy the opportunity to compare notes about communicating information, and perhaps end some of the isolation they might be experiencing. I invited Robert Orr to co-lead the group, having known him around the centre and having read his book (Orr, 2003), based on his experience in special education and running a residential school for the Royal National Institute for the Blind for children with multiple disabilities.

My daughters were using the nursery. The booklet on Hope, who has achondroplasia, was written so that I could bypass the squillionth request for information on my child's history, prognosis and needs from professionals, friends and other centre users. In my role as a parent-governor (and user of a Home-Start volunteer) I had come across Robert, who had been facilitating the parent group and group psychology courses, and we got talking about the centre head's suggestion that we got together another parent group but with the specific task of producing such booklets so that new people could readily reach an understanding of each child.

Figure 4.1 Learning the IT skills required

Moving forward

We knew we were not going to narrowly pursue the first practical objective (producing the booklets), but would take our time to discuss, at the speed the participants could manage, the intricacies of the children's conditions and the impact these were making on them, their social networks and the public services. We knew from the outset that we would want to take an emancipatory and participatory 'action research' approach (Boog, 2003) to publishing our findings in what promised to be a research project with a therapeutic subtext.

The first five people who responded to personal requests to pilot the project were variously forthright and militant, shy and accepting, angry and belligerent: all were staggeringly perceptive about their own child as well as funny and interested in the idea of spending time together to thrash out individual conclusions. Scales fell from our eyes as the stories unfolded and we came to an understanding of how stirring our companionship was becoming. We were good for each other.

It is amazing how the mother of two boys with autism can contribute to the discussion of a boy who uses sign and breathes through a tracheostomy – and vice versa. The effort of explaining to each other taught us how we would need to communicate to an even more naïve audience. We had pictured ten weeks of talk and word processing, but the first cohort stretched to 12 weeks and not everybody finished up with a booklet as envisaged. For some of us, sickness, the trauma of diagnosis or treatments during the course of the project meant that the work was not always sustained to completion. Some made the booklet and did not use it, some distributed multiple versions to different audiences – their child's peers, the school staff, medics. We learned to manipulate many photographs and little text and had IT support to achieve it. We invited community health specialists and psychologists to address us on topics we chose collectively.

Example from practice
Example from practice

Cassie's story

I have two boys with autism. Walter is 14 and the older brother; he is governed by routines and delayed in his personal care skills. Allan is the younger brother and rarely speaks to children or adults – it was for his network of contacts that I wrote an illustrated booklet explaining his silence. The boys and their father are Asian. I brought the boys to the UK so that they could get specialist help in their schooling. They travel to see their father infrequently because of the cost. Both will be called on to do National Service there when they are 18, one in the police and one in the army. I am a Home-Start volunteer and also care daily for my young niece, who is developing typically. I work part-time for the NHS and attend Robert's other groups at the children's centre on psychology and relationships.

What was the impact of your experience in the group? Tell me about the difference it has made.

It has enabled me to demonstrate to people that Allan has a distinct personality with interests and experiences of his own. By talking to the other group members I was able to clarify just what it was I needed to tell people and how simple it needed to be, with more pictures than words.

I made new friends and asked all the awkward questions about their children that I would never normally have the opportunity to ask, and they did the same with me. I now know about tracheostomies, for example. Allan's teacher refers to his 'silent stutter' and selective, not elective, mutism but I wanted to stress his normality, that he can hear and that his silence does not mean he does not like you.

I had several weeks to talk through my experience and listen to the others' experiences before we embarked on the writing on computers. There was no rush and we were free to say as much as we wanted to say. We talked about our pet hates and the struggles we have dealing with people's reactions to our children.

It was so good to speak to people who did not judge you but could acknowledge difference without seeing it as *less than* – as Temple Grandin puts it (Grandin, 1996; Jackson, 2010). Each time I watch the film about her I am struck by Allan's similar experience to her shoe reaction – when you mention the word to her she pictures every shoe she ever wore and it takes time. When Allan hears a girl ask if she can open a window, he visualises every window he has ever dealt with, all the types of fastening and opening. Mind boggling!

I felt a bond with the other parents – a bond that cannot be found with parents whose children are not having the sort of difficulties ours were encountering. Other parents cannot readily empathise. Meeting this group brings it all home. I thought that Robert understood because of his long involvement with special needs (Orr, 2003), although he has not had children of his own with special needs.

Why would anyone feel sorry for me? I am not sorry I had these beautiful boys I love, they are my normal children. We can laugh and joke about them as a way of overcoming the frustration and alienation – we are entitled to be ironic. I am frustrated by Walter's brightness (he wants to be a forensic scientist) yet he can take 18 months to learn to use an electric toothbrush and manipulate it with arm movements. I don't want him to be useless, in a bedsit, on the dole. I want him to be a contributor. He will, like his dad, love the army and its regimentation but I fear he may be placed in civil defence and his brother in the army where he will want to drive tanks – his present obsession.

I have used the booklet about Allan which I made on the course at airports, scouts, at school transition. I feel I have succeeded in communicating that he has a personality all his own. After a year in his new class he has begun to speak to a teaching assistant.

In the group I got a clearer understanding of how others perceive our children. It turns out the others love to be questioned, anything rather than be stared at and looked away from!

I came to the subsequent group that was run in order to offer my experience and show how a book might turn out. I saw the same calming effect where we were put at our ease and allowed time to explore ideas about our children and how to communicate our knowledge to others. I loved to hear how Joanne had helped Hope's classmates appreciate some of her difficulties when she challenged them to open a door using their elbows to simulate having very short arms. It was so unlike listening to specialists who can be amazingly unaware of the everyday complexity of living with disability.

The many different parents I met had a huge range of difficulties and contrasting sets of priorities. The blunt questions showed how we knew absolutely everything about our own children and absolutely nothing of each other's. The internet cannot tell you about your own child, our own expertise can.

If I were running a group I would focus more on catering – food can be such a social lubricant. People are usually willing to bring food and share it. I'd have a ready-made example of a book, perhaps of a fictional child.

I am delighted with my end product – the booklet does not mention autism, just my boy Allan.

Themes emerged that drew on people's new-found expertise in their areas. Cassie, for example, runs a support group for parents of children with autism and was a mine of information on diagnoses and various doctors' usefulness. We would assist each other on making appointments. It seems easier to be assertive for someone else than to clamour for medics' attention for our own needs. We were full of useful tips for each other – the sort of stuff that makes you miss the participants when the time is up.

Example from practice

Mary's story

My name is Mary and I have two children. I have Jenny who is seven and Thomas who is six. I have been coming to the Pen Green Centre basically since they were born. I used to use all the groups – Baby Massage, Growing Together, 'Drop-in' – and then both children went through nursery at Pen Green.

I was asked to join the Hope Project by Joanne because Tom was about to start school and was showing signs of and has traits of Aspergers, as yet undiagnosed. He finds social interaction and social situations difficult. He has some problems with sensory issues – he can't bear labels on clothing, or people touching him when they are wet, for example. I found the Hope Project group very interesting because I was able to talk to other people who had the same issues and people who found it difficult to explain what was going on with their special children to people. If you look at Tom most of the time he looks quiet and angelic but when he does go off on one it can be quite violent and disruptive. There were other people in the group who had children with other disabilities and it was good to bounce ideas off each other. People would tell me what they thought might be important to know or might help people know how to deal with Tom and how to keep him calm.

In the book I started off with stories about Tom – what he likes, what makes him happy, his favourite topics like Spiderman, Batman (anything superhero). I put some pictures in of him playing in his home environment and then I told them what he didn't like. What would set him off, what would make him angry, what could make him cry, and gave ideas on how to defuse the situation and calm him down and make him feel a bit better. I found the group interesting and I would encourage other people to join it if they are having problems or they don't know how to explain to people about their child. I used it because Tom was going to school and I made a little book for the teachers so they were aware of some of the issues that Tom may have. I've been using Pen Green forever so I kind of know that Pen Green is giving me that sense that I can stand up for my child and I can say what I want done for him and I don't need to accept what teachers may say, I am not afraid to speak up and tell them what I expect for my child. The Pen Green 'image of the child' (McKinnon, forthcoming) is that they feel strong, in control, able to question and able to make choices. This way of working makes us, the parents, also stronger, more in control, able to make the right choices and question what we do not understand or agree with. The Hope Project sessions reinforced my sense of being in control (see Malaguzzi, 1993: 10).

As group leaders, we encouraged people to gain the view of their close relatives who also have a refined sense of the child and family's unique needs; they can, and did, contribute to the content and style of the booklets. It became apparent that a parent might need to join in more than one set of sessions if their work was not done, if they had not reached a 'Gestalt' cycle (Perls, 1969) of resolution and accepted the issues they were chewing over in the company of this peer group.

Example from practice

Example from practice

Martha's story

Martha was assured by Robert that 'if at any time you do not wish your account to be included at all you need only say to Joanne or me and that will be absolutely fine, there is no need to believe that you have to agree to be involved if it later turns out that it is not what you want to do'.

Martha has a son Bill and younger daughter Elsa. Martha has difficulty with walking and balancing because of a motor problem associated with muscular dystrophy. She describes her condition as a 'manifest carrier' of the gene as she is both affected by it and can pass it on to her children. Recently it has been confirmed that Bill has Duchenne's muscular dystrophy, which is life-threatening. She is in contact with adults with the condition and has seen how profound the effect on Bill will be. At six years of age, he is not yet aware of the nature of his illness though he knows his movements and posture are different from his peers'. He has a close friend at school who is very small for his age and both of them have adapted seating. Many of Martha's friends and family seem to avoid spending time with them, apparently finding a deteriorating condition too much to bear. It seems Elsa is not affected.

How did you get involved in the Hope Project?

I met Joanne in a sewing group at the Pen Green Centre and she invited me to join the Hope Project when we discussed my concerns about Bill's motor problems and her concerns about her daughter Hope with achondroplasia.

What was the impact on you of being in the group?

When I joined I no longer felt alone. We talked to each other about our special children and I felt understood – we were all in the same boat. I felt able to include Robert with his experience though his own children do not have special needs. When I talk to my partner or my parents we get upset but in the group I found strong people who didn't cry. They were strong enough to listen. I didn't feel alienated. I was able to say all the things that other people back off from. Even close family avoid spending time with us – perhaps muscular dystrophy is just too awful for them to contemplate.

We worked well together, smoothly, I felt it come alive, felt welcomed and wanted to stay longer after the job was done. Another mother in the group has a boy in Bill's class so we are always in touch. She doesn't avoid the important topics and is happy to answer my questions – I hate people avoiding me.

I was able to describe my limb-girdle dystrophy and the significance of being a manifest carrier, meaning that I am affected and can pass the gene on. At the time of our meetings I was going through tests and discovered the diagnosis was not confirmed – I lost my sense of identity and discovered that Bill had Duchenne's, a life-threatening condition. My daughter is a nimble climber and is not affected; my sister tells me she has been tested and is clear too. I cried with relief, not envy. My brother walks oddly but is not seeking to be tested. I can tell you all about XX and XY chromosomes now.

Every day I wake up is a nightmare – two months ago I was expecting to be told of a cure but have been disappointed. Instead I am offered only steroids.

I liked my time in the group. I was not judged, no fingers were pointed. We promised not to gossip about what we learned about each other, we understood and supported each other. The contrasting conditions involved made a good mix. I am ready to produce a booklet but am waiting until Bill becomes aware of what his form of dystrophy implies. I would hate people to have more knowledge than he has of himself. His peers speak of his 'poorly legs' or 'poorly back'.

What else would you like to add?

I am in contact with a young man with Duchenne's who I saw on *Embarrassing Bodies* on TV (Maverick TV, 2012) – he is my hero! He works in computing, has a great sense of humour and recently posted a two-word message online: *Duchenne's sucks*. He has a knack of knowing what to say!

My mother is always online researching the disease but talks to me very little about it. I struggle seeing my partner's family leaving us out of events, spending more time with the other grandchildren. My sister can hardly manage five minutes with us. I see more of Bill's best friend and his delightful mother. Nobody's coming round. I want to get it sorted but I don't know how – but I have discovered that shouting at my mother and throwing things, telling her I wish she hadn't had me, are not the answer!

Thank goodness for my Pen Green Family Support worker and the brilliant Growing Together sessions where the staff knew Bill and keep asking after him while I am there watching how Elsa learns. My Family Worker in the nursery and the head are like old friends and I have new ones from the Hope Project group now as we bonded over what was happening to our children.

It took time to decide what to write, getting the ideas of what to do. The group was just one more of the many things that help me get through each day.

Robert on leading the group

At the centre we run a masters level stand–alone unit on groupwork in which the leadership of groups is unpicked. There is an emphasis on the relationship between the facilitating pair and other pairings within the group (what Wilfred Bion calls 'basic assumption *Pairing*'). Joanne and I took the Freudian view that people internalise the male/female partnerships they witness as children and then see new couples in the same terms, so we would have to deal with the ghosts of other couples in our relating to each other, and also in relating to the participants who would view us unwittingly as they viewed couples in the long past (what is sometimes called 'the unthought known' [Bollas 1987]). The same happens with other pairings that emerge, moment by moment, between one member and one of the facilitators or between two group members. Another activity in any group is task avoidance (Bion's 'basic assumption *Fight/Flight*') where people inadvertently steer conversation away or resist the task. Then there is dependency ('basic assumption *Dependency*'), often on the leaders or sometimes on other members who offer an alternative to the leaders for people to follow passively, instead of doing the work themselves (Bion, 1961).

Joanne and I unpicked our relationship and roles after each meeting, with nods in the direction of psychodynamic theory and the possible implications for the members of the Hope Project group. We were aware of the intensity of the content and the birth-to-death themes explored. There were tearful and stressful moments and the constant throb of imminent revelations about parenthood, couples and disability. There was discussion about member attendance and absence and we detected a tone of grieving for the adults that these children would not become. We reconfirmed our determination that we would allow attention to stay on the *process* of what was happening with the participants and us, rather than on the *end product* of the informative booklets (see, for example, Aram *et al.*, 2009; Collarbone & West-Burnham, 2008; Whitaker, 1998).

We observed how there was plenty of talk in the group about resistance to labelling, not wanting the children to be defined by their diagnoses, and talk about when and how much to confide in them the extent or prognosis of their disabilities.

Tales were exchanged about the crass insensitivity friends and neighbours (and professionals) can blunder into and the contribution the booklets might make to enlightening the ill-informed. We discussed the burden that falls on the parent to explain to all who ask or stare or pry or evade or retreat.

Key information

In any human group there is a complex tide of emotional tensions that are mostly hidden from participants' awareness; there is usually someone who is sensitive to the dynamics and responds to the unspoken communication. Wilfred Bion and Donald Winnicott, who were both psychoanalysed by Melanie Klein, represent a tradition now maintained at the Tavistock Institute and the Anna Freud Centre in London. They attend, at times, to the psychological flow of groups as if it were a single entity beyond the individuals who constitute it.

Points for discussion

- What have you learned from the examples presented in this chapter?
- How can you ensure that all families are thought about and included in your service?
- What sorts of professional development might help workers to work more effectively in groups with parents?

References

Aram. E., Baxter, R. and Nutkevitch, A. (eds) (2009) *Adaptation and Innovation: Theory, design and role-taking in group relations conferences and their applications*, Vol. II, London: Karnac.

Bion, W. (1961) *Experiences in Groups*, London: Tavistock.

Bollas, C. (1987) *The Shadow of the Object: Psychoanalysis of the unthought known*, New York: Columbia University Press.

Boog, B. (2003) 'The emancipatory character of action research: its history and the present state of the art', *Journal of Community and Applied Social Psychology*, vol. 13, pp. 426–38.

Collarbone, P. and West-Burnham, J. (2008) *Understanding Systems Leadership: Securing excellence and equity in education*, London: Network Continuum.

Grandin, T. (1996) *Thinking in Pictures*, New York: Vintage Press.

Jackson, M. (director) (2010) *Temple Grandin*, HBO home video.

McKinnon, E. (forthcoming) *Improving Practice through Research* [working title], London: Routledge.

Malaguzzi, L. (1993) 'For an education based on relationships', *Young Children*, vol. 49, no. 1, pp. 9–12.

Maverick TV (2012) *Embarrassing Bodies*, produced by A. Fraser, Channel 4, 16 Apr. 2012.

Orr, R. J. (2003) *My Right to Play: A child with complex needs*, Maidstone: Open University Press.

Perls, F. S. (1969) *Gestalt Therapy Verbatim*, Gouldsboro, ME: Gestalt Journal Press.

Whitaker, P. (1998) *Managing Schools*, Oxford: Butterworth/Heinemann.

5

Home-visiting from an education and care perspective: getting to know, supporting and working in partnership with families

Margaret Myles, Laura Kiff and Katherine Clark

In this chapter we present:
- the theory underpinning the practice of regular home-visiting of children and families
- how that happens in nursery for all families
- how part of the 'nurturing' in Nurture Group happens through home-visiting.

Introduction

We will be presenting how Pen Green Children's Centre supports all nursery families through home-visiting, but particularly supports the most vulnerable children within the town through our Nurture Group and intensive home-visiting service. We will identify the significant difference from similar groups that are common in schools and express our commitment to working with families who may find services difficult to access, going beyond expectations to enable them to have positive experiences and trust in us as professionals.

Evidence from research

Desforges and Abouchaar (2003), Feinstein (2003), the EPPE study (Sylva *et al.*, 2004) and Gutman and Feinstein (2007) show us clearly that when parents, mothers and fathers, 'have the knowledge, skills and confidence to provide the kind of relationships and experiences that children need in the early years, it makes a real difference to children's futures' (Roberts, 2009: 6).

The introduction to the Statutory Framework for the Early Years Foundation Stage (DfE, 2012: 2) states that the EYFS seeks to provide 'partnership working between practitioners and with parents and/or carers' and it is perhaps helpful at this point to consider all that 'partnership working' entails.

Gillian Pugh makes it clear that partnership 'does not mean professionals dictating the terms of the relationship but rather a more equal approach based on respect, trust, empathy and integrity' (Pugh, 2010: 2).

The *Concise Oxford Dictionary* (Allen, 1992) defines 'partnership' as a 'venture with shared risks and profits'. For parents the 'risky' elements of working in partnership with early years practitioners might include the fear of being judged as a parent, of being patronised, the fear of feeling out of your depth and caught up in the mire of trying to make sense of professional jargon, the fear of admitting you are struggling or sometimes getting it wrong for your child.

Some of the perceived 'risks' for early years practitioners of working in partnership with parents might include having to consider the power imbalance in the relationship. As early years practitioners we have a duty/responsibility to continually build on our knowledge, understanding and skills in working with young children and their families, and while we might have a great deal of expertise in this area, we must recognise and acknowledge that parents/carers are the experts when it comes to their child. As Athey says, 'Parents and professionals can help children separately or they can work together for the greater benefit of children' (1990: 66). Easen makes it explicit that 'The roles of professional experience and parents' everyday experience are seen as complementary but equally important' (Easen et al., 1992: 285).

For some early years practitioners unused to working closely with parents it may feel very threatening or scary to have to articulate and share our knowledge and working practices; as Athey also points out (2007: 18) 'human beings are territorial and part of a person's territory is their knowledge'. It is sometimes difficult even for experienced professionals to offer up embedded 'practice wisdom' for discussion and question with parents, and even harder to admit that practitioners don't have all the answers and need to ask parents what they think.

Athey (2007: 66) continues, 'but perhaps the greatest benefit to a teacher in working with parents is the spur towards making their own pedagogy more conscious and explicit'.

The practitioners who cling to the jargon of their profession often do so in order to maintain control in relationships with others and protect themselves against having their (often) weak practices exposed and questioned. Working in partnership can take us into the unknown and that can feel scary – maybe we have never worked with families who are travellers or speak a different language to us, where the family is affected by a particular disability or struggling or resistant to working with services because of the complexity of their lives.

There is much we can do to find out more about particular cultures and disabilities for example, and professionally we have a responsibility to do so, but if we truly believe that children, parents and practitioners are all co-constructors of knowledge then we should be asking children and parents to teach us all we need to know about working with them and their family. As Whalley says, 'the quality of the relationship which develops between staff and parents really seemed to depend on the openness, clarity and warmth displayed by each individual member of staff' (1994: 15).

The Early Learning Partnership Parental Engagement group details a principle for engaging with families that 'recognises and builds on parents' expertise, where professionals and parents really listen to and learn from each other in ways that are valued and evaluated by parents themselves' (Pugh, 2010).

- As a practitioner you need to reflect on your relationships with children and their families on your own, with colleagues, and in regular supervision sessions where you may gain other useful perspectives on your work.
- Many practitioners find it extremely useful to study communication and counselling skills as they begin to work more closely with children or their parents.
- Research by Wheeler and Connor (2009) into parental involvement identified many of the barriers which have to be overcome at the 'service/practitioner level' and at the 'parent level' before a true partnership is forged.
- When practitioners adopt a principled approach to working with families it seems only natural that we should be offering parents the first opportunity to share their knowledge about their child with us in the place they feel most comfortable, and for most parents that is their home. It is through home visits that children, parents and practitioners 'profit' most.

Visiting nursery children at home

All children due to start at Pen Green nursery will be visited by their Family Worker prior to their starting and will receive regular home visits thereafter. This has been our practice since the nursery opened in 1983 and a culture of home visits has become well established. Meeting children and their carers in their home is an important first step in beginning to understand each child and their home context.

If fathers or mothers who have contact with the child do not live in the child's home then all attempts should be made by the practitioner to start to build a relationship by visiting each parent when the child is at their home. In this way they can share their different perspective on their child with you.

If you are at all apprehensive about a home visit you must talk to your supervisor about your concerns. In some instances it may be appropriate to visit the family with a colleague but as a general rule you should visit on your own.

In her research on nursery home visits, Greenfield (2012: 109) found that practitioners interviewed felt that they would have benefited from some training on home-visiting beforehand. Your setting may want to organise this.

When you telephone a parent to make an appointment to home-visit at a time convenient to the family, be prepared to offer information about why your setting believes in home-visiting all children prior to them starting in nursery. Give parents some idea about how long the visit will last and what you would like to find out about their child and their family, and offer the visit as a way that the family can find out about you, your setting and the way you will be working with their child in nursery.

This initial contact may make you aware that you and the parent might need support if you don't speak the same language. Often families who are learning English as an additional language can call on the help of other family members to translate or use other people from their community to help them overcome language barriers. There are also professional interpreter services you could contact – most local authorities have a bank of interpreters they can call on.

Maybe in your setting you could offer training/support and Criminal Records Bureau clearance to other service users interested in volunteering their services working with families who speak their language.

Example from practice
Example from practice

Max

Max and his family were of Romany descent. His parents Viktor and Anna came to Corby with extended family members from Holland where they had spent much of their youth. Originally the family were from Serbia. Their home language was Romany/Serbian. Viktor could understand some Dutch. He had a brother Alek who had been in Corby for one year and had got work locally. His brother Alek had taught himself some English. Anna had never been to school and spoke and understood only her Romany dialect.

I first met Max, Viktor, Anna, Alek and one of Anna's younger sisters when they were brought into the centre by a health visitor. Anna was quite far on in her pregnancy with her third child. By chance there was a student in nursery, Lena, whose family were Serbian (Corby has had a well-established Serbo/Croatian community since the 1940s) and I asked her to join us.

Between us we established that the family wanted medical care for Anna and were keen for Max to go to 'school'. Alek and Viktor had also been told that they needed to attend an ESOL (English for speakers of other languages) class, which was held at the centre. They also needed help with their benefits claim.

Lena could only understand a little of what the family were saying as she was unfamiliar with their particular Serbian/Romany dialect, but I was very grateful for her help as, like many British people, I have never prioritised learning to speak another language. Together we toured the nursery and many of the community spaces in our centre. I could already see that this family had complex needs and that they needed the support of a translator. Lena explained to them that I would contact a local translation service and asked if they would be happy to pass on their contact details and a brief family history to them in order that they in turn could contact the family to arrange a convenient time for us all to meet in their home.

The translator arranged a time, then telephoned me. At the family home I introduced myself and began to describe how our nursery operated and some of the principles which underpinned how we worked with children and families.

It became apparent very quickly that the translator who had been engaged was translating my words and responses from the family in the briefest of terms. He seemed to be translating only the areas he felt were relevant. I spoke to him about it afterwards and he felt that 'he needed to keep things simple' for the family, which I felt was patronising. It is really important for families to fully understand how and why we work in certain ways with their children and the importance we attach to working in partnership with them.

I decided to go back to the translation service and ask whether they had another translator with an interest in and some experience of working with families, and they were able to put me in touch with someone else who instantly 'connected' with the family and in subsequent home visits I was able to gain a much richer picture of Max in the context of his family.

Language translation services can be expensive but by liaising with the family health visitor we co-ordinated our visits to the family and split the time with the translator to cover the important areas we needed to discuss and divided the cost.

The initial home visit can be the start of a good working relationship with the child and their family and you should do all you can to convey the fact that you respect parents as the experts on their child and you are genuinely interested in what they are telling you.

We need to start with the firm belief that all parents are interested in the development and progress of their own children.

(Pen Green Centre team, 2004)

Think about how you present yourself to new families. It is highly likely that you will find yourself playing with the child – probably on the floor. I am not suggesting you wear your old ripped jeans, neither would I advocate a business suit, revealing clothing, 'team' shirts, old trainers or high heels, but first impressions are important and you should consider this.

You also need to think about the information you need to gather to start working with this family. At Pen Green we have devoted many of our training days to thinking about our information-gathering paperwork and asking for only the information which will be helpful in building up a picture of the child in this family. Your questions should be sufficiently open-ended to enable parents to tell you about their child and their family. As Greenfield (2012: 108) states: 'The arrival of teachers carrying clipboards holding structured questionnaires and wanting to find out information certainly creates an image of officialdom.'

The home visit is a two-way information-sharing opportunity and it should be sufficiently flexible in its structure to enable parents to work through their own agenda for the visit. Information about the child's and family's interests – things they enjoy doing, favourite TV programmes, songs or stories – will help you start to think about planning a meaningful curriculum for each individual child in your care, and it is good practice to have something the child is interested in or familiar with planned for the child's first session in nursery with you. It lets children and families know that you have held in mind all that they told you on the home visit and that this information-sharing is important to you, and that information you seek will be seen to be used for the greater good of the child and their family.

If children and families are happy to have their photographs taken, having their photographs displayed at the child's height on their first day lets the child and their family know that there is a place for them in this nursery.

During the first home visit essential information about the child's health and dietary needs is sought from parents. It is good practice to ask parents to tell you all that you need to know in order to look after their child. Parents can also be invited to share their concerns about their child coming into nursery. When parents are encouraged and supported to be strong advocates for their child in nursery – sharing their knowledge about their child, contributing ideas for planning for their child with their worker, contributing to any assessment process about their child – then workers can plan in a more focused way for the child and the child will blossom and grow in all areas of their development.

We also know that parents who have become their child's strongest advocate in nursery take their advocacy skills with them and use them as their child moves to primary school and then on to senior school (Whalley *et al.*, 2012).

Raven (1980), when reviewing The Lothian Region Educational home-visiting scheme, found that some of the lasting effects on the mothers involved in the study were that they felt more tuned in to their children's interests, more confident in their abilities to influence their child's development, and had higher expectations of their children.

Parents can be asked about their child's week: who are the other important people in their lives that they spend time with? Do children spend time in other homes? This information will help you to understand the complexity of some children's lives and to be able to offer the level of service each child and family needs.

The home visit is a time for the worker to ask the family about their hopes and aspirations for their child, and to talk about the principles and ethos that underpin our work with them. When children see their worker welcomed into the family home by their parents, the seeds of trust in the worker can be sown, especially if you engage the child in talking about themselves and things they like to play with. Some children might be open to you playing with them on the first visit, others might want to sit alongside you and do some mark-making on the spare paper you have taken along with your paperwork.

At Pen Green Nursery, families are informed when they first register their child that all children need to be 'settled in' to our nursery: supported by a trusted adult for the first two weeks. Working families may need to save holiday for this. The settling-in time is a hugely important time for children and their parents, as they start to form a relationship with you and the nursery setting. The attachment process is complex and needs to start from the point where the child feels secure.

Through his studies of infants and their primary caregivers, John Bowlby developed the concept of 'attachment', which describes how children and adults form and develop reciprocal relationships (Bowlby, 1969).

From birth, babies need to be physically close to their primary caregivers and their needs for food, comfort, support to survive periods of distress, companionship and love need to be consistently met. When babies experience this consistency of care they develop a secure belief in their carers' abilities to care for and protect them, and in their own abilities to survive brief periods of distress.

From this secure base as they get older the child develops the confidence to explore their world knowing that, although at times they may not be physically close to their carer, they will feel psychologically close: held in the minds of those who love them. Having a parent or carer around while the child finds out about you, others in nursery, this new place and its routines, really benefits children and enables this process to develop. During the settling-in period, parents can observe our practice and daily routines, and develop confidence in our abilities to care for their child; children then 'borrow' their parents' confidence.

During this time staff at the nursery plan regular sessions which we call our *key concept* sessions. These are informal group discussions where we encourage parents to come along to find out more about how we will be working with their children and, just as importantly, how they can become involved in their children's learning in nursery. We offer sessions in the morning, afternoon and early evening, and either arrange a crèche for other children or plan to accommodate them in the same room, setting up an area and having a worker in the room to play with them.

The key concepts we discuss in these initial parent sessions are: *well-being* (Laevers, 1997), *involvement* (Laevers, 1997), *schemas* (Athey, 1990) and *pedagogic strategies* (Whalley & Arnold, 1997). They are important lenses through which we study and become informed about some of the different aspects of children's learning (see Chapter 3).

Athey, reflecting on her ground-breaking Froebel Educational Institute Project (Athey, 1990: 49), showed how valuable such ways of working in partnership are.

> The programme was based on a new kind of collaboration between parents and professionals. The professionals did not deny their specialised knowledge but made it freely available to parents without fear of loss of status.

Once the child has started in nursery it is really important to make yourself available to welcome children and their families every day and make time for daily chats about what the child has been interested in or doing at home. If shift patterns or planned absences from nursery mean that you are not in nursery then you should inform children and their parents beforehand. Maybe you could help them to make links with a colleague in nursery to talk to and for the child to be with in your absence. Parents may also want to talk to you about other important things that are happening in their lives which are having an effect on their child. At these times it is more appropriate for parents to be able to talk to you at length, and arranging a home visit will give them the opportunity to do this.

Staff at Pen Green Nursery are allowed time out of nursery for home visits. Termly home visits, when the child's nursery record of achievement can be shared with their family and when workers can find out more about the children's current interests at home, are really important ways of deepening your understanding of the child in their family. Deep meaningful discussion will lead to more accurate assessment of where the child is now in their development – information on which you will base future planning.

Figure 5.1 Margaret on a home visit

We create a 'developmental partnership' (Easen *et al.*, 1992), in which parents and practitioners contribute their expertise in constructing a meaningful curriculum for the child. As Meade and Cubey point out, 'we know that young children achieve more and are happier when EY educators work with parents and share ideas about how to support and extend children's learning' (Meade & Cubey, 1995, in ELPPEG, 2010: 13).

Where children's fathers do not live in the family home but do have regular contact with their child it is good practice to do all that you can to home-visit children when they are with their dad as well. Not only is it fathers' and children's rights to have fathers involved in their education and other aspects of their life, but it also offers fathers the opportunity to tell you about their child – another view which contributes to your understanding of the child.

Research by Hobcraft (1998) and Flouri and Buchanan (2001) shows that children do better in school when their fathers can be actively interested and involved in their lives (see Chapter 12 for more on work with fathers).

As your relationship with the child and their family develops you may find yourself taking on the role of 'resourceful friend' (Holman, 1983). It is important to remember that you have a duty of care to the child and the responsibility to work within the safeguarding procedures of your setting. If you are working with families who have complex lives then it may be important to be honest with them from the start that some of the information they choose to share with you may need to be shared with other professionals in the interest of safeguarding their child.

A word of caution about social networking sites. It is not advisable to have children's parents or other family members as contacts: the boundaries between your professional life and private life should be clear and unambiguous to parents. Your work with children and families is confidential and should never be discussed in the public domain.

Key information

Safe working practices are of course common sense, and in England they are also an OFSTED requirement. You should ensure that a system for logging home visits is in place in your setting: who you are going to home-visit, the address, and the times you intend to arrive and leave all need to be left with colleagues. You should also carry a mobile phone and its phone number should be left at your setting. If you intend to go home at the end of your visit you should telephone your setting to inform them that your visit has been completed and you are on your way home.

It is helpful to have the telephone number of a senior colleague and, if any issues arise on the home visit which leave you concerned for the safety or well-being of the child(ren), you need to talk these over with them as soon as you can after the visit.

Visiting Nurture Group families at home

In this section of the chapter we will be presenting how Pen Green Children's Centre supports the most vulnerable children within the town through its Nurture Group and a more intensive home-visiting service. We will identify the significant differences between this and Nurture Groups that are common in schools, and express our commitment to working with families who may find services difficult to access, going beyond expectations to enable them to have positive experiences and trust in us as professionals.

The significant differences between Nurture Group at Pen Green and those commonly found in schools

Our Nurture Group began 20 years ago, originally named 'Early Intervention and Support Team', with funding from Social Care and Health. Two skilled practitioners were employed to work closely with four to six families who were considered very vulnerable. All the children were on the brink of being taking into the care system, on long-term 'Child Protection Plans' and considered at risk. Practitioners were paid for eight hours per week but often the intensity of the role meant working into their own time.

Nurture Group has developed, and currently two Family Workers are employed for 16 hours to work with four children, aged from 18 months to three years, and their families. These families are considered the most vulnerable in the community. We have a crucial role in safeguarding and work closely with the 'Every Child Matters' framework (DCSF, 2004). Children attend the nursery for two morning sessions per week, where they are given intensive support on a ratio of one Family Worker for two children.

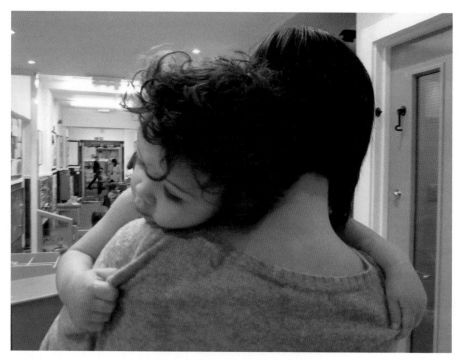

Figure 5.2 Worker and child (Nurture Group)

We provide transport into the setting, regular intensive home visits, attend and support parents at a range of meetings including 'team around the child', family case conferences and network meetings. We may also take on a lead professional role for the Common Assessment Framework (CAF); although we are often supporting families who would be considered above CAF level, we refer on to appropriate services. These may include health, speech and language, counselling, drug and alcohol agencies, support for homelessness or domestic violence. We regularly accompany parents to these services and provide care for their children while they access them.

Children no longer have to be working with social services to access Nurture Group; we now allocate children and their families a place from a range of referrers, including:

- social services
- drug/alcohol support services
- Home-Start
- health visitors
- general practitioners
- county council/housing
- local children's centres.

Nurture Group: a special service for families in need

Children who are the most vulnerable are thought about very carefully at Pen Green. We understand that their parents may find accessing services difficult. Often the historical context for these families can mean that professional involvement brings with it the fear and anxieties of previous generations, where social services and/or health authorities may have previously become engaged.

We believe that all parents want their children to have better experiences and more life choices than they had. Experience has demonstrated to us that parents often feel that life events – daily life – can get in the way. We hope that when we are with families we can 'contain' some of these daily anxieties. Through building strong and trusting relationships with parents, we enable them to access our service successfully, and find the strengths and skills their particular family needs to begin the transition from living in crisis to living in hope.

Recent government papers (e.g. Field, 2010; Munro, 2011) indicate that children aged birth to three years are the most at risk of their life opportunities being affected by the disadvantages of poverty, domestic violence, neglect, emotional abuse or drug or alcohol misuse. Feinstein (2003) identified the gap in achievement between disadvantaged young children in poverty and their more affluent peers. Blanden (2006), using the same data as Feinstein (the 1970s birth cohort data), identified that parental involvement is key to disadvantaged children achieving. These thoughts are the foundations of our practice. We aim to stand alongside parents and assist them to provide a more positive future for themselves and their children.

Standing on the shoulders of giants: theories and ideas we consider when supporting families

We recognise the importance our position holds for the emotional development of the children and their parents. When working with families either in the home or the setting we have strong values and beliefs regarding our practice. Bowlby's theory of attachment (1969) and his ideas regarding children needing a secure base (1988) suggest that children need to develop loving and nurturing relationships with significant adults, which then enable them to reach out and explore the world around them. Bion's theory of containment (1962) and the notion of 'holding' (Winnicott, 1965) are concepts we draw on. Our interpretation of containment is that a child projects unmanageable thoughts and feelings to an adult, who would help them to process these states, which then become more manageable for the infant. We understand 'holding' in the sense that a person would experience it, when being either physically or emotionally supported by another person, often referred to as being 'held in mind'. These ideas are transferable to adult relationships and interactions. Focusing on these ideas has meant these theories have become part of our thoughts and practice when engaging with children and parents. We are continuously aiming to understand play and relationships at a deeper level, considering how parents and their children might experience the Nurture Group service and how this may influence their future interactions and relationships.

Home-visiting: going beyond expectations to enable positive experiences and trust

We want to provide an accessible service, as we understand this is the most effective long-term. Often we meet parents for the first time within their own home. We would intend to present ourselves in a friendly, relaxed manner. We would not want to intimidate or patronise parents. There is a fine line between being condescending and interested. Often, until we know families well we can feel a little like we are walking on eggshells. The early stages of building relationships with families may influence the success of the service we provide. However, we do not let this deter us from having difficult conversations with parents from very early on. We would always ensure parents are aware that any concern for a child's safety will be discussed with them directly and with any other relevant agency. This may include social services.

Over time we share celebrations, sorrow, frustrations and anger with families. We 'contain' (Bion, 1962) many emotions of families. At times these interactions may feel like friendships but this relationship is professional, it is focused and it has a purpose, which is to support parents to think about their children, the way they parent them and their family context. This can be considered through the Johari Window model (Luft & Ingram, 1950).

Figure 5.3 On a home visit (Nurture Group)

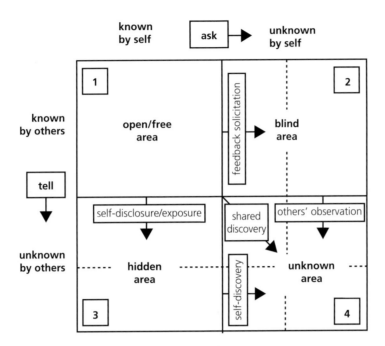

Figure 5.4 The Johari Window model

The model depicts four areas, each representing the aspects of ourselves we share with, or conceal from, each other. Parents expose previously hidden areas to us as we develop connections with them. In our relationships we support parents to discover and explore areas, while keeping many of our own hidden. Maintaining formal relationships, such as the Johari Window depicts, enables professionals and parents to engage in safe relationships with clear boundaries. We have used clinical supervision to help us keep children safe, to prevent us from becoming absorbed in the accounts parents share, and to effectively separate our experiences and feelings from those of others. Supervision sessions also help to guide the direction of our practice.

Once a child has a place within Nurture Group, we will go beyond normal expectations to ensure they attend their weekly sessions and the families receive the service they are entitled to. For example, we will use our own cars to collect them, call and text families regularly, visit families out of typical working hours, enter homes that may be considered unsafe, insanitary, have violent partners present or where drug misuse is evident. Of course personal safety must be considered in these circumstances:

- We carry work mobile phones.
- We inform colleagues where we are going.
- We may avoid conversations that we believe are confrontational if we feel parents may respond aggressively, and instead have these conversations with parents in a safer environment.
- Although rare – we may choose to visit in pairs.

Formal risk assessment should always be considered, but should never deter us from facing the emotional celebrations and challenges that we may experience with families.

We believe that the positive experiences children receive in the nursery warrant going the extra mile to bring them here, and that for vulnerable families the service we offer is vital for supporting them to create change and better life opportunities.

Example from practice

Example from practice

Sarah and Jack

Our community social worker was visiting all families in our reach area with children who could access our service but who were currently not using our provision. She 'happened' to meet Sarah and her son Jack.

Sarah recalls this visit as 'changing everything; if it hadn't been for that visit I don't know how things would be now'.

Jack was referred to Nurture Group after the community social worker had been supporting the family at home and through respite crèche provision for Jack. At that time Sarah had separated from Jack's father. Sarah was feeling emotionally run down and physically worn out from looking after a very demanding toddler. She was grieving the loss of another child and suffering from frequent bouts of low mood.

Sarah felt Jack was isolated from other children and wanted him to be able to have early experiences with peers. She had concerns regarding his development – having worked with young adults with autism previously, she wondered if this was what Jack's demanding behaviour was due to.

Sarah recalls, 'I could see the warning signs … the way he was with other children and when he stacked his food when we were out for lunch one day … I just knew he wasn't right.'

The family was allocated a Nurture Group place. Jack attended for ten months before his nursery funding could be accessed and he took a place within Pen Green Nursery. A CAF was already in place for the family. A Nurture Group Family Worker took the lead professional role and led six weekly meetings for Sarah and Jack. A range of professionals including specialist services had became involved to support the family through the autism pathway to diagnosis. This had begun following a paediatrician appointment where Sarah was able to share her concerns regarding Jack.

While Jack attended Nurture Group we offered him intensive support within the setting. This often involved him having one-to-one time with his worker. We focused on engaging him in social interactions and on supporting his emotional development, as these were the areas of concern that Sarah had identified. An individual educational plan (IEP) was set, with a target of 'social interactions with adults he trusts' agreed as the most suitable for Jack. We filmed Jack in the setting engaging in play, exploring the nursery and even caught the first beautiful moment that he invited a peer to play alongside him. As with all children who attend the setting a Celebration of Achievements file was created for Jack, which documented his learning and special events and experiences. All these experiences were shared with Sarah during daily contact.

During home visits Sarah and the Nurture Group worker shared dialogue regarding Jack's development, sharing stories of experiences and magical moments we had all observed with Jack. Sarah borrowed the setting's video recorder and filmed Jack extensively, films which were happily exchanged with clips of Jack in the setting.

Sarah recalls the clip where Jack first invited a peer to play alongside him: 'I loved that piece of video … it brought tears to my eyes. I couldn't wait to show his dad … we still watch it now.'

When referring to how information was shared with her, Sarah says, 'I was always being updated with daily chats, copies of DVDs, having his file at home, which has been great, and home visits.'

Frequent home visits led, built and maintained a trusting relationship between Sarah and her Nurture Group worker. Conversations on these visits covered a range of topics, including communicating worries about Jack's development, sharing exciting news about holidays and magical moments, and sometimes even political debates!

When reflecting on her time with Nurture Group, Sarah reports:

'On the days he went I got a break. When I collected him he was happy to see me and we would always have a good day together. It gave me a chance to get the housework done … It gave me a break … It was reassuring to have my fears confirmed by them that it wasn't all in my head, that it wasn't something I had done wrong.'

'His speech came on amazingly and socialising with his peers. He became a lot happier in himself and more confident. He changed so much.'

'Everything was amazing, it made such a difference to us.'

'Targeted early intervention in the early years tends to mix a focus on deep structures in parent–child relationships, such as attachment and coercive parenting, with attention to practical problems' (Allen, 2011: 73). Regular CAF meetings, frequent home visits, developing a productive relationship with Sarah and giving attention to the practical problems she faced helped Sarah to get the needs of her son met, while giving her the time she needed to talk and think about what her family needed.

Sarah and Jack's dad have resumed their relationship, and are enjoying being a family. Sarah has decided that it is in Jack's best interests for her to remain a full-time mother, and with useful support in place she is able to make the most of her time with Jack, relishing being with him. Jack did change and develop during his time with Nurture Group. As he left us the process of a pathway to diagnosis was in place. Although Sarah was in no hurry to 'label' Jack, she was relieved that the professionals supporting her family were able to understand what he might need to continue this progression.

This is a real success story for Nurture Group. We were able to build positive relationships with the family and work within a multi-agency team, which ensured long-term change for Sarah and her family. The case study identifies how our ideas, values and beliefs translate into practice and enhance the possibility of positive outcomes for children and families.

Related professional issues: expressing our commitment to engaging with families who may find accessing services difficult

This is not the case for all families who attend Nurture Group. We have supported children who left us while going through statutory legal processes. We understand that we may always encounter challenges with children and families, that confronting parents with concerns is difficult – but it is vital in order to keep children safe. We accept that we are on a learning journey ourselves and are privileged to share the journeys of the families we meet. We also understand that becoming emotionally involved is sometimes unavoidable; however hard we try, we will always encounter children we fall in love with and parents who make us smile. These are the joys and the heartaches of the role. This is where regular and consistent supervision is essential, in order to discuss and air these feelings and issues with a manager and/or your peers.

As families move on, we may be left wondering if we have had enough impact to change the path for their children. We may not have – but we can be reassured that the experiences, support and care we have offered is genuine and unique for each child and parent. We hope that it is this that resonates through the future for each of them.

Points for discussion

- Share any experiences you have of being visited by professionals and of visiting families as professionals.
- What are the advantages of visiting all children who attend your setting, at home?
- How might you minimise the power differential when visiting vulnerable children and families in their homes?
- How might an organisation manage the burdens this approach puts on workers?

References

Allen, G. (2011) *Early Intervention: The Next Steps, an independent report to Her Majesty's Government*, London: Cabinet Office.

Allen, R. E. (ed.) (1992) *The Concise Oxford Dictionary* (8th edn), Oxford: Clarendon Press.

Athey, C. (1990) *Extending Thought in Young Children: A parent–teacher partnership*, London: PCP.

Athey, C. (2007) *Extending Thought in Young Children: A parent–teacher partnership* (2nd edn), London: PCP.

Bion, W. (1962) *Learning from Experience*, London: Heinemann.

Blanden, J. (2006) 'Bucking the trend: what enables those who are disadvantaged in childhood to succeed later in life?', *Working Paper No. 21*, London: DWP.

Bowlby, J. (1969) *Attachment and Loss. Vol. 1: Attachment*, London: Hogarth Press.

Bowlby, J. (1988) *A Secure Base: Clinical applications of attachment theory*, London: Routledge.

DCSF (Department for Children, Schools and Families) (2004) *Every Child Matters: Change for children*, London: TSO.

Desforges, C. and Abouchaar, A. (2003) 'The impact of parental involvement, parental support and family education on pupil achievements and adjustments: a literature review', *Research Report No. 433*, London: DfES.

DfE (Department for Education) (2012) *Statutory Framework for the Early Years Foundation Stage: Setting the standards for learning development and care for children from birth to five*, Cheshire: Crown Copyright.

Easen, P. P., Kendal, P. and Shaw, J. (1992) 'Parents and educators: dialogue and developing through partnership', *Children and Society*, vol. 6, no. 4, pp. 282–96.

ELPPEG (Early Learning Partnership Parental Engagement Group) (2010) *Principles for Engaging with Families: A Framework for local authorities and national organisations to evaluate and improve engagement with families*, London: NQIN.

Feinstein, L. (2003) 'Inequality in early cognitive development of British children in 1970 cohort', *Economica*, vol. 70, no. 227, pp. 73–97.

Field, F. (2010) *The Foundation Years: Preventing poor children becoming poor adults*, London: HMG.

Flouri, E. and Buchanan, A. (2001) 'Fathertime', *Community Care*, Oct., no. 40, pp. 4–10.

Greenfield, S. (2012) 'Nursery home visits: rhetoric and reality', *Journal of Early Childhood Research*, Feb., vol. 10, no. 1, pp. 100–112.

Gutman, L. M. and Feinstein, L. (2007) *Parenting Behaviours and Children's Development from Infancy to Early Childhood: Changes, continuities and contributions*, Research Report No. 22, London: Wider Benefits of Learning.

Hobcraft, J. (1998) *Childhood Experiences and the Risks of Social Exclusion in Adulthood*, London School of Economics STICERD (Research Paper No. CASEBRIEF08).

Holman, B. (1983) *Resourceful Friends: Skills in community social work*, London: Children's Society.

Luft, J. and Ingham, H. (1950). 'The Johari window, a graphic model of interpersonal awareness', *Proceedings of the Western Training Laboratory in Group Development,* Los Angeles: UCLA.

Meade, A. and Cubey, P. (1995) *Thinking Children – Learning about schemas*, Buckingham: Open University Press.

Munro, E. (2011) *The Munro Review of Child Protection: Final report, a child-centred system*, London: Department for Education.

Pen Green Centre team (2004) 'Rules of engagement', *Nursery World*, 3 June.

Pugh, G. (2010) Foreword to ELPPEG above.

Raven, J. (1980) *Parents, Teachers and Children: A study of an educational home-visiting scheme*, Edinburgh: Scottish Council for Research in Education/Hodder & Stoughton.

Roberts, K. (2009) *Early Home Learning Matters: A good practice guide*, London: Family and Parenting Institute.

Sylva, K., Melhuish, E., Sammons, P., Siraj-Blatchford, I. and Taggart, B. (2004) *The Effective Provision of Pre-school Education (EPPE) Project Final Report. A longitudinal evaluation (1997–2004)*, London: DfES.

Whalley, M. (1994) *Learning to Be Strong: Setting up a neighbourhood service for under-fives and their families,* London: Hodder & Stoughton.

Whalley, M., Arnold, C., Lawrence, P. and Peerless, S. (2012) 'The voices of their childhood: families and early years practitioners developing emancipatory methodologies through a tracer study', *European Early Childhood Education Research Journal,* vol. 20, no. 4, pp. 519–35.

Wheeler, H. and Connor, J. (2009) 'Parents, early years and learning: parents as partners in the Early Years Foundation Stage', *Principles into Practice*, London: NCB.

Winnicott, D. W. (1965) *The Child, the Family and the Outside World*, Middlesex: Penguin Books.

6

Developing a groupwork programme to respond to the needs of local families

Lorna MacLeod and Elaine Young

In this chapter we introduce ideas about:

- why we began running groups for parents at the Pen Green Centre
- what kinds of groups we run currently
- the professional development and support needed for adults running groups
- how we continue to evaluate our groupwork.

Introduction

In this chapter we will include information relating to the groupwork programme in the Pen Green Centre. It will cover how groupwork evolved within the centre over the last 30 years, why we value working in groups with families, and what groups we currently run. Training and supporting group leaders is an important aspect of groupwork, so we will describe how we support this and how we regularly evaluate the impact of our services. We provide examples from practice as well as challenges for the future.

Why groupwork?

Pen Green started as a nursery in 1983, providing an early years setting for local children and their families with nursery places for two- and three-year-olds. At this time very few nursery schools or nursery classes offered places to children under three years of age. Families would engage with the nursery but would find that there were very few additional services available for them to access if they had another baby or toddler. It is our belief that children cannot be considered nor worked with in isolation from their parents. Parents, like their babies and toddlers, have different needs and wants. One effective way of providing for parents' needs was to run groups that could offer:

- practical support in a welcoming environment
- companionship, a chance to meet other parents and have some time for themselves
- a stimulating play experience for their baby or toddler and a chance to share the care.

We found that it was a better use of staff time to work with a group of parents, rather than parents individually. Pen Green offers a range of groups and courses that are run by members of staff, external workers, adult tutors and, more importantly, parent volunteers who are trained and supported by staff members. We have found that we would not be able to offer these kinds of services without the support from volunteers or other agencies with whom we work in partnership.

It is important at this point to think about how families access the services provided by children's centres. Our experience has shown that a wide variety of opportunities enables choices to be made by the family as to what best suits their needs at that time. However, workers will need to be mindful that families' needs change, develop and grow, and the services provided will need to reflect this. Parents may start off using a universal group and then, when they have built up trusting relationships with staff, they may feel able to acknowledge difficulties with other issues that could be met in a targeted group, or vice versa.

Universal	Targeted
These tend to be open-access groups that families can drop in to	These tend to be specific closed groups around a particular issue or concern. Families make a commitment to attend for a certain period of time.

Table 6.1 Universal and targeted groups

Example from practice

Example from practice

Trudi shares some experiences of attending both universal and targeted groups:

'I'd had depression before and I was about four or five months pregnant and I could see my symptoms coming back: I didn't want to go out, to do much, to be honest. I withdrew again and because I'd had it before, I knew what was coming and I wanted to snip it because I knew I was going to have the baby. Everything was meant to be great so I went to the midwife. She referred me straight to "Great Expectations" and I think I came the week after seeing her. I spoke to the group leader on the phone and she met me at the couches and I wasn't really thinking. I just knew that I needed this to stop from happening, so she took me into the group and I sat there, and these ladies were a lot more heavily pregnant and you couldn't really tell that I was pregnant. I must have been nearly six months because I was on crutches so I had got down here on my crutches and I think that was when my depression had kicked in 'cause I was housebound but I had come out to here.'

The group that Trudi was referring to is a targeted group which is co-led by a midwife and an experienced centre worker. The group offers women a chance to explore issues they may be experiencing in their pregnancy, while their health care needs can be met by the midwife. Women attending this group are referred either by other professionals or themselves.

Within the groupwork programme there are certain criteria for when a group may end. This is not always an easy process for families.

Example from practice

Example from practice

Trudi reflects on her feelings as she prepares to move on from Great Expectations, which was a targeted group (where she experienced individual support with familiar, regular group members), to a universal drop-in group with a fluctuating membership:

'My baby was about six months old and I had started another group because we went from Great Expectations, and being there was starting my anxiety feelings. It was like people were constantly watching me and, although they weren't and I knew logically they weren't, I felt that everyone was watching to see how I was with the baby.'

At Pen Green we offer a responsive groupwork programme that is tailor-made to reflect the immediate concerns and needs of our families, alongside groups that we are required to provide and that are seen as our 'core offer or purpose' as decided by government or policy makers.

Groupwork is about creating an environment which allows choice and flexibility and takes into account the philosophy of the centre, which respects the individual rights of children and adults.

Within the centre we have a crèche which supports the groupwork programme. This enables us to offer a diverse range of groups, so adults can attend educational or therapeutic groups while their children are receiving a high level of early years care (see Chapter 14).

Our groupwork programme

Groupwork and community education values

All groups and courses that run at Pen Green work towards the same shared values, for everyone to:
- have access to and be offered the same opportunities and choices
- respect each other's beliefs, behaviours and values
- offer a welcoming place where individuals feel safe, included and able to express themselves with confidence
- be sensitive and take time to understand each person's learning journey and life circumstances
- learn from each other and value what each of us has to offer
- be concerned about and support individual learning routes and help sustain learners on their journey
- enable learners to realise their own potential and feel safe enough to take risks
- encourage people to feel they have the power to challenge and change things.

The rationale for our groupwork programme is informed by the use of national, local and centre data, alongside parents' voices and the needs of the local community. In Corby:
- 19.5 per cent of children live in poverty, compared to the county average of 15.4 per cent.
- Three-quarters of the children in poverty live with a lone parent and half the families in poverty have a child under the age of four.
- There were 919 live births in 2010.
- 16,850 people live in one of the 20 per cent most deprived areas in England.

(Corby Local Strategic Partnership)

Our groupwork programme consists of the following three categories: Community Education, Groups for Adults with Children, and Groups for Adults and Healthy Lifestyle. In some ways this approach of categorising the groups can cease to be useful as we believe that all groups can be educative, supportive and to some degree therapeutic.

Community Education	<ul><li>The provision of accessible routes back into education</li><li>Adults re-engaging with their own learning, especially if they have had poor experiences of schooling</li><li>Building community capital</li><li>Building economic capacity</li><li>Overcoming inequalities due to educational experience</li></ul>

(Continued)

Groups for Adults with Children	• Opportunities for parents or other carers and children to spend time together • Encouraging secure attachment between those adults and children • Opportunities for mothers, fathers, grandparents, childminders and other significant adults all to have time with the children they care for • Reducing social isolation
Groups for Adults and Healthy Lifestyle	• Providing specific interventions related to adult well-being and mental health, and to parent–child well-being and mental health • Providing a safe environment for parents to reflect upon and discuss their own situations

Table 6.2 Three categories of groups

The groups we currently run at Pen Green are:

Community Education	Groups for Adults with Children	Groups for Adults and Healthy Lifestyle
Adult Numeracy	Childminders Support Group	Freedom Programme
Functional Skills in Maths	U2 Can Be Messy	Great Expectations
Adult Literacy	Social Baby	Parents' Involvement in Their Children's Learning (PICL)
Computer Literacy and Information Technology (CLAIT)	Social Toddler	Counselling Skills
Children and Young People's Workforce Certificate/Diploma	Community Drop-in	Parents of Children with Additional Needs/Special Rights
Introduction to Childcare	Singing and Music	New Pathways
Introduction to Counselling Skills	Infant Massage	GAP
Introduction to TA (Transactional Analysis)	Young Parents' Massage	Story Sacks
Mood Mapping	Breastfeeding Support	Sewing
English for Speakers of Other Languages (ESOL)	Dads' Massage Saturday	Roots to Routes
Home-Start Preparation Course	Growing Together	Smoking Cessation Programme
New-Start Course	Young Parents' Drop-in and Tea (under 19 years)	All About You
	Young Parents' Drop-in and Tea (under 25 years)	Baby'cise
	Get Together	Tiddler'cise
	Stay, Play and Have Lunch	Tots'cise
KEY	Dads' Club Saturday	Parents' Involvement in Their Children's Learning (PICL)
Evening groups	Dads' Club Sunday	Women's Aerobics
Weekly groups	Health Visitor Clinic	Men's Circuit Training
Term-time/Specific number of weeks		

Table 6.3 Current Pen Green Centre groups

Groups for Adults with Children

From the feedback from parents and carers on our recent evaluations it is clear that they value the groups that we provide. One such group is Growing Together. This group is for parents and carers with children aged birth to three. It runs as a weekly drop-in group. The aim of the group is to encourage 'reflective parenting' where the adult is filmed alongside their child. They then spend time with a worker thinking about the video material and produce a portfolio to print off and take home (see Chapter 10 for more information).

Example from practice

Example from practice

Donna shares her experiences of attending Growing Together. Donna lives with her husband John and their two children: Luke, who is five years old, and Ellie, who is two years old. She attended the group initially with Luke from when he was six weeks old and now with Ellie. Donna points out: 'We have been coming to the group virtually every Friday since!' John comes to the group whenever he has a Friday off – he was able to attend quite regularly with Luke but it is more difficult now he works six days a week. Donna says, 'Every opportunity that he gets he will come along.'

Donna shares that watching herself on video affirms her parenting skills and boosts her confidence as a parent. Watching her interactions with her children confirms that what she is doing is right. She states, 'As a mum you sometimes think that you are probably not the best at it, then you see yourself on camera and you see how you *do* respond to them and that you *do* react to them, you see that they are happy and you think you can't be doing that much of a bad job.' Donna says that she appreciates talking about the video with the group leaders and finds their comments helpful and supportive. 'It's nice to talk to someone who is really interested in my child and how she is developing and to have someone there to point out, "That's really nice what you are doing." Sometimes when people have something to say about your children you could feel criticised but I have never felt like that, they use language that offers suggestions and is supportive and point out things that I have never noticed before.' She often thinks about the dialogue she and the group leader have had when she's back at home later in the day or even a few days later before she comes to the group again the following week. 'I think – oh! So-and-so said that today and that makes perfect sense. I definitely take it home, or they do something a few days later and I think ah! It's all linked in with the conversation we had during the filming, it kind of clicks.' Donna shows her capacity to reflect between the dialogue at the group and the link to her own child's behaviour and development. Donna enjoys the whole process of attending the Growing Together group, from spending time thinking about her children's development to meeting other parents. Her final comments sum up her thoughts about the experience. 'I have made a good circle of friends at the group, we have similar-aged children, so have a chance to talk about our week and any issues we may be having. I love the process of filming. The portfolios are a lovely reminder of what my children enjoyed at various stages of their development.'

Some important thoughts to take from this case study are:

Donna's experience of working together with the group leader and sharing a mutual interest in her child's interests and behaviour links with Easen (Easen *et al.*, 1992), whose work focuses on the parent and educator's partnership in dialogue and learning. He and his colleagues conclude that one of the advantages of working in partnership is that 'Through the validation of their experience, parents' self-esteem and confidence in their role as a parent and as an individual is enhanced' (p. 294).

Donna enjoys the whole process of attending this group and the use of video enables her to explore her growing relationship with her children. Woodhead points out that mothers who participate in the filming process have the 'unique' opportunity 'to talk at length about their baby, their emotions and their experiences of motherhood', which is something 'they appear to relish' (Woodhead *et al.*, 2006: 14).

Infant massage

Infant massage is becoming increasingly popular and is promoted by health care professionals as an early intervention because it enhances early interaction. Parents attending infant massage are spending time tuning in to their children. As well as making physical contact with their babies and toddlers in a whole new way they are also gazing intently at them, talking to them, singing to them, reassuring them with language as well as touch. Current research conveys the crucial role that gentle touch plays in the development of neural connections (Glaser, 2000). Infant massage programmes are now offered regularly during the postnatal period in many different settings such as Sure Start and children's centres.

Infant massage has been running each week at Pen Green Centre for over 20 years. Originally the group was set up after a health visitor who worked at the centre observed parents struggling with the idea of physical touch and communication with their children. Staff attended a ten-week aromatherapy and massage course before co-leading the massage groups. These groups focused on a parent being given individual instruction in basic massage techniques. The co-leader would massage each baby and then support the parent to continue to massage their baby. Although the groups were popular and well attended the team felt that they needed some more in-depth training that would reflect the beliefs and values of the centre in addition to what they were already offering. A member of staff explored the training material of the International Association of Infant Massage (IAIM) and found that the approach they taught incorporated reciprocity, which was a concept that was deeply embedded in all of our work. The concept of reciprocity comes from child development theory and is the process by which the parent is sensitive to the needs and feelings of the child and the child responds to the parent in a two-way flow of communication (Stern, 1971; Schore, 1994; Trevarthen & Aitken, 2001). The other key difference with IAIM was that the instructors demonstrate the strokes on a doll and the parent watches and massages their own baby. The approach also reflects our philosophy when working with parents, as we too advocate valuing parents, recognising parents' expertise and empowering families.

Figure 6.1 An instructor demonstrating baby massage

Examples from practice

Parents' thoughts

We get a lot of helpful feedback from parents about what we offer.

Monika shares her thoughts about the U2 Can Be Messy group:

'The group is important to me because it is an opportunity for my son to socialise with other children. We can try out new ideas, get messy and bring a nice painting back home.'

Sarah explains why she came to Growing Together:

'I came to the group when my daughter was three months old and I was struggling with things, not leaving the house, etc. Once I came to the group I turned a corner, meeting other mums and the facilitators made me feel so much better about being a mum. It really helped and changed things for me.'

Groupwork challenges

Some of the challenges and dilemmas that face us when co-leading these groups are:

Parents may attend U2 Can Be Messy with their child and keep taking their child away from the water tray or a particular messy activity, which creates tension between parent and child. The child naturally goes back to the water or activity and gets frustrated when their parent takes them away again. Group leaders need to approach this situation with sensitivity, listening to the parent's concerns while acknowledging the needs of the child and the aims of the group. Group leaders would talk with parents about the learning opportunities for their child when they play with these 'messy 'resources. We offer aprons, the use of a tumble dryer and spare clothes if needed to enable parents to support their children as they explore the resources available.

Similarly, group leaders need to be sensitive enough to have an awareness of when a parent may be feeling vulnerable. An incident that a worker may feel is insignificant could be very anxiety-provoking for the parent.

Example from practice

A parent's point of view

Trudi shares her experiences of attending a toddler group while she was coping with issues relating to anxiety and depression:

'I really struggle with toddler groups 'cause once I went and a little girl nipped Alan's hand and he got really upset, but I felt like I had lost control because I couldn't get that little girl off him, she wasn't mine; it's stupid … but then there's certain times when I think I haven't been back 'cause one of the mums made me feel like I hadn't done it right … It made me feel like I did at school … Alan wasn't sleeping at the time so everything upset me.'

Training

To support this comprehensive ever-changing piece of work we have also developed a training and supervision model for all group workers in order to offer the best possible service for adults and children. It is rare for a worker to come ready-trained and equipped to facilitate groups of adults. We argue that professional development must include an accumulation of theoretical and practical skills in managing such groups. The Pen Green approach to groups expresses an appreciation of the complexity of human relations and the wisdom of experiential (process-oriented) learning rather than didactic (curriculum-driven) teaching. We propose a three-tiered structure for professional development in groupwork: an introductory level, a maintenance level and an advanced academic level.

Introductory level

Every worker and volunteer taking on a group leadership role needs to appreciate the mechanics of running a group, what to expect when doing so and what is expected of them in return. One day will be set aside for initial groupwork training, where potential group workers have the opportunity to become familiar with the programme that Pen Green offers. They explore the embedded philosophy that underpins all of our groupwork. They are also introduced to the organisational aspects of running groups and what is required of them when facilitating the group. These include:

- familiarising themselves with the organisation's policies and procedures
- understanding the importance of completing all the paperwork involved, for example e-start forms, registers, and planning and reflection sheets as they directly relate to the centre data collection
- booking rooms, providing supplies, arranging settings, inviting participation, taking responsibility for the running of the event, operating a time boundary, clearing up and evaluating.

Group leaders find that as families attend a well-run group and get what is advertised, there is an opportunity to go more deeply into people's life experiences, to build relationships. When a group follows a curriculum there can be little time left for self-discovery: in a process-oriented group such undercurrents become the currency, the content instead of the asides. One effective model is for a more experienced group leader to work alongside a new worker and alternating roles with them, either in taking the lead or intuiting the below-surface issues, picking up the tensions, noticing the differing levels of involvement and well-being among participants. It is about reading between the lines more than just the surface social behaviour, responding to hints and oblique references to needs or troubles. A period of debriefing after every group will allow group leaders to reflect on the subtleties they noticed while the group was running. An outsider's take on what is happening for the group leadership is also essential. Being able to talk through group issues in a supervision session is essential and will be discussed in the next section.

Maintenance level

This tends to be called supervision. Group leaders are offered monthly supervision sessions with their co-leaders and it is about ensuring that the workers can manage to continue through difficult times and develop their own skills as well as foster the skills of the participants; it is a process where group leaders have the opportunity to reflect on their practice and voice any worries and concerns. This model favours group supervision as separate from the normal organisational review of individuals and would be for the pair or more who jointly run the group. Karen John writes: 'The primary focus of group supervision is the support of the group members practically and emotionally, assisting them to share and develop their understandings and skills in working collaboratively with children and families' (John, 2008: 32).

Supervision needs to be regular and contractual, with a time and place set aside and taking high priority. The atmosphere needs to be one of debate and challenge as well as reassurance. Supervision is an integral part of running a group. It values the complex and important role group leaders undertake when running a group. 'Supervision can be the means of communicating to staff that they are important assets and that they are valued for their special contribution' (Rodd, 2006: 168).

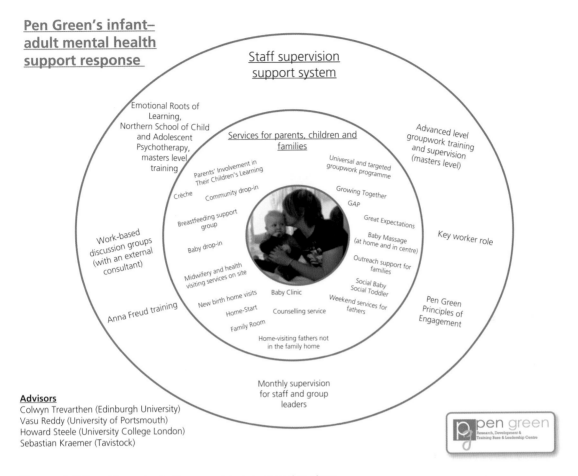

Pen Green's infant–adult mental health support response

Staff supervision support system

Emotional Roots of Learning, Northern School of Child and Adolescent Psychotherapy, masters level training

Advanced level groupwork training and supervision (masters level)

Services for parents, children and families

Parents' Involvement in Their Children's Learning

Universal and targeted groupwork programme

Crèche   Community drop-in

Growing Together GAP

Breastfeeding support group

Great Expectations

Work-based discussion groups (with an external consultant)

Baby drop-in

Baby Massage (at home and in centre)

Key worker role

Midwifery and health visiting services on site

Outreach support for families

Social Baby Social Toddler

New birth home visits   Baby Clinic

Weekend services for fathers

Pen Green Principles of Engagement

Anna Freud training

Home-Start   Counselling service

Family Room

Home-visiting fathers not in the family home

Monthly supervision for staff and group leaders

Advisors
Colwyn Trevarthen (Edinburgh University)
Vasu Reddy (University of Portsmouth)
Howard Steele (University College London)
Sebastian Kraemer (Tavistock)

pen green
Research, Development &
Training Base & Leadership Centre

Figure 6.2 Pen Green's staff supervision support system

Advanced academic level

This third element acknowledges the history and tradition of published material on the facilitation of groups, and stems from the Leicester/Tavistock human relations tradition. It provides an opportunity for sophisticated practitioners to reflect upon their own membership of a group with their fellow course members on a university masters level accredited module, and to consider how their experiential learning enlightens their own approach to the leadership of their groups. The course at Pen Green develops the participants' capacity to carry out ethical 'action research' with their group members and their co-leaders. The course takes place over a ten-week period in evening sessions that are three hours long. There are two tutors and a non-participant observer present. The number of participants varies from ten to 15. The tutors sometimes spend the first half of the session sharing groupwork theory. Then the rest of the time is the experiential group with the tutors in a consultant role. Members of the group sit in a circle and have to take responsibility to contribute and participate in the group process. Leaders emerge in the group – the group functions as each person says something. The tutors comment only occasionally on what they observe happening and link this to theory. By participating in this experiential group, participants have the opportunity to study group dynamics at first hand. They can explore the interactions and behaviours of different people in the group, including themselves, and observe how their behaviour may influence other group members. David Armstrong in his paper stated that 'If the group is potentially an arena for transformations, what is it that is being transformed, what does the process of transformation involve and what is its value?' (Armstrong, 1992: 263).

As a result of this personal experience what develops is a reflective practitioner who continuously revises and refines their leadership role on a secure evidence base and has a deeper understanding of what it feels like to be a group member.

A group leader reflects on her experience of taking part in the advanced module: 'Being part of an experiential group was a very different but powerful way of learning for me. I gained valuable insights into group relationships and processes. I was able to analyse my own learning rather than only reading of other people's experiences in books.'

Evaluation of the groupwork programme

As an organisation we recognised that in order to provide services for families, we need to establish what current service users feel about the groups that they currently attend. We compiled a questionnaire for participants to fill in asking for their thoughts on the group that they were attending. In previous consultation with families some of the feedback regarding the questionnaires was that families felt limited in how they could respond. So, before the evaluations of spring 2012, a working group of parents and carers, volunteers and staff met together to co-construct a comprehensive programme for the evaluation process. This consisted of:

- looking at the appropriateness of the previous questionnaire
- discussing how the questionnaire would be used
- considering the timescale of evaluation
- planning for outcomes from the evaluation.

The outcome of these planning meetings enabled us to approach the evaluation process in a more inclusive and user-friendly mode.

- We devised a questionnaire which included open-ended questions.
- A process for parent volunteers to go into each individual group with the questionnaires rather than the group leaders asking the questions.
- A three-week block was identified for the evaluation process to take place.
- Parents or carers have been given the opportunity to take part in further evaluations of our services. We are linking this to a data document which will give us qualitative and quantitative information on our entire groupwork programme.

Key information

Themes from parents' and carers' voices

- Reduction in isolation, getting out the house and having something to look forward to in the week
- Socialisation relating to adults and children, building relationships, making friendships
- Children happily engaged and parents or carers being able to have some time to themselves, for example time to drink a hot cup of tea
- The opportunity to use all of the spaces and resources within the centre
- Recommendations and signposting from professionals and other parents or carers
- Support which can be experienced by providing a listening ear, being available for parents to talk to, providing families with choices and being aware of what is going on for families
- Safe environment, which does not only mean creating a relaxed safe physical environment but also creating an emotionally safe environment too. Group leaders try to provide an emotionally safe environment by tuning in to parents' body language and being aware of the mood in the group. Initially group leaders would get a good indication of how parents were feeling by greeting them and offering them a hot drink and engaging in conversation with each other. This approach to groupwork relates to Bion's concept of 'containment' (1962), which he describes as the parent acknowledging the baby's feelings of distress, being able to understand them and responding to the baby.

Where next?

We constantly review our groupwork programme, both to evaluate what has happened and to decide what we now need to do. The challenge for us now is to continue to:

- balance the needs of our community and what we can offer against staff skills, funding and venue availability
- balance the findings from local, national and community data against what we can offer in terms of staff and parents' skills and knowledge base
- promote the groupwork programme for families in our community who do not currently access the centre – promotional literature being more available within the community, such as leaflets in local doctors' surgeries, community centres and shops
- widen our information via social networking sites
- continue to work alongside and make links with other workers and professionals from partner agencies to co-lead groups within our centre
- continue to support the skills and expertise of parents, volunteers and staff.

Points for discussion

- How do you decide which groups to run in your setting?
- What sorts of professional development do you provide for workers running groups for parents?
- How effectively are you able to evaluate your groupwork?

References

Armstrong, D. (1992) 'Names, thoughts and lies: the relevance of Bion's later writings to the understanding of experiences in groups', *Free Associations*, vol. 26, no. 3, pp. 261–82. Available from: http://human-nature.com/hraj/lies.html.

Bion, W. (1962) *Learning from Experience*, London: Heinemann.

Easen, P., Kendall, P. and Shaw, J. (1992) 'Parents and educators: dialogue and development through partnership', *Children and Society,* vol. 6, no. 4, pp. 282–96.

Glaser, D. (2000) 'Child abuse and neglect and the brain: a review', *Journal of Child Psychology and Psychiatry*, vol. 41, no. 1, pp. 97–116.

John, K. (2008) *Leadership Mentoring and Staff Supervision in Children's Centres. Guidance on Policy and Practice*, unpublished, Corby: Pen Green Centre.

Rodd, J. (2006) *Leadership in Early Childhood*, Maidenhead: Open University Press.

Schore, A. (1994) *Affect Regulation and the Origin of the Self: The neurobiology of emotional development*, New Jersey: Lawrence Erlbaum.

Stern, D. (1971) 'A micro-analysis of mother–infant interactions: behaviours regulating social contact between a mother and her three-and-a-half-month-old twins', *Journal of the American Academy of Child Psychiatry*, vol. 10, pp. 507–17.

Trevarthen, C. and Aitken, K. J. (2001) 'Infant intersubjectivity: research, theory and clinical application', *Journal of Child Psychology and Psychiatry*, vol. 42, no. 1, pp. 3–48.

Woodhead, J., Bland, K. and Baradon, T. (2006) 'Focusing the lens: the use of digital video in the practice and evaluation of parent–infant psychotherapy', *Infant Observation*, vol. 9, no. 2, pp. 139–50.

7

The Family Room: providing a space for the community to drop in
Sandra Mole and Caroline Griffiths

In this chapter the workers currently involved in the Family Room:
- introduce themselves
- introduce examples from practice to communicate the value of the Family Room
- offer reflections on their work.

Introduction

We begin this chapter by outlining our own experiences as parents, as this informs our work with other parents in the context of the Family Room at the Pen Green Centre. We explain what the 'Family Room' is and how it is used by families. Most of this chapter is given over to hearing real examples from parents about their lives. Finally, we reflect on our work and on the progress made.

Sandra

I am mother to four children. I had my first three in the town I grew up in, surrounded by friends and family. Following our twin boys' birth I moved to Corby, an hour away from home. To avoid isolation I was determined to get out and meet some new people, and found Pen Green within weeks of my arrival. I use the centre most days and my enthusiasm for it rarely wanes. What started as an opportunity to play and meet new people became a chance to have a say, shape services and educate myself. As I met more and more other parents I would encourage them to get involved too, I was so excited to meet others who thought like me about children.

As my children progressed through school I started making tea for others at groups and volunteering to help out when staff were absent. As my confidence grew so did my opportunities and in the summer of 2010 I was offered the chance to work in the Family Room. I bring with me memories of being a young parent and of being spoken down to. I can recall feeling lonely and unsure of myself, and I have four children awaiting my arrival home from work who are happy to confirm I am not the perfect parent!

Caroline

I began using Pen Green in September 2000 when my first daughter was just six days old. My midwife explained about the groups on offer and I was warmly welcomed. I became pregnant for the second time while still breastfeeding and found it incredibly hard to have to stop. The support I received was invaluable and the group leader who had welcomed me so warmly to Pen Green went on to deliver my second daughter. Importantly for me, I began to make friends with other parents in the centre and was shocked to learn that I had become pregnant for the third time in three years. Pen Green was my safe place where my children could be free spirits. As a family we began fostering children and Pen Green remained somewhere that held the same beliefs as me about children. It was a safe, secure place to be, which had everything, and more, on offer for me as a mother. The facilities were second to none and my children, along with the six I have fostered, have had the freedom to play, explore and learn. When my youngest started school I was asked if I would consider working some hours within the Family Room and before long I decided to take the plunge and applied for the post permanently. I have now had the role for two years. I am passionate about my job and enjoy the day-to-day challenges it brings. The centre feels like a second home to me, it certainly was when my children were little.

What is the Family Room?

It takes a whole village to raise a child.

(African proverb)

Britain is a nation of tea drinkers; cafes, coffee shops and pubs offer the community the opportunity to come and go with easy access to 'water' – the watering hole is what has bound communities for centuries. Every community represented on television features somewhere anyone can go and get a drink: the Queen Vic in *Eastenders*, the coffee shop in *Friends* and the café in *Neighbours*. Each of these is essential in the lives of the cast and often hosts the drama and delight of everyday life. The Family Room is the watering hole of the Pen Green community. Residents can come and go and have easy access to a drink. We have regulars, one-off visitors and people who come on a particular day. Some families we know a lot about and get very involved with, others we know nothing about. Everyone is welcome but, like any other community space, newcomers are looked at and wondered about.

A community drop-in resource, the Family Room was part of the original Pen Green plan and is its longest lasting group. As McMillan envisaged over 80 years ago:

Every order of society appears to evolve certain institutions that show the nature of the society – what it is founded on, its relations to groups and classes of persons, and to reflect their mutual powers or weaknesses, privileges or needs.

(McMillan, 1930: 131)

It is open to all families but tends to be used regularly by some of our most vulnerable families; the mood of the room is often thought to reflect the mood of the community at any given time. Usage of the room has ebbed and flowed over the past 30 years; at present users must have a child under school age or be volunteering or working within the centre.

As a unique space within Corby, the Family Room offers families the opportunities Gilkes envisioned 'to meet on neutral ground, to get them out of the isolation of their homes, to help them create new friendships and a network of support outside the extended nuclear family' (Gilkes, 1987: 111). Alongside the families there have always been staff on hand. It would be impossible to write an accurate job description but 'support' would be a key word to include: we support families in their everyday lives, in their interactions with each other, in communicating with outside agencies, in planning for the future and in dealing with their past.

We arrive in the room about 8:45 a.m. and are usually tidying up the areas as the first families arrive. Hot drinks are the first thing parents head for and we very much encourage making them for yourself and anyone else in the room. Often the room is very busy and loud until about 9:45 a.m, when those with things to do in town, or groups to attend, will drift off. While there are toys available at all times we will not usually set up an activity until this time – any earlier and we will upset those children who are not staying. For the rest of the morning the room will be busy with activity and conversations.

Food is a very big part of life in the Family Room. Every day, lunch is cooked from scratch using fresh and healthy ingredients. The menu and rota of chefs is planned the week before, with regular users taking it in turns to cook for each other. So, during all the hustle and bustle in the room, someone will be in the kitchen busy preparing the feast of the day. To cover costs we ask for £1.50 for adults to eat and 50p for children, and endeavour to create fresh, tasty, cheap and healthy meals which families can then replicate at home.

Sample menu

Monday – Vegetable soup

Tuesday – Spaghetti bolognese

Wednesday – Jacket potato with beans and cheese

Thursday – Chinese vegetable noodles

Friday – Homemade fish fingers and chips

With families in and out all morning, there is little time to clear away before lunch is served. As workers, we tend to sit round a small table with all the children, while the adults sit on the large chairs around the room. Our wish would be to have a dining area created so we could all dine together.

After lunch we encourage the children to play in the garden. In summer this is well received, but it can be a real bone of contention during the less fine months. Parents take it in turns to clear up after lunch and wash up.

At 1 p.m. some children leave to go to nursery, so again we tend not to put out an activity until after that. Families will come and go all afternoon but just before 3 p.m. all will go quiet as many leave for the school run, before reigniting for the 'late shift', as the room fills with noisy and boisterous school-age children.

We find it difficult to plan, never knowing which children will come in or whether they will or won't be allowed to participate in activities like messy play or being in the garden. The beauty of a community drop-in space is that we can be responsive to whoever chooses to come in but as families come along regularly there is an expectation to develop a timetable. Parents want to know for practical reasons whether the activities will be messy or outdoors. We have to tread a fine line between organic development of services and being realistic about what parents can cope with. We have in the past planned activities and felt under real pressure when the child is desperate to join in and the parent is not allowing it, even if yesterday it was okay. This is when we need to represent the voice of the child, while managing the practicalities for the adult. Some of our most successful activities have been those with an adult and child element, from carnival preparation to bracelet-making. Many of our parents have never had those opportunities so struggle to be enthusiastic about offering them to their child.

We need to provide a safe and welcoming space. The room itself must be attractive and welcoming to adults while remaining pedagogically appropriate for the children. We have a well-fitted kitchen, seating and play areas, and a large garden. In making the room enticing we must make sure we 'blend the best aspects of home and institution' (Gilkes, 1987: 45). The room is open all day long, so activities flow from one to another with little time to clear up or reflect. With a fast turnover of users we have to remain reactive throughout the day and balance the needs of the adults with those of the children using the space. Families can use the room before, after or instead of other groups in the centre, and reasons for use vary from day to day and family to family. Some come for a cuppa and a sympathetic ear, others because it's the only place their children can get messy, some because they want to catch up with their friends, others because their child just won't stop (moving, arguing, crying, etc.). Kirk found that 'through contributing to the development of support networks and building relationships with families, early years centres can help provide a foundation for future resilience' (Kirk, 2003: 96). We know that many families stay in the Family Room because it is the place they feel safest.

Key information

- The Family Room offers a safe, welcoming environment for adults and children.
- It is open all day for people to come and go as they please.
- It is attractive to adults and pedagogically appropriate for young children.
- Anyone can make drinks and parents take turns to make a healthy lunch for each other.
- Staff are there to support families in their everyday lives.
- It is difficult to plan provision, and staff need to be responsive to whoever chooses to use the Family Room each day.

Figure 7.1 A mother with children in the Family Room

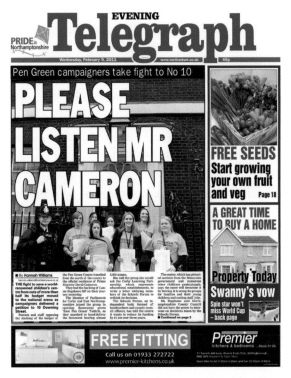

Figure 7.2 Newspaper headline and photo at Downing Street (courtesy of Northants Telegraph)

Example from practice

Mairi (mother)

Mairi has been using the Family Room for over 14 years. She first attended on the advice of her health visitor when she was pregnant with her second child and has been a key part of the room ever since. 'I had quite bad postnatal depression so wasn't into new people or groups, in fact I've always had a bit of a group phobia.'

Mairi went on to have four more children, setting up a group for non-breastfeeding mums along the way, 'that was a major issue, so we nipped the head's ear for a couple of weeks'. Holman recognised 'one of the dangers of modern social work is that by continually doing things for or to people they are made to feel even more inadequate and isolated' (Holman, 1983: 21). Mairi sensed the head didn't really think they would take it seriously, 'but he told us to go away and make a plan and he was pleased and gave us some funding to do it'.

Bastiani points out that 'what matters to most parents … is not the guarantee of immediate success, but the genuineness of a school's efforts and the spirit in which things are attempted' (Bastiani, 1989: 22).

Mairi uses the Family Room as a comfort zone, somewhere to come and relax without the demands of the home: 'There is someone there to step in, take over for a few minutes, interact with your child; there is always something going on, parents don't need to go anywhere else, it offers friendship, and support.'

Mairi has been at the forefront of many campaigns on behalf of the centre. In February 2011 when Pen Green was facing a huge cut to funding, Mairi was instrumental in collecting signatures for a petition and raising the money to visit London, presenting the petition to Downing Street. Having enjoyed a tour of the Palace of Westminster, and seeing the point of politics, she joined us at the Family Room at the Labour Party Conference, an event where different professions came together to think about family policy in the UK.

Community development and action begin when those in power meet members of the community as equals, respecting, valuing and trusting them to identify and build on their individual and collective strengths and to exercise choice about things that really matter to them.

(Trodd and Chivers, 2011: 145)

With her sixth child a year from starting school, having completed an Open University course and recently been voted a parent-governor, Mairi is still reluctant to move on from the Family Room and would like the opportunity to give something back to Pen Green. 'The Family Room is unique and other children's centres don't have things like it. Everyone comes from different places, no one knows what their problem is – they can just come in, then go home. We all have different home lives and come here, maybe my life would be a little bit different if I did not have somewhere to go, I would be stuck in the house, depressed.'

It is our hope to be alongside parents as their confidence grows while fostering a belief in their own abilities. As Whalley asserts:

Too often families become known to professional agencies because of their tragedies or their vulnerabilities. Many have been labelled for so long that they have forgotten where their strengths and interests lie, or have never been given the opportunity to discover them.

(Whalley et al., 1997: 67)

It was our job to inspire Mairi's citizenship and sense of community, increase awareness of her political voice, acknowledge and contain her anxieties and build upon all her existing skills and attributes. One of the keys of the success of the Family Room is that parents decide when they use it and for how long: had Mairi been offered a six-week parenting course one wonders whether her passion would still have been ignited!

Example from practice

Tom (baby)

We could not fail to notice Tom in the Family Room, his high-pitched cries echoed through the centre. When his mother held him it was at arm's length, as far from her as possible. Feeding was a fractious and emotive affair, and more often than not unsuccessful. As mothers we both wanted to try and soothe Tom but knew to do so successfully would undermine the confidence of his obviously depressed mother. In the event Tom could find no comfort from any of us and his cries continued to tear through the centre.

'I absolutely hated Tom, I thought he was the most evil child because everybody else's child would eat and be happy and there was mine screaming.'

As professionals we talk a lot about attachment problems (Bowlby, 1969) but to witness it day after day was mentally and emotionally draining. We both knew what was happening, what the impact could be but had to bear the pain of not being able to rescue mother or child.

Because Tom struggled to feed, he failed to gain weight and his mother would ping-pong from professional to professional, being seen by doctors, nurses and health visitors, as well as other colleagues in Pen Green. As the weeks went on the feeding got worse and our observations of mother and child became more alarming. Tom refused to allow bottles in his mouth or seemed to vomit what little he had been fed. We felt scared that no one was joining up or seeing how much both were suffering. We recognised that they needed support but felt unsure where to start. Quinton points out that 'it's easy to respond to a problem by saying that we should put in more support, without being at all clear on what we mean by that or what we want to achieve' (Quinton, 2004: 21).

With his mother's permission we liaised with the local health service so that whenever Tom presented for treatment they would alert us; sometimes this was four times in a week. Often Tom would need to be seen by a doctor on a Friday and through talking with his mother we realised this was because the prospect of a whole weekend with him was terrifying. Tom was admitted to hospital a few times, and to ensure a joined-up approach we would visit in the evenings, sharing our concerns with the doctors.

Sometimes we felt unheard, but with courage in our convictions we pushed boundaries and challenged other professionals we perceived to be far higher up than us in the pursuit of ensuring Tom's voice was heard.

'I remember that Sunday, you knew I was struggling and you were my voice because I just did not have one – I was a million miles away; you were both saying "you need to take her seriously because she is going to end up in the system" to the doctors; I was literally going to give him up, I was ready to walk.'

When in the Family Room we would focus on the positive and encourage benevolent experiences (Lieberman et al., 2005), having time together in our snoozelen for calm cuddles, or using a sling, so Tom could hear his mother's heartbeat, a reminder of their bond. On film we endeavoured to catch those tiny glimmers when mother and child looked at each other, affirming that only she was qualified to offer the love he craved.

As help was put in place, Tom found feeding easier. He never lost his affection for his mother and we were able to witness a change in their relationship. We do not see Tom very often anymore, but his mother is making up for lost time, attending lots of Pen Green groups and going on outings with new friends. She feels like they are getting their relationship back.

'For me if the Family Room wasn't there I would not be in the same place I am, it was my sanctuary when I was having so many problems, they gave me my backbone when I had none.'

Because the Family Room is open all day, Tom and his mother were able to come and stay, day after day. An appointment in a doctor's office, or even a morning playgroup, offers only a time-limited snapshot. We saw the reality of life for Tom, rather than saying you should do this or do that, we held and fed Tom, holding and feeding as we would have held and fed our own babies, a coming together of three adults to love Tom. If Tom did not come in we would pop out and see him at home. Daws points out that:

Paying attention to parents may help them to find resources from within themselves. Often, parents come describing complex and fraught feeding situations and may then calm down simply with the experience of being listened to and taken seriously.

(Daws, 1999: 271)

Example from practice

Example from practice

Denise and Sandra (mother and worker)

I met Denise on a sunny day, my first day working in the Family Room. It was hard to see what she looked like as all I could see was a young woman under a baseball cap, which was under a hoodie, which was under a coat which was wrapped with a scarf. She was sitting with her knees to her chest and her arms folded across them. I am not a body language expert but she gave the impression she was not open to a conversation!

Carrying on regardless, over the weeks, as her son warmed to me, so did Denise and I learned that, like me, she was a mother of four. She shared with me the grief that was overshadowing her life; soon after her youngest child was born her brother tragically died in a car accident and things spiralled out of control. Unable to cope with the grief, her relationship with the children's father became more and more volatile. Eventually he left, leaving Denise in a downward spiral of drug-taking, beginning with cannabis and ending up spending hundreds of pounds feeding a cocaine habit.

Having weaned herself off cocaine she had been using the Family Room for about a year. As with most individuals her journey through parenthood had been varied and it would be unfair to characterise it by attaching one specific label; at different points in the last ten years she has worked full time, claimed income support, been part of a couple and been a single parent.

Sometimes she would appear exhausted. My instinct was that the best thing we could do for her, and her children, was to allow her the space and time to catch up on some sleep. We found an unused room, a relaxation CD and a blanket, and would wrap her up for a rest. In time she confided that she struggled with sleeping and could not go to bed without a few joints of cannabis. We got talking with the local well-being team about their sleep management courses. Reluctant to go alone, Caroline (worker) joined her for the weekly sessions. After their completion she told us she was down to one joint a night.

However, with the anniversary of her brother's death approaching, Denise confided in me that she had been struggling more and more and was using a lot more cannabis again. As the Family Room was relatively quiet I suggested we pop along to CAN [drug and alcohol agency]. We were seen immediately and an appointment was made for acupuncture therapy the following week. Denise was keen to attend but adamant that I join her. In the actual session she was brilliant at taking care of me, a lifelong needle phobic, while receiving her treatment. I felt it strengthened our relationship for her to see my weakness. Maslow talks about how when we 'give people affection and security, they will give affection and be secure in their feelings and their behaviour' (see, for example, Bronstein, 2009).

I noticed that the better our relationship got, the fewer layers of clothing she wore. I was shocked to see how slim she was the first time she walked in wearing a vest top and jeans. Munro notes that 'the quality of the relationship between the child and family and professionals directly impacts on the effectiveness of help given' (Munro, 2011: 23). I could tell when something was wrong because the layers would be piled back on. As we got closer I could spot when Denise was angry and likely to lose control; I would kneel down and suggest we go outside to cool down. We got good at popping out for a fag when things were about to get heated and over time she did not need me to go with her.

Denise could be very loud and aggressive at times and some staff seemed reluctant to work with her. But 'it is not a failure to fear a powerful, aggressive parent. These parents need a strong, caring staff member to help them as much as the depressed and inadequate parents' (Gilkes, 1987: 49). I felt able to see beyond the bravado and noticed a kind but vulnerable woman who was really keen to try new things. Taking the time to include her in all activities meant she was able to take more risks and challenge herself to grow and learn. In a report about parents who use drugs we are advised that we 'should develop interventions that focus on parenting strengths and on confidence building, helping parents to recognise their own areas of competence and vulnerability' (Hogan & Higgins, 2001: 32).

Denise was one of our most regular lunchtime chefs and successfully undertook the food hygiene course. As her youngest child was approaching school age she completed the New Start course so she could start volunteering within Pen Green and she has not used any drugs for over six months.

People who are properly listened to and appreciated for who they are and what they have to face may then be able to take on the ideas about themselves ... then start thinking for themselves and perhaps create some of what was missing.

(Daws, 1999: 278)

Figure 7.3 The carnival float

Example from practice

Example from practice

Ashley and Alan (mother and father)

'We both really enjoy the Family Room and groups at Pen Green, but with Alan working shifts it is mostly Ashley that gets to have all the fun with the children.'

Ashley remembered years ago Pen Green doing a carnival but, having grown up on the Isle of Man, Alan had never seen one. The couple thought it would be something great to do with other parents in the Family Room, 'with the new blood of Sandra and Caroline we saw an opportunity to try something a bit different; as it was Oliver's last year at nursery he could go out with a bang'.

When they suggested it to us, we encouraged them to find out all the information and see who else would be interested. Ashley emailed the committee about all the rules etc.: 'It felt like ages trying to get everything finalised but once it was done it was full steam ahead. It was amazing because everyone wanted to help make stuff and get creative.'

Having found out that the Dads' Club was also interested in doing a float they worked in partnership to create one fabulous float. The whole thing was decked out in pieces made by the children and parents from across the centre, the Family Room and the Dads' Club, 'it felt like a real accomplishment'.

It was fascinating for us to be alongside the families while we prepared for the carnival, often some are reluctant to take part in messy play or arty endeavours but with a clear focus everyone worked hard all day. Some even came back after school with their older children, to design, create and decorate pieces. 'By talking together, comparing ideas, discussing common experiences, and perhaps undertaking some kind of joint activity people come to understand and trust one another' (Gilchrist, 2004: 42). Having a clear direction and goal inspired parents to join in activities with their children and gave others what they needed to take risks, take part and try something new.

On carnival day the float was packed, Ashley sat proudly with Oliver while Alan walked beaming alongside with baby Ava. Their efforts were recognised when the float was given a trophy and for the remainder of the year parents talked about the next one.

Ashley and Alan could not come to this year's carnival. They were getting married. The carnival evoked the same enthusiasm and looks set to be a regular feature of the Family Room calendar for years to come, Eisenstadt, when reviewing Sure Start, comments that 'just doing what parents ask for will not work. But never doing what parents ask for will create a centre that no one wants to use' (Eisenstadt, 2011: 157).

Reflections

Underpinning everything we do is a belief in the power of people. Mezirow advises that 'critical reflectivity is fostered with a premium placed on personalising what is learned by applying insights to one's own life and works as opposed to mere intellectualisation' (Mezirow, 1981: 133). We both remember how it feels as a young mother to be made to feel you don't fit someone else's agenda. The parents do not need the Family Room or the centre to fix them; we aim to be 'really human, empathetic, loving, communicative, and humble' (Freire, 1972: 139) and certainly don't believe that our payslips make us holders of an ultimate truth which we need to impart upon those families using the space.

We know that all of the parents using the Family Room try their best and want their children to succeed. We also recognise that, however hard any of us tries, sometimes life just gets in the way. Our role is to embrace the whole family and be alongside them through whatever, whenever.

On a good day we are a community of people who really care about each other and share discoveries. On a bad day we are a rivalrous group competing to have unmet needs satisfied. The room can be loud and intimidating to those on the outside, with difficult emotions often rife. Staff and families alike can get a bad feeling and be reluctant to use the space. For those families who do, however, the room becomes an important part of their lives. We hope to:

> recreate some of the advantages of family life on a wider community base ... a relaxed informal atmosphere, acceptance of people for what they are, encouragement to develop potential to the full and the provision of basic needs of physical and emotional care, continuity and security.
>
> (Phelan, 1983: 38)

Much is made of the behaviour of the women in the Family Room but actually a lot of it is very ordinary: scapegoating, leadership, complaining and falling out about men is what can be seen acted out by groups of women in so many communities, in the coffee shops, pubs and watering holes on the TV and in the real world.

Figure 7.4 A mother and child in the Family Room

Points for discussion

- Are you able to offer a space for parents to drop in anytime of day?
- Which of these stories resonated with your experience of working with parents?
- Think about the progress each family made over time – which families do you know who have been supported to grow in some of these ways?

References

Bastiani, J. (1989) *Working with Parents: A whole school approach*, Windsor: NFER–Nelson.

Bowlby, J. (1969) *Attachment and Loss. Vol. 1: Attachment*, London: Hogarth Press.

Bronstein, S. F. (2009) *Maslow's Hierarchy: Safety needs* [online]. Available from http://stanleybronstein.com/maslows-hierarchy-safety-needs/ (accessed Jan. 2013).

Daws, D. (1999) 'Parent–infant psychotherapy: remembering the Oedipus complex', *Psychoanalytic Inquiry: A Topical Journal for Mental Health Professionals*, vol. 19, no. 2, pp. 267–78.

Eisenstadt, N. (2011) *Providing a Sure Start*, Bristol: Policy Press.

Freire, P. (1972) *Pedagogy of the Oppressed*, London: Penguin.

Gilchrist, A. (2004) *The Well-connected Community*, Bristol: Policy Press.

Gilkes, J. (1987) *Developing Nursery Education*, Milton Keynes: Open University Press.

Hogan, D. and Higgins, L. (2001) *When Parents Use Drugs*, Dublin: Children's Research Centre.

Holman, B. (1983) *Resourceful Friends: Skills in community social work*, London: Children's Society.

Kirk, R. (2003) 'Family support: the role of early years centres', *Children and Society*, vol. 17, pp. 85–99.

Lieberman, A., Padron, E., Van Horn, P. and Harris, W. (2005) 'Angels in the nursery: the intergenerational transmission of benevolent parental influences', *Infant Mental Health Journal*, vol. 26, no. 6, pp. 504–20.

McMillan, M. (1930) *The Nursery School*, London: Dent.

Mezirow, J. (1981) 'A critical theory of adult learning and education', *Adult Education Journal,* vol. 32, no. 1, pp.3–24.

Munro, E. (2011) *The Munro Review of Child Protection. Final report – a child centered system*, London: HMG.

Phelan, J. (1983) *Family Centres: A study*, London: The Children's Society.

Quinton, D. (2004) *Supporting Parents: Messages from research*, London: Jessica Kingsley.

Trodd, L. and Chivers, L. (2011*) Interprofessional Working in Practice: Learning and working together for children and families*, Maidenhead: Open University Press.

Whalley, M. (1994) *Learning to Be Strong: Setting up a neighbourhood service for under-fives and their families,* London: Hodder & Stoughton.

Whalley, M. and the Pen Green Centre team (1997) *Working With Parents*, London: Hodder & Stoughton.

8

Family Support for families with young children

Sheena Griffiths-Baker, Carol McFarlane, Rebecca Elliott and Judy Potts

Key points in this chapter on Family Support are:

- The most effective Family Support for families with young children is 'early intervention'.
- Children's centres provide the ideal venue for multi-disciplinary, multi-agency integrated services, with local families and local volunteers providing Family Support services alongside professionals.
- Families with the most complex challenges require targeted services; they prefer these to be alongside universal services.
- Families value relationships with workers based on genuine partnership and recognition of their uniqueness; these relationships enable real and sustainable change.
- Regular, robust supervision is vital for the well-being of workers supporting families with overwhelming difficulties, and to ensure children are always safeguarded.

Introduction

This chapter draws on current research findings and government policy that the most effective Family Support for families with young children is 'early intervention'. This has two meanings: services need to start as soon as there is a pregnancy in the family, and services need to be offered before problems become overwhelming. Children's centres are the best place to locate these integrated services, as they are within the local community and they provide a venue for a range of disciplines and agencies. Children's centres must provide specialist support to those families with the most complex challenges. Research shows that such families are more likely to take up these services if they are offered alongside universal services by workers with a principled approach, who believe in building relationships of trust, honouring each family's unique circumstances, respecting their priorities and choices. This requires highly skilled practitioners, who have regular supervision and training, so they are able to empower parents while safeguarding children. The case studies, particularly from the parents' perspectives, illustrate these principles in practice.

Family Support

Family Support for families with young children responds to a range of needs and is provided by a range of integrated services across professional and agency boundaries. The focus is on early intervention, antenatally as well as postnatally. Graham Allen's report demands that all parties accept that early intervention is the most effective way of delivering services:

> *The central objective of Early Intervention is to provide a social and emotional bedrock for the current and future generations of babies, children and young people by helping them and their parents (or other main caregivers) before problems arise.*
>
> (Allen, 2011: 6)

Children's centres are becoming the hub for welfare agencies, health services, early years education services, and Family Support services delivered by children's centre workers and through voluntary sector services located in the centre.

The core purpose of children's centres is stated as being:

> *Focused on improving outcomes for young children and their families, and reducing inequalities particularly around:*
>
> - *child development and school readiness*
>
> - *parenting aspirations, self-esteem and skills*
>
> - *family health and well-being.*
>
> (http://www.foundationyears.org.uk, 2013)

Family Support has always been a central element of the work of Pen Green and is practised across domains with Family Workers in the Nursery, Baby Nest and Family Room and in the groupwork programme, offering support to families alongside the outreach Family Support team and a range of voluntary sector agencies both within Pen Green and in the local community.

Our Family Support team includes social workers, Family Support workers, a maternity assistant, a sessional health professional and a deputy head. A universal, early intervention service is provided in partnership with health services. Our team visits all families with new births who agree to contact with their children's centre. We are able both to tell families about the huge range of services on offer and invite them to visit, begin a relationship with them, and pick up on families needing enhanced support.

Family Support is not just about professionals and families working together; we believe in the contribution that local families make to supporting each other. We encourage families to get together by providing supported spaces throughout the centre where families can meet together informally. They also meet together in the groups they choose to attend as well as when using services provided by local parent volunteers. Family Support aims to build resilience, by strengthening family and community-based support networks.

Frank Field's report on poverty and children's life chances states:

> *In general, the most effective and cost-effective way to help and support young families is in the earliest years of a child's life. By the age of three, a baby's brain is 80 per cent formed.*
>
> (Field, 2010: 7)

> *Sure Start Children's Centres should re-focus on their original purpose and identify, reach and provide targeted help to the most disadvantaged families. New Sure Start contracts should include conditions that reward Centres for reaching out effectively and improving the outcomes of the most disadvantaged children.*
>
> (Field, 2010: 9)

Through Integrated Working Procedures (Northamptonshire Children and Young People's Partnership, 2012) all agencies providing services for families with children operate within the same framework. The Vulnerability Matrix defines the four levels of need. For each level, the expected developmental milestones of the baby or young child are stated, alongside the expected parenting abilities and the available services relevant to families.

Children's centres are expected to offer support to families at:

- Level 3 – Needs causing concern requiring a targeted response
- Level 4 – Needs require specialist and/or statutory services.

Families prefer and are more likely to access intensive support when it is offered within a universal service. Carmel Devaney (2011) emphasises the importance of the relationships formed and the support required by workers engaged in this complex work. She states that this work should be mediated by an enabling, empowering relationship between worker/volunteer and the family, and that reflective practice and high-quality supervision are essential.

The government literature review, the *Think Family* report (Social Exclusion Task Force, 2008: 3), reveals the complexity of providing this intensive support across diverse family structures and difficulties. It notices that marginalised families may be demonstrating significant strengths which might go under-recognised if services focus on risk and responsibility. It notes that approaches such as the 'ethic of care' and supporting resilience are relevant to all families, and may provide a model for developing preferred ways of working between (public) professionals and (private) families. It finds that positive interdependency within families requires recognition and support, and the components of the working relationship between families and professionals (trust, openness, respect, responsivity) are crucial, regardless of the actual service type (whether 'specialist' or 'mainstream').

In 2010 the National Quality Improvement Network published a framework for local authorities and national organisations to evaluate and improve engagement with families. Gillian Pugh, while acknowledging that the concept of partnership is not new, states: 'Partnership should be based on a "principled" approach that recognises and builds on parents' expertise, where professionals and parents really listen to and learn from each other in ways that are valued and evaluated by parents themselves' (Pugh, 2010: 2).

A consultation conference held at the Pen Green Research Base, on 9 November 2009, provided a forum for the formulation of ten such principles for engaging with families.

The essential principle is that:

> **Successful and sustained engagement with families is maintained when practitioners work alongside families in a valued working relationship.**
>
> (ELPPEG, 2010: 9)

The key elements of this are:

1 Practitioners and parents are willing to listen to and learn from each other.
2 Practitioners respect what families know and already do.
3 Practitioners find ways to actively engage those who do not traditionally access services.
4 Parents are encouraged and supported to become decision-makers in organisations and services.
5 The quality of this relationship enables families' views, opinions and expectations of services to be raised and their confidence as service users increased.
6 The whole family is supported.

7 More intensive, specialist services are available within a universal setting.

8 This type of Family Support, specially created for each family's unique circumstances, requires regular effective support and supervision for staff, encouraging evaluation and self-reflection.

9 Family Support with families living with complex challenges requires practitioners to be constantly mindful of safeguarding and honest in sharing concerns.

It seems that it is not 'family support' as a concept in itself that encourages people to seek help, instead it is a network of relationships, and the quality and nature of those relationships, that brings people into contact with the team at Pen Green.

Key information

To support families struggling with multiple challenges workers need to be flexible, persistent, patient, meet families on their own patch, and make equal efforts to engage fathers and mothers.

Families are more likely to take up services where the principle of partnership working through respectful relationships is central, and where families feel that their unique history, culture and strengths are being valued. In turn, families come to listen and respect workers' knowledge, expertise and child-focused perspectives, and let these inform their choices of how to change and grow.

Family Support in practice

Below are accounts of one of our workers' involvement with four families with very different situations and needs. However, they all illustrate many of the above key qualities and the key component of creating trusting, encouraging relationships.

Example from practice

Family 1: family with complex family relationships and multiple challenges

Mother Louisa had four children aged birth to six with partner Cam. She was pregnant. Father Cam had serious mental health problems, drug use, historic trauma, requiring specialist services. Dual diagnosis services and forensic mental health services were unable to provide ongoing support. Cam rarely left the house. He had complex family issues with his ex-partner and their two children. With safeguarding concerns about these children, children's social services became involved. Cam was too unwell to participate actively in meetings to address these concerns. Support lasted two years with this family.

When Louisa first came into contact with the Family Support team she was pregnant with her fifth child, living with Cam and their four young children. Carly (Family Support worker) was recommended to Louisa by a friend. The mental health problems suffered by Cam for many years prompted Louisa to make contact with Carly when she felt that she needed support to cope. This was to be her first contact with Pen Green. She found the courage to contact

Carly by telephone and to ask if she would come out to visit the family in their home. When Carly and Steph, the centre's mental health worker, visited the family, they were prepared to give Louisa as long as she needed to talk everything through and to explain what she felt the family needed in terms of support.

At first Carly visited Louisa at home, but gradually, on Carly's suggestion, she began to access the Great Expectations group in the centre. As Louisa says, 'It was a bit scary because I'd never done group stuff or anything like that but I think after a couple of weeks I started to get used to it.' With Carly's encouragement, she went on to complete a counselling course and has plans to begin a literacy course also on offer at the centre.

For Louisa, the success of her involvement with the Family Support team lies in the quality of her relationship with Carly. At first it was hard for her to discuss sensitive issues with someone outside the family, as she explains, 'Before Carly started coming out, I didn't really go anywhere or talk to anyone. It was just me, the children and Cam.' This gives some measure of the degree of isolation she experienced coping on her own. Gradually a trusting relationship developed. Louisa says, 'I would never believe a support worker would be so easy to talk to and so helpful. She is really helpful.'

Carly supported Cam when he went to Child in Need meetings and mental health appointments. Cam had previously not been able to leave the house and go to CAN for drug/alcohol counselling. Carly arranged for these appointments to be at Pen Green which enabled Cam to access this service. Louisa explains, 'Cam's one of these that doesn't really listen. He listens to the bits that *he* wants to hear. Carly explained it a lot to him so he knew where he was going.' Louisa said that support was available for 'the family as a whole, the whole unit'.

Carly says, 'I learnt an awful lot about drugs and mental health issues. I learnt lots from the partner's point of view. How it was for Louisa to hold it all together. And as a support worker, to hold all the parts of the whole in mind: the pregnant mum, who was also the partner of a person with serious mental health problems, the children, and the father with these problems. I discovered how inadequate services are for those with a dual diagnosis of both mental health and drug use. Adult services are compartmentalised and sometimes the safeguarding of children can be lost.'

Carly found that Abel, their two-year-old, had a very insecure attachment to both parents. Carly worked closely with the crèche team at Pen Green to support the child's gradual separation from his parents and growing ability to enjoy play in the crèche.

Cam's mental health problems were too disturbing for him to feel confident to look after his children alone. Carly supported his attachment by introducing Parent's Involvement in Their Children's Learning (PICL) techniques during her home visits. She encouraged Cam to film his children's play. He was seeing his child through a lens – one step removed – and this felt safer for him. Later, he had time and brain space to look at the video clips, often with Louisa, and develop his understanding of his child's play.

Alice, their four-year-old, was given a high-staffing-ratio 'Nurture' place in her Reception class. This involved play sessions at their local children's centre, which Louisa was not comfortable to go into. Carly supported Louisa's introduction to this centre and Louisa was subsequently able to support her daughter's play sessions there.

Reflection

Marginalised families often do not trust services enough to risk their involvement. It was only on the personal recommendation of a friend that Louisa took the risk of contacting Carly.

Adults with serious mental health problems and significant drug/alcohol use find difficulty in accessing appropriate services, as do their carers. Cam was very apprehensive about being truthful about how he felt as he feared how agencies would react to the perceived risks.

Adult services and children's services find difficulty in coming together informally or having meetings about their concerns. The interagency aspect of this work involved:

- Children's Services – Child in Need team
- primary and secondary schools
- Community Mental Health team
- Dual Diagnosis team (briefly)
- Forensic team (referral but didn't provide a service)
- health visitor
- mental health worker at Pen Green
- principal social worker at Pen Green
- CAN (drug/alcohol counselling)
- local children's centre
- crèche and groupwork programme at Pen Green.

The simple skills of slowly building trust through listening, preparing parents for meetings by explaining procedures and building their confidence, being alongside parents at meetings and going through what's happened afterwards, all allowed this disenfranchised father to take a more positive, active role in the care of the children from his previous partnership. Through the PICL work, Cam now has a very positive, hands–on relationship with both his little boys and all his children from his current relationship.

Louisa was no longer isolated and dealing with all the complex challenges herself. As Cam became stronger, she could find more space to prepare for her pregnancy and to be with her children. She began to build her self-confidence and to participate in her continuing education.

Example from practice

Family 2: support for a travelling family

The family are Irish travellers. They had just arrived in Corby. The father William came with four children, aged two to 18. Later, the mother came with another of William's children and two of her own, making seven children in total. The family wanted a plot on a local site but the site had been closed. They had to park illegally on the verge where there were no domestic services for the family. The family wanted school and nursery places, and wanted to register with medical services and get appropriate benefits for the family's new circumstances.

New to the area, William, the head of the family, sought help from the Citizens Advice Bureau in the town and was re-directed to the children's centre and Family Support. William explained, 'I was in a caravan and things were very difficult. It was okay coming in here. They (Carly) helped me straight away. If it wasn't for this place I'd have cracked up to be honest with you.' He continues, 'They help me with paperwork, forms, things like that. They're helping with the doctors and we're hoping to get the children into the school over the way.' As the family were parked illegally and had no basic services, Carly prioritised getting the Traveller Liaison service involved.

Reflecting on the experience of walking into the children's centre and what it was that enabled him to connect with the people he encountered there, William says, 'I'm the kind of person, if you're straight with me, I'm okay with that … I'm straight with you. They (Carly) were straight from the beginning and I like that.' Straightforward honesty is a key factor for William in forging a successful relationship, as is acceptance. Victoria, William's eldest daughter, said of her experience, 'Within the first day we felt very welcomed. Everyone was very friendly, not judgemental, not seeing us as portrayed on the TV, but seeing us as the people we are. They chat with me, chat with the kids.'

The relationship with Carly is central. Victoria says, 'She is very friendly. She will let us know what we can do … if we want to do something like bake cakes she will tell us if it's okay or not.'

William also felt that this would be a good place for the children to mix with children from outside the travelling community, settled children. William's children range from two to 18 years. They enjoy the opportunity to play within the centre.

Ten-year-old Lily says that it is 'kinda fun here … making stuff like cakes and things'. Monty, aged eight, spotted a poster in the cloakroom at Pen Green Nursery, which showed a traveller family. As he toured the centre, he said to his sister, Lily, 'Do you see, they like travellers here.' Later on, he said, 'They like me.'

While their two-year-old and four-year-old were settling in to Nursery, their eldest daughter talked with their Family Worker and showed interest in the EYFS. She commented how the four-year-old's language had improved after a few weeks in Nursery, being with other small children.

Initially, the older children had no school places and, while the younger children were in Nursery, they spent time in the Family Room, Beach and Gardens. Often the family stayed till 6 p.m.

Reflection

Traveller families face discrimination from both institutions and individuals. This case study illustrates that when a Family Support worker can interact with *all* members of a family so they feel really listened to and accepted, and the organisation has taken care to promote positive images and become knowledgeable about specialist traveller services, then real barriers can be overcome and the family can access universal services.

Our initial response was crucial. William first talked to a very welcoming parent volunteer at Reception, who immediately fetched Carly who was straight away able to listen and plan with William how best to respond and involve other agencies.

Family Support needs to be flexible and tailor-made to each unique family. This family appreciated the use of the washing machine at the centre and the chance to bake cakes, just as much as help with engaging with the many other agencies.

The interagency aspect of this Family Support involved Carly supporting William to engage with the following agencies:

- Traveller Liaison officer and Community Support worker for Northamptonshire
- health visitor
- Pen Green Nursery and Family Room
- Job Centre to update benefits
- Corby Borough Council housing officer
- school liaison officer
- assigned police officer.

William's first visit to one of these agencies was on his own. On his second visit to one of these agencies, Carly accompanied him but sat apart while he discussed his needs with the worker. He said, 'That was very different from the first time I came.' Was this because he was feeling more encouraged or did Carly's presence in the background make a difference?

Example from practice

Example from practice

Family 3: long-term support and a good ending

Mary is a single parent. She had a stormy relationship with her East European ex-partner, and they parted when their only child, Connor, was small. Mary has used Pen Green services and Home-Start since her son was born over four years ago. Her health visitor has given a lot of support, her son was in Nurture Group (see Chapter 5) and Nursery at Pen Green. There have been safeguarding concerns on several occasions, and at one point Connor lived with the extended family for a few months.

Mary asked for a Family Support worker even though Connor was at Pen Green Nursery and she was in contact with the centre daily. She particularly asked for Carly because Carly had been a group leader in the group Mary had recently attended – a group to support the parenting of drug- and alcohol-misusing parents.

Mary said that things were difficult at home and with Connor's behaviour. During the group Mary spoke a lot, 'I'd go in and speak very fast. Carly would break it down, so I could see it, so I could see what was happening to Connor. I was just – oh my God; I couldn't understand what was going on in his head. I wanted to *understand* more, instead of thinking he was naughty.'

When the group finished, Mary was allocated Carly within a few weeks.

At first they met in Pen Green while Connor was in nursery. That meant Mary had two workers, Carly and Connor's Family Worker in nursery, with the potential of splitting. Mary said, 'When Connor was in nursery I felt I was being told what to do all the time but with Carly, I could make my own decisions. They were completely different relationships – I saw my nursery worker every day but she only came to visit every six to eight weeks, whereas I saw Carly every week at home. The nursery worker was more supportive of Connor, I understand that.'

Then, at the end of the summer term, Connor left Pen Green Nursery, and Carly visited at home. Mary said, 'I found that really nice. It was my own territory, so it was more relaxing for me, more meaningful.' Mary explained that it was significant to her that Carly was taking time to come to her house. Connor was in bed and it was a good time for Mary to speak without distractions. Mary said, 'I felt special and important.'

They talked about 'loads of stuff'. Mary says Carly did more than just listen and help her sort out her thoughts. 'There would be times when Carly would challenge me; she would say, 'What do you think Connor would feel?' I would be having a moan, saying Connor's done this or that. Carly would say, 'You can get your head round that, you're an adult.' It helped me, it meant I could sit and understand stuff about Connor.'

Mary also felt Carly helped with her confidence and self-esteem. 'Carly would reassure me because I kept doubting myself; she challenged my negative thought patterns.'

Then Mary had a very significant bereavement, which she had been dreading – her grandmother, whom she had lived with as a young child and again when she was a teenager, died. Mary said, 'When Gran died, Carly's visits helped me a lot to cope with my feelings. It meant I was able to hold it back for Connor, and with Carly I was able to say whatever was in my mind.'

Carly also helped Mary to understand and reflect on all the other services she was then engaged with. At this point, Connor had a Child Protection Plan and involvement with a Children's Services social worker, CAN counselling, Corby Home-Start, counselling at Pen Green and primary school. 'Carly was able to break it down, to take it step by step, so I was able to see things differently.'

Carly went to some interagency meetings with Mary. 'It felt like she was on my side and if I got a bit muddled she would either help me get it straight so I could speak or would say things on my behalf.' Carly came to one of the Child Protection Conference meetings with Mary – this made a big difference to her. She said, 'I just felt I was being judged a lot – which I can understand as there were problems – but it was nice to have a friendly face there.'

Mary said Carly's particular role in safeguarding Connor was to support Mary as she made the transition from Pen Green, where she had had support all Connor's life, to school. Mary said that the transition went very well, she has made a good relationship with the school and Connor is doing very well there.

What difference did Carly make?

Mary said, 'There was a lot of bad stuff happening and it felt all negative. Carly kept reminding me of the little positives that were also happening. This has helped my self-confidence. I now know I can make the right decisions, I know things are going fine, I don't need to keep questioning myself, I now don't need constant reassurance.'

Carly finished supporting Mary a few months ago. Mary said: 'I think differently now: I take a lot more things on board, I used to let my emotions run riot, now I can put my son first. I know I can make the right decisions. I'm not doubting myself as much, I can understand Connor more, where he is coming from, his behaviour, his feelings. I can deal with him more appropriately. Before I always put my feelings first, I forgot what was going on for him, I pushed him away. Now if something goes wrong, I deal with it at the appropriate time. I make sure that Connor is sorted; I don't hide away or push things away. I am more available to him. I see and acknowledge how well he is doing but I'll also deal with the negative stuff, not let it overwhelm me. I used to think it was the end of the world [when something awful happened].'

How are things now for Mary?

Mary was able to go to the last Child Protection Conference by herself. She feels confident about going into school and feels able to discuss anything with the school. Mary said: 'It's the right time, I trust myself to make the right decisions.'

Mary felt the services which had supported her most were her health visitor – 'she was fantastic when Connor was small', the Nurture Group at Pen Green 'helped a hell of a lot with me and Connor and with housing', and Home-Start, which led eventually to Mary going to the Relaxation Group where she is now a volunteer. Mary also used the Family Room and Growing Together group. Mary said, 'For me the most important service would be Carly – she helped when Gran died.'

Also important was the Adult Education, 'I got qualifications in English and maths. And doing PICL, it helped me understand a lot, I had to stop when Nan became very ill but I continued the PICL work in the group I was in with Carly. I did a portfolio there about Connor, and Carly is going to make sure I get accredited for that. And counselling – well I wouldn't be here without that. When the bereavement happened, I was a mess. I beat myself up. But my counsellor said I was allowed days when my heart breaks, it's okay to have bad days. I can now deal with bad stuff. I can deal with emotions. I can handle it. I can contain myself. I can keep a lid on it.'

Reflection

Endings are very important, especially when significant relationships have been formed. These relations may happen in groups, with other parents, with volunteers or with Family Support workers. Workers at Pen Green were aware of the significance of coming to the end of over four years of intensive involvement for Mary. Carly, Home-Start workers and Mary talked together often about this and planned how Mary could move on in a positive way.

Family Support for Mary and Connor has involved almost every aspect of Pen Green services, as well as health and children's statutory services. There have been many times when workers have had to share honestly their concerns for Connor's well-being. Mary used to react angrily but has become increasingly able to reflect on the issues raised, and throughout we have always been able to maintain a working relationship. Carly's support included Cognitive Behavioural Therapy techniques, often advocating on behalf of Connor, which Mary was able to hear because of the strength of their relationship.

Mary is clear that this support has encouraged her to be an autonomous, confident parent.

Example from practice

Example from practice

Family 4: family Support seen from the perspectives of separated parents

Evie had a daughter of 20 months from a previous relationship. Then Evie and Robert lived together and had a son, Ross. Robert left when Ross was about 10 months old. Evie was a long-term drug user and Robert was a recreational drug user.

Evie's story

Evie first came into contact with the Family Support team after the birth of her second child; she was referred by her health visitor. At first Evie was highly resistant to the idea of having a support worker but felt that the circumstances of her referral (concerns about the welfare of the young children and imminent eviction) gave her little choice but to comply. She remembers, 'I started thinking "social services" and all that kind of thing and I was like "no, no, no".' At the time, she and her then partner, Robert, lived four miles across town from Pen Green and were able to access the centre with their children through the Family Support team's transport budget.

Evie and Robert separated shortly after moving to within walking distance of the centre. Subsequently, Ross went to live with Robert. Both parents decided that they still wanted Carly to continue to support them both separately.

Evie said, 'I really did need the support then because I didn't really have a solid support network. I was quite depressed at the time. Some mornings I'd wake up and just wouldn't want to answer the phone or talk to anyone and Carly was the only one I'd answer the door to. I was just finding it really hard on my own to get both kids up to Pen Green on time every morning and Carly used to come and collect Daisy and take her up for me, and she'd phone me when Daisy was finishing to see if I would come and collect her or if I would like her to bring Daisy home.'

When Evie reflected back over the six years she had been receiving support from the team, and Carly in particular, she felt that this involvement had made a positive difference to her life.

'When Carly first met me I was a drug addict. I had been for about 15 years but I was in denial and Carly sort of helped me. Put me in touch with CAN [drug and alcohol agency] and I had a worker there who I got to know and trust. I could just phone her. It turned out she was just a friend in the end. So yeah, Carly pointed me in the right direction and I've been clean for two years now, thanks to her.'

When Evie was unable to find the strength within herself, Carly helped her to manage the practicalities of life. Carly's support included stepping in to make phone calls to sort out rent, gas and electricity. 'I knew that if I didn't phone them I'd get into trouble but I still didn't phone them. Carly realised what I was doing and sorted it all out, rang them all and sorted out all my debt … She even had my landlord come into the centre and I didn't want to face him on my own so she came with me and he was brilliant. I didn't have anything to worry about but in my head at that time, because of where I was, I wasn't seeing it that way.'

Evie has not always had a good relationship with Carly. Reflecting on her feelings about Carly, she said: 'We didn't always have a good relationship because when I was in that place I wasn't who I am now, I wasn't co-operative … We didn't get on but it was just because of me you know, what I was doing, what I was taking … I was like – I really hate you, don't come into my house again. But, she's good at her job and she didn't let go of me … No matter what you say or how much you shout at her she just says "Okay Evie, whatever."'

Gradually, this level of support enabled Evie to gain the confidence to take control of her life and to stop feeling scared. 'Now I do it all on my own and it's good.'

Evie had another baby with a new partner, but participating in any of the groups on offer was more than she could cope with, so Carly and Steph, the mental health worker at Pen Green, went to Evie's home and taught the family baby massage, including her little daughter, and Evie was able to gain a certificate in Baby Massage.

Subsequently, Family Support ensured that the children had access to the Summer Playscheme when Evie was pregnant with her fourth child and videoed their play so that she could enjoy the experience of focusing on her children in a positive way at home.

Robert's story

Robert's involvement with the Family Support team began when the health visitor referred Evie to the Family Support team. 'I didn't know she had postnatal depression. The health visitor came round and was like "you're depressed", and Evie said "yes". I just looked at her and was like, "you didn't tell me, am I just sitting here for nothing?" That's where it started and how we met Carly.'

Robert found this early period of involvement bewildering. Struggling to come to terms with Evie's depression, he at first perceived Family Support as a service focused solely on Evie. 'I thought the help was supposed to be for Evie but it seemed like she just took a back seat and everyone else got the support. It was supposed to get her out and get her back into normal, but it just didn't happen like that.'

To begin with Robert would bring the children across town to Pen Green on his own, 'I think Evie came once or twice and then that was it. I kept coming up with the kids and it went from there.'

When Evie then took an overdose Robert took Ross to live with him. Their relationship came to an acrimonious end and a court case ensued. As Robert acknowledges, Carly's involvement with both adults continued 'because of the kids'. During this time Robert used the centre as a neutral place to allow Evie access to their son.

'Carly supported me as well during that time. I used to phone her and be able to sound off at her and she'd just calm me down and go through everything with me and try and make me see things a bit differently. It didn't always work but most of the time it did. She used to say to me "just phone me and talk to me instead of going round there and shouting at Evie and going mental and doing something stupid". So Carly really helped me with that and really helped me through it.'

Carly also took Robert to another children's centre closer to his house. 'She took me down there and basically helped me with everything I needed, told me where I could get things and who to go to for help. Made things available for me and really helped me a lot.' Having access to help outside his family gave Robert the perspective he needed in order to think and act rationally throughout a time of great stress and confusion.

'Carly was great because I had someone else's point of view and someone who is not on the inside or on anyone's side to look and tell you what they can see. I was angry at the time and Carly always had a way of making me see things differently, which calmed me down.'

Carly used contacts and colleagues within the centre to involve Robert in as many new experiences as possible: 'She got me roped into all sorts in here. That's how I got the job in the kitchen.' Carly supported Robert to make an application for Ross for a place at Pen Green Nursery.

Reflecting on the experience of being involved with Carly, he said, 'I've had plenty of cross words but it was just me shouting at Carly. She must've had the phone away from her ear half the time waiting for me to finish shouting! She has been really good. I've never fallen out with her and she's always helped me when I needed it.'

Reflection

This family study shows how important dads are and how, with support, Robert was able to sustain being Ross's main carer.

It also illustrates the pressure that a worker can be subjected to when working closely with parents who are disturbed and angry because of the extremely stressful situation they are in: poverty, relationship breakdown, attempted suicide, substance misuse, extreme social isolation. Both of the above parents stated what a hard time they had given Carly. They targeted their anger and frustration at Carly, which allowed them to just about keep enough contact with each other to ensure the children saw both their mum and dad regularly.

For Carly, in managing her relationship with parents who are in the midst of conflict, keeping confidentiality and impartiality to the forefront is essential. As she explains, 'It's not about loyalty to one adult or another, it's about the children.' She is able to manage the complexities of supporting families by always holding the children firmly at the centre of her thinking. Parents may find that they can only focus on the difficulties *they* are experiencing and Carly will always give them the time and attention they need from her but as she says, 'I always think about where the children are in it.'

Even when parents are in the throes of difficult and distressing situations, Carly will suggest some kind of family activity that will give the children an opportunity to be with their parents in a relaxed and un-pressurised way. In creating spaces such as these Carly says, 'It's as though a little light comes on which is them thinking about their children, if only for a moment in a week.'

Visiting the family regularly helps to create the space for that 'little light' to occur with increasing frequency until the needs of the children gain more and more presence in their parents' minds. Ultimately, in Carly's experience, the parents she works with eventually demonstrate a shift in their ability to find a space for their children and to hold them in mind.

The importance of the relationship between family member and worker has traditionally been a key factor in social work. Sudbery says that whatever the focus of the work, whether advocacy, practical help, welfare rights or safeguarding concerns, 'social workers have a core responsibility for outcomes which are therapeutic, empowering and developmental' (Sudbery, 2002: 149).

He views the key components of these relationships as:
■ attention to basic need
■ response to aggressive impulses and
■ the lessening of punitive self-criticism.

Aspects of the mediating relationship between the parent and worker can be conceptualised within the psychodynamic framework of transference, counter-transference and the punitive self-ego. The worker has feelings projected on to them, aspects of their own family relationships can be evoked and they can take on the parent's highly critical self-perception. Good supervision is absolutely essential so the worker can attend to and identify these feelings, attribute them to their rightful source, and reflect on the state of mind of the parent, which will then inform how to proceed in the relationship for maximum therapeutic benefit.

Andrew Cooper, one of the current leading advocates of relationship-based practice, spoke about how workers are exposed to so much distress and pain when working with marginalised and hurt families. He asked, 'How deeply and directly can we bear to know?' He continued:

> We can only come to know properly by being able to be in relationship with other persons, and that at heart is also a painful process for us. Enlarging our capacity to bear such pain, while protecting ourselves sufficiently to be capable of continuing to engage with the work is the heart of relationship-based practice.
>
> *(Cooper, 2012)*

Pamela Trevithick takes this a step further. By experiencing the distressing circumstances of many families' lives, Family Support workers 'can bear witness and report on "social ills" as they impact on the lives of service users' (Trevithick, 2003: 167).

Being exposed to the pain of families for whom the many inequalities in our society bear down so harshly gives Family Support workers a special responsibility and also hard evidence on which to base future service planning.

Points for discussion

■ Government justifiably demands rigorous evaluation to provide evidence for effective interventions. How can such complex interactions as described above be measured? And on what timescale? The parents above report increased self-confidence and self-esteem, managing their feelings better, increased understanding of their role and confidence to be active advocates for their children, increased ability to hold their child in mind, to see things from their child's perspective and not just from their own, learning to enjoy being with their children. These changes will transform their children's lives. But these are long-term outcome measures, whereas many evaluation frameworks look at more concrete short-term achievements that may not endure over time. Pen Green has published a PICL self-evaluation tool, co-produced with parents, that uses these longer-term fundamental changes as outcome measures (Pen Green, 2012).

- Children's Services increasingly require children's centres to provide Family Support at Levels 3 and 4, but pressure of referral numbers may lead to short-term interventions that do not give the necessary time for trusting relationships that lead to life-changing changes within parents. Do children's centres have access to the appropriately skilled supervision necessary for this work?

- How can workers maintain a child-focused aspect of their work when parents are overwhelmed with their own difficulties?

References

Allen, G. (2011) *Early Intervention: The next steps. An independent report to Her Majesty's Government*, London: HMG.

Cooper, A. (2012) 'The self in social work practice: uses and abuses', paper for the CSWP/Essex University day conference *How to Do Relationship-based Social Work*, 13 January.

Devaney, C. (2011) 'A family support approach to protecting children: current issues and perspectives', paper for the UNESCO *Child and Family Research Centre Conference*, 16 June.

ELPPEG (Early Learning Partnership Parental Engagement Group) (2010) *Principles for Engaging with Families: A Framework for local authorities and national organisations to evaluate and improve engagement with families*, London: NQIN.

Field, F. (2010) *The Foundation Years: Preventing poor children becoming poor adults. The report of the Independent Review on Poverty and Life Chances*, London: HMG.

Northamptonshire Children and Young People's Partnership (2012) *Integrated Working Procedures* [online]. Available from: http://www.proceduresonline.com/integratedworking/index.htm (accessed January 2013).

Pen Green (2012) *Measuring Impact on Parents*, unpublished evaluation tool, Corby: Pen Green.

Pugh, G. (2010) Foreword to ELPPEG above.

Social Exclusion Task Force (2008) *Think Family: A literature review of whole family approaches*, London: Cabinet Office.

Sudbery, J. (2002) 'Key features of therapeutic social work: the use of relationship', *Journal of Social Work Practice*, vol. 16, no. 2, pp. 149–62.

Trevithick, P. (2003) 'Effective relation-based practice: a theoretical exploration', *Journal of Social Work Practice*, vol. 17, no. 2, pp. 163–76.

Websites

Foundation Years [online] http://www.foundationyears.org.uk

Home-Start: integrating voluntary sector support for families within a children's centre

Maggie Mackay and Elaine Young

In this chapter we will be introducing:
- the history of Home-Start Corby, which began as Family Friends in 1984
- the transition from Family Friends to Pen Green and Home-Start Corby Integration
- the preparation course for volunteers
- the importance of supervision for home-visiting volunteers
- examples from practice
- current challenges and points for discussion.

Introduction

The aim of this chapter is to explore the history of establishing a voluntary organisation in a children's centre and how the work is being continued currently. It will consider the achievements, challenges and the future development of integrated partnership working.

Background

Origins of Family Friends at Pen Green Children's Centre

In 1984 Family Friends was introduced to Pen Green by the head of centre Margy Whalley alongside a steering group, after listening to and responding to the needs of families living across the town in the 1980s. Hughes and Read (2012: 8) describe the different relationships parents have experienced in different decades with professionals: the 1960s were a time when professionals gave their advice to parents, suggesting that professionals knew best. The 1970s were a time when the views of parents were beginning to be heard. However, the 1980s was more about hearing the wishes of parents. Parents were encouraged to discuss policies and procedures and be part of any consultation about their children's welfare and learning. Margy Whalley (1994: 4) believed that creating an environment within the local community where all parents with young children would feel equally welcome and valued was paramount to the success of the building of relationships between professionals and parents both within settings and at home.

Family Friends was a way of building relationships with children and their families. Professionals, parents and volunteers had the ability to learn from each other and appreciate that all parents find parenting a challenge at times. The status of the parent doesn't provide protection from these challenges when they arise.

The steering group consisted of professionals from health and social care backgrounds, local business and parents. It was formed to look at the needs of the community and how the project could be funded. It was firstly funded by the Manpower Services Commission and the European Social Fund.

From this Family Friends became a parent volunteer service which provided friendship and information to local parents at various stages of parenthood. Its aim was to value parents as key people in their children's development.

Family Friends was led by a co-ordinator and co-worker with administrator support, who recruited and prepared local parent volunteers through appropriate courses to work alongside families. These parent volunteers supported families both within the children's centre and at home. Volunteers were often parents who had children who attended Pen Green nursery or who came from the borough of Corby so understood the community and knew the families well.

Example from practice
Example from practice

Lynne Hammond, former co-ordinator of Family Friends, who is now chair of Corby Home-Start, speaks of her experience:

'I wasn't around at the very beginning of Family Friends but think it probably started soon after the centre opened. I joined Family Friends in 1987/88 as a co-ordinator and I worked with a co-worker. We were very much part of the centre staff team and training was offered as part of professional and personal development and in response to the needs of families at the time. We operated very much the same as Home-Start Corby does now. We ran the course one day a week for ten weeks. The course was always one of my favourite parts of the job, meeting these very keen new volunteers whom you would build strong relationships with and who would visit families for a while. Some of them progressed on to successful careers and so left us behind. Nothing has changed in this respect.

'Thinking back, the family centre as it was then was much smaller, the staff team was only between 20 and 25, not the hundreds that there are today. I really enjoyed that time. It was a real learning curve for me. I loved my job. I have never doubted the value of being able to offer support to families in their own homes, encouraging them and hopefully enabling them to make any changes they may wish to make. Family Friends or Home-Start – whatever it may be called – is such a great principle. The simple thing of one parent helping another can make such a difference to the lives it has touched. I am very happy to have been involved in its evolution and very happy to still be playing some part.'

Volunteers' knowledge of the local community during the early 1980s enabled parents to build trusting relationships. Members of the local community rallied together and people within the changing community had a real empathy with each other's positions. Corby was in a unique situation in the 1980s.

The future was worrying for parents of young children who wondered what the opportunities for their children would be, as Corby sank deeper into a recession due to the gradual closure of the steel industry from 1979/1980 and of many other industries at the time. The years that followed were tough for parents and children as poverty increased.

> As the steel redundancies hit home – 5,500 in the first wave and then some batches of 600 at a time over the next few years – whole families (in some cases a father and perhaps three sons in the same household) found themselves on the scrapheap with no immediate prospects of other work … unemployment stood at nearly 30 per cent, the second highest in the UK.
>
> (Shakespeare & Lewis, 1989: 59)

Figure 9.1 Steelworks, Stephenson Way (Corby Community Arts Archive)

The family support provided was vital during this time. Quinton (2004: 59) states that research has consistently documented the strong associations between poverty and problems with health, family life and children's development. He goes on to say that, although the priority must always be to alleviate poverty and disadvantage, improving informal and formal support to parents has a major part to play. As well as support parents received, the volunteer training provided an opportunity to undertake adult learning and to gain knowledge from local professionals. This gave much-needed hope.

Home-Start UK

Home-Start UK is an independent charity which provides support to 327 schemes nationally and overseas. There are six schemes in Northamptonshire: Corby, Kettering, Wellingborough, East Northants, Northampton and Daventry.

Home–Start originated in Leicester, founded by Margaret Harrison in 1973. In her book *Hooray! Here Comes Tuesday: The Home–Start Story* (2003), she talks about the origins of Home–Start and her passionate belief in volunteers being able to provide emotional support and practical assistance to children and their families, usually at the start of family life. This is when families can feel overwhelmed by the demands of meeting the needs of a small child or children. They can feel emotionally tired and criticised by other people. Support during the formative years is important to ensure the long-term success of children and their development, health-wise, educationally, emotionally and socially.

The Home–Start approach is to reach families through home-visiting volunteers. Margaret Harrison was clear that Home–Start would be based on human qualities rather than on qualifications. She believed that this support should take place within the home to provide support, friendship and practical help for the whole family where their difficulties exist and where their dignity and identity can be respected and protected.

A three-year study into a Home–Start scheme in Wakefield, called *Negotiated Friendship: Home–Start and the delivery of family support* (Frost *et al.*, 1996), details some of the challenges Home–Start has faced in becoming firmly rooted in service provision to children and their families. One of the findings of this study (p. 208) was that Home–Start contributes to the continuum of family support under Section 17 of the Children Act 1989, in that it can deliver clear, positive outcomes for the families it is supporting.

The transition from Family Friends to Pen Green and Home–Start Corby integration

Family Friends evolved into Home–Start Corby in 1994.

Example from practice

Mary Champion, the first co-ordinator of Home–Start Corby, recounts:

'When I joined the admin team at Pen Green in 1990, Family Friends was already offering support to families with young children … Home–Starts were being established nationally and the management team at Pen Green, recognising the need to expand the services of Family Friends in Corby, decided to apply for the necessary funding to become Home–Start. The ethos of Family Friends matched perfectly the aims and values of Home–Start UK. The only downside was losing the name Family Friends, which many believed to perfectly promote everything the scheme was about.

'It was an exciting journey and probably evolving still. I can think of many people, volunteers, staff and parents who became more confident, learnt new skills and how to enjoy life by joining Home–Start Corby. That includes me.'

Home–Start Corby remains in Pen Green for many reasons. It is part of the centre's history and is known locally and remembered generationally by families. Pen Green remains a generous funder and supporter of the charity locally and the opportunities for choice it offers to both volunteers and families. This helps to strengthen strategic and operational relationships between the organisations within the community, keeping an overview of challenges both at a local and national level.

Home-Start Corby provides a quality-assured service through stringent policies and procedures issued from Home-Start UK. These are put in place to meet standards in service provision, and respect and value the privilege of working alongside children and their parents. Ensuring that safeguarding of children is a priority in practice is an ongoing training and communication concern. Each scheme is overseen by a Board of Trustees and Advisors which has representation from professionals across the community.

Gill and Jack (2007: 82) believe that, through joint discussions and the sharing of ideas between professional workers and community members, effective and coherent community practice is developed. One aspect of this approach is that it needs to be based on the particular issues facing the individual community. The success of working closely together for the ultimate well-being of the families is paramount. This has been demonstrated in the Laming Report following the sad death of Baby Peter, which stated that 'much more needs to be done to ensure that ... services are as effective as possible at working together to achieve positive outcomes for children' (Laming, 2009: 9, para. 1.1).

The support network of local schemes is an extremely valuable resource in relation to recent (2012) funding issues. We hold regular county funding meetings which are attended by all Home-Starts and the regional consultant. We also hold more generic support meetings. By being able to work strongly together as schemes, we can plan for the future and share knowledge as a team to provide an effective service for children and their families.

Pen Green appreciates the support systems in place for Home-Start Corby and continues to offer its support too.

Home-Start Corby shares a space with the Community Development team in a building on the Pen Green site called Little Jimmy's. This is now the base for the outreach support team which provides outreach support and training to the community of Corby. Maintaining their own unique identities and ethos as different organisations is important due to providing choice for families, volunteers and external agencies. 'The most effective joined-up working emerges from actual practice, working together on joint activities with parents present, each contributing their own specialist knowledge and expertise' (Anning et al., 2006: 108).

Preparing Home-Start volunteers

When working with families and children it is important that volunteers are ready professionally for the role. Margaret Harrison called the course 'A course of preparation' and the first course was facilitated for volunteers in 1973 in Leicester. As recounted earlier, Family Friends also found training to be vital for home-visiting volunteers. The Home-Start course materials are produced in Home-Start UK and individual scheme co-ordinators attend training in order to facilitate the course of preparation in their individual schemes. The beginning of the relationship between co-ordinator and volunteer starts with a home visit to the volunteer's home, to get a sense of who they are, and it also forms part of the training later on when they consider how they felt with a stranger visiting them at home.

This gives new volunteers the opportunity to make an informed decision as to whether home-visiting is the right volunteering for them. If they prefer the prospect of working in a children's centre, then centre staff are available to discuss this option. Opportunities to meet with staff and current volunteers begins the process of team-building. If the potential volunteer demonstrates a capacity to work alongside children and their families, they are invited to attend a course of preparation.

Once the course is successfully completed continuous professional development sessions are provided. This consistency is essential for new volunteers to practise safely and, while building their confidence, they can learn from their peers. The course of preparation consists of the following:

Week 1: team-building and getting to know about Home-Start, Pen Green and the other children's centres in town

Representatives from each of the four children's centres in Corby will attend to meet the new volunteers, who will essentially be informing families of the services across town. This ensures that families have an informed choice from the outset. This helps the volunteers feel comfortable and part of a bigger team of people so that they can confidently signpost parents to the best sources of information for them. Pen Green Community Development workers and existing volunteers also attend to look at volunteering in a wider context. This provides volunteers with choices too.

Week 2: listening skills

It is vital that volunteers have the ability to listen to families well so that parents feel heard and feel that their situation is respected. In this session there will be exercises and role playing and experiential learning which will look at how parents feel when they are not listened to.

Week 3: confidentiality

This is explored with volunteers in an in-depth session which relates to times when confidences have been broken and the damage caused to people and to any trust built up. It is also the beginning of looking at policies and procedures to ensure that, although they are volunteering, there is still an ethical responsibility to adhere to policies and procedures.

Week 4: what is a family and family law?

We have a representative from a family law firm come in to work alongside the volunteers solving case studies of typical situations that might crop up in their work. The solicitor is an advisor on the trustee and advisor panels and provides free legal advice to families once a month at Pen Green Children's Centre. This is a valuable service for families in the town and a useful resource for volunteers.

Week 5: time to play

We look at play and family life from the position of the children. Volunteers reflect on memories of their play and recount stories to share from their own pasts. This session also looks at child development and a health visitor comes in to share issues affecting children's health and well-being.

Week 6: diversity

This is a very interactive session based on the diversity of the people within our community. Corby has a richness of culture and diversity which has its origins in history. We try to make our services inclusive and celebratory of each individual in our community.

Week 7: safeguarding

We have a local social worker from a Family Support team who comes and shares his knowledge of what is happening in our own community. This session has been updated over the years at Home-start Corby to cover the CAF process and those children who are being supported on a Child in Need plan. A skilled member of the Pen Green outreach team comes and shares her knowledge of CAF in practice with the volunteers. This helps volunteers to understand processes and their role in these situations. It also helps them to hone their natural skills of empathy to support families sensitively at these times.

Week 8: self-awareness

A member of the Pen Green research team who is trained in psychotherapy and counselling facilitates this session and focuses on volunteers learning more about themselves and why they may have come into volunteering. He encourages people to think about what motivates them and why some issues may affect them more than others. Quite often volunteers go on to the Introduction to Counselling course held at Pen Green after the Home-Start preparation course.

Week 9: limit setting and endings

This session is facilitated by a Home-Start trustee alongside the co-ordinator who has previous experience in supervisory training. She has a wealth of knowledge of Home-Start Corby and Pen Green Children's Centre. This session demonstrates to volunteers the necessity to put boundaries in place in their role for the safety of themselves and the families they support.

Week 10: it's not about the money

This session looks at ways to support families looking at finances and budgeting and managing resources. It includes where to go for help with debt and all things to do with managing household finances.

Week 11: healthy eating

This looks at healthy eating within families from birth to five years.

(An overview of the autumn 2012 course of preparation at Home-Start Corby using materials provided by Home-Start UK.)

An existing volunteer from Home-Start Corby states: 'The course gives you an opportunity to learn about yourself as a parent and to use this knowledge to support families. I enjoyed the course and made good friendships with the team I did it with. The training is good.'

The commitment from agencies and professionals who facilitate the sessions within the course ensures that families receive quality support from their volunteer in a way that is safe and tailored to the individual. It also assists volunteers to understand that they do not need to know everything and that there are professionals in the community, more skilled in certain issues, who can help the family more effectively. Volunteers who are self-aware and who have built up their skills are better able to be consistent and congruent with families.

The sharing of resources at Pen Green by way of the crèche and rooms for course facilitation is also essential to the success of the individual volunteer as a learner. Recently the current community social worker or development worker facilitated some training on safeguarding which was extremely informative and this enabled volunteers to be confident in asking questions that they may not otherwise have asked of a trainer who they did not know. Siraj-Blatchford and colleagues (2008: 140) explain that a shared community of practice within children's centres enables early years practitioners to have the opportunity to engage in mutual interactions, and share their own professional knowledge with others when working with young children and their families. The development of such a community requires a high level of agreement among members in the formation and safeguarding of a shared vision of practice.

Once the course is completed and the volunteer has been cleared by safer recruitment processes the volunteer will be matched to a family. This is an intricate process which successfully matches a parent with the most appropriate volunteer for them. The co-ordinators at Home-Start will have knowledge of both the family and the volunteer and this knowledge helps the link to work. If the family is receiving support from other agencies Home-Start Corby will have continued dialogue around practice-based discussions.

Key information

Volunteer support and supervision

Supervision is a way of connecting with volunteers to ensure they are working with families in a healthy and constructive way where both parties are receiving what they need in order to progress. There are three ways in which volunteer supervision and support is given:

Weekly group support

This is where volunteers interact with each other and share their experiences. They share information, challenges, highs and lows. Co-ordinators facilitate these sessions and offer ongoing support and training. Volunteers can learn a lot about their role from each other.

(The value of using the same space each week is encouraged by colleagues in Pen Green so that consistency of support and identity of role is maintained. Inclusivity means that support sessions can be offered in the evenings or at weekends.)

Individual supervision

Family support and family dynamics are talked through and information shared on which services might be suitable for the family they are supporting. This is also an opportunity to look at training aspirations for volunteers or to listen to their challenges to practices. Supervision is every four to six weeks.

Volunteer supervision is held as a priority so that volunteers do not feel that they are working in isolation. Retention of volunteers is vital and celebrations about their work can be shared. Regularity of supervision will also depend on the family the volunteer is working with. For example, if a family is going through a crisis or safeguarding processes, the volunteer will be supported more frequently as they may experience greater anxiety.

Informal supervision

A volunteer may drop in to the office and have a discussion with a co-ordinator. This may reveal issues concerning the volunteer or the family they are supporting. This is also a time to complete office requirements, such as timesheets and expenses.

Extra support

If there is a time when a co-ordinator for Home-Start Corby is not around and a volunteer needs a bit of advice on services, the Community Development team at Pen Green always help and support them where they can, while remaining ethical and confidential to the family and volunteer. This extra reassurance for the volunteer and passing of the information to the co-ordinators is vital in ensuring families' and volunteers' needs are responded to quickly.

The family support role

Home-Start Corby volunteers will visit families in their homes for two hours per week on average. Historically Home-Start Corby has always received referrals for families with varying levels of need so the Hardiker Model is used by Home-Start UK (Hardiker *et al.*, 1991). This was developed in order to help understand different levels of need within a population of children. A basic interpretation of the levels follows:

- Level 1 – This refers to *universal services* available to all children, such as health care, education and other services provided in communities.
- Level 2 – This represents children who have some *additional needs*. For example, behaviour support or parent support.
- Level 3 – Services here are provided through a *complex mix of services,* usually as a result of crisis being experienced. The services need to work together to provide specific and relevant support.
- Level 4 – Represents support for families and individual children where the family may have *broken down temporarily or permanently.*

Families will move across levels regularly. For example, a family referred for support at Level 3 will move to Level 2 and vice versa. The levels are useful as a guide but humans are much more complex.

Home-Start Corby receives referrals for families where the level of need is 2 or 3. Families at this level quite often require time, patience, understanding and encouragement. Families at level 3 and above may be receiving support from colleagues in statutory agencies such as Health and Social Care or Children-and-Families teams.

At times such as these, families may be resistant to these services and feel very vulnerable or misunderstood. Tracy was aware of Home-Start Corby as an organisation from a professional perspective; below she talks about her experiences as a service user.

Example from practice
Example from practice

A parent's story

What happens when the bomb goes off in your family, which you thought was normal, and the bomb keeps exploding with every new professional and agency that becomes involved, with their jargon and ways of working that differ so much from each other? All I wanted was answers to my questions – how can this happen and why me and my family?

I made a phone call to the Home-Start Corby office and the support from the co-ordinator became my containment, the consistency of the home visits, advocacy in meetings and the speed of other agencies' responses to a phone call from her rather than me. To be able to talk through what decisions others are making about your family, and support with the understanding of these processes, became really important for me. Not just in the beginning but also towards the end of the supportive relationship. I remember that we went for a meeting at the Criminal Prosecution Service and then we challenged the minutes from the meeting – I would never have been able to do that for myself.

To know that a service will include support to all of the family not just the under-fives, for us all to go on an outing or attend an event, to start to be a family again and to have fun, to have special times together.

A Home-Start volunteer or co-ordinator who knows a family's story and who can advocate on their behalf in meetings about the positives that are going on is vital. As a result of integrated working practices Home-Start volunteers may know the roles of the other workers or know them through joint working experiences. This will further enhance their supportive role in enabling families to feel less fraught in stressful situations. Families quite often ask for their volunteer to attend these meetings with scheme co-ordinators. Volunteers will attend these family meetings and play an active part in developing plans. Colleagues from external agencies will often be happy to undertake joint home visits to further benefit the families. Family Support workers within all four children's centres in Corby are very familiar with Home-Start volunteers and regard them as valuable colleagues.

The health visiting team in Corby and all four children's centres and Home-Start Corby are committed to ensuring families receive an informed choice as to the array of services available to them. A benefit of working closely together is reaching those families who may need vital support. Regular communication meetings between health visitors and children's centres across town ensures inclusivity. Families can self-refer to Home-Start Corby. This is the second most frequent way referrals are received, with health visitors being the first.

The diversity of families we visit has changed over the years with the influx of migrant workers to the town. The need for volunteers who have English as a second language has risen since 2004. Pen Green is a service which newcomers to the town learn about very quickly owing to the nursery provision available at Pen Green. It has been recognised that some people are very wary of agencies, so having a Home-Start based in a children's centre such as Pen Green has helped families receive vital support that feels safe for them. Barbara's story demonstrates the challenges of moving to a new country and the need for support.

Example from practice

A parent's story

I came to Corby from Poland in 2007. I completed a Home-Start course two years ago. As I didn't speak English very well, I was worried if the people on the course would accept me. My worries were based on not only my English language skills but also on a few racist incidents I experienced when I moved with my partner and son to Corby from Poland.

These experiences made me feel vulnerable at the beginning but, because I usually do not give up easily, I did not go back to Poland but instead decided to fight for my rights and improve my English skills, find out where I can look for help in such situations and how to support others who may go through similar experiences and are not strong enough to move on their own.

When I went on my first interview with Maggie and Elaine I felt this was the course I needed. They made me feel welcome and were happy to have on board a volunteer from another country.

On the course there were people from different backgrounds and they also made me feel welcome and that my voice was as important as the others (which was my big worry – if the group would accept me and my different views about some things).

On the course we shared our experiences, the problems we struggle with sometimes and the ways based on our own experiences we would support families. I shared with the group how the family support system works in my country, what the differences are. I shared information about how we celebrate Christmas and other holidays. I explained why the people from my country worry about getting in touch or asking for support from any agencies if they need it. In Poland we do not have so much support for children and families; we do not have voluntary organisations such as Home-Start or children's centres. There isn't any kind of early intervention. When social workers are involved the situation is very serious and there are too many problems within the family.

I am very happy that I had that opportunity and tried something new – my education I gained in Poland is different in nature, as I hold a masters degree in economics. Unfortunately, the degree from my country is not recognised by employers in England and only people who are confident, strong enough and have the opportunity to start a new career or gain skills in England in their occupation may achieve it.

On the Home-Start course I found out lots of very important information about safeguarding children, working with families, supporting them in difficult moments in their lives, how to support Home-Start to raise the money for families in need.

The information, skills I gained, new friends I met on the Home-Start course and voluntary work I have done opened the door and gave me confidence to start my new career – working with children and families – which I still do on a daily basis and really enjoy it.

I love to be a Home-Start volunteer and support families as much as I can. I always promote the Home-Start organisation within my community and others as it is very important to understand how much children and their families can benefit from being involved with Home-Start, especially for families that have limited English, are new in the town, do not know where they can go with children to support their development, socialise and get support when they need it.

Some of the families I have worked with so far needed just a little help: making sure that they understand their rights and responsibilities in England, such as the education system that varies from the one in my country, translating of some documents, making phone calls or giving advice on what groups parents may attend with their children, and what groups parents may attend such as adult education or others to meet new friends.

I had the opportunity to attend some trips with my son which was great especially as we did not have many friends around.

I also attend other courses organised by Home-Start and I will attend more in the future to be up to date with all policies and improve my knowledge to be more successful when supporting families.

Children and their families in Corby are very lucky that they can have support from the Home-Start team and volunteers who work so hard to meet the needs of all the children and families that need it.

Home-Start is a universal and inclusive home-visiting service which means that volunteers visit families who feel they need support regardless of their background. Steve Duncan is one of Home-Start's trustees and here he recounts his story.

Example from practice

Example from practice

A parent's story

In 2010, when our daughters arrived, we were in our late 30s/early 40s. Both highly trained and experienced military professionals, my wife a nurse while I'm aircrew. Own house, good salaries, well educated, why would we need help?

We assumed that as my wife was a nurse she would have some advantage when it came to dealing with babies, and that as we were both used to dealing with complex problems in difficult situations we would have an advantage. How wrong can you be? Even my regular exposure to sleep deprivation had not prepared me for the onslaught to come. While twins had seemed like such a good idea at the time, having two hungry crying babies who were completely out of synch soon took its toll. To compound things Nikki knew that as soon as my paternity leave was over I would be flying out of the country, and due to my job, repeatedly doing so for the foreseeable future. Like many Corby families we were recent immigrants to the area, having been here less than a year, and so we did not have the support of a wider family or group of friends. When I was away Nikki would truly be left to cope on her own and the prospect frightened her. Of all the many tasks we've completed in our military careers none was as important or vital as looking after our daughters; at no time had the repercussions of getting it wrong been as serious.

At this stage luck played its part and we were introduced to Home-Start. Shortly after, our volunteer – the amazing Elaine – came. Having her own children she brought the experience and perspective that we were lacking. Providing a reassuring voice to Nikki she helped her to see that in fact she was doing well and that it was normal to feel overwhelmed. She came when I was away and looked after the girls so Nikki could have a decent shower and later on helped with the swimming lessons when I couldn't make it. Through Elaine we were introduced to the excellent facilities at Pen Green. This gave us, as a family, much wider options in terms of things to do and a place where Nikki felt she could take the girls when I was away. In a fairly short period of time we no longer needed Elaine's assistance, though we do still like catching up and she remains very interested in the girls' development.

So that's where it ends then? Well no, it's just where it begins. Home-Start made such an enormous difference to us at a critical time in all of our lives that I wanted to give something back. Like most charities Home-Start is constantly looking for volunteers and requires a committed and active Board of Trustees to allow it to function. Responding to an advert I volunteered as a trustee and have been serving as one for almost two years now.

I get to assist families like mine; I get to support the best people in the world, our volunteers. I'm learning all the time, not just rules and regulations but how charities, boards, welfare actually work. Volunteering brings such an amazing array of rewards, volunteers are such amazing people – it is a privilege to work alongside them and one that is open to all.

Volunteers know about services in the town and can quickly signpost families to services that are of use to them. The following case study demonstrates one of the reasons why Home-Start Corby is still based in Pen Green and why families need the familiarity of people and consistency of services over time to receive quality support. I approached Jane to ask if she wouldn't mind sharing her experience of Pen Green and Home-Start Corby. Jane is clear these services are part of her history and future.

Example from practice

A parent's story

My daughter is at seniors now so I have been using Pen Green for a long time. I remember coming to Pen Green when I was little with my mum and my brother. We used to go into the Family Room when it was a room in the old school building, not like it is now. My mum would have a cup of tea there and we used to play with the toys that were put out. My mum used to go there all the time and stay for ages. The staff were really friendly. My mum liked it there. When I grew up, left home and had children of my own my son attended the nursery. The staff helped me to get a 'statement of additional needs' for him and brought his speech on. He goes to big school now and is doing well. Pen Green got me in to Home-Start, they told me they were there and could help me with my children. My experience of Home-Start has been fantastic. They helped me over the years. I'm doing the prep course to become a volunteer to help other families in the same position as me. Some of the staff I used to know are still at Pen Green now. Angela was my brother's group teacher and she is still there now.

My experience of Pen Green made me feel comfortable to ask for help and to tell people if they weren't helping me.

The common theme here is that by knowing how services work families feel safe and advocated for.

Integrated working within Pen Green

Home-Start Corby and Pen Green, while very different organisations, see the value of sharing joint occasions. Family Fun Days can be a time when Home-Start and Pen Green come together to just have fun alongside children and families using the facilities in the centre. These events happen during the weekends and school holidays, and provide those families who may not be able to access the services during normal times of opening with a chance to have fun with their children. These occasions can also be useful in informing families what we do and by being accessible means we can reach families we may otherwise not meet. Home-Start being visible in this way is a good way to celebrate volunteering and recruiting volunteers. Pen Green recognises Home-Start volunteers for their professionalism and welcomes opportunities to work alongside them.

The New Start course for all centre volunteers

Part of developing and strengthening volunteering within Pen Green has been the recent development of the New Start programme. This six-week training course was designed by Home-Start Corby as a way to share knowledge of working with volunteers. At Pen Green it is facilitated jointly by Pen Green staff and Home-Start co-ordinators. The benefits of the course are that volunteers all receive the same information around safeguarding, confidentiality and groups and services that are vital to support families.

Working in a similar way across the centre provides reassurance that families receive consistency. Sharing experiences and highs and lows is important to volunteers. Both Home-Start Corby and Pen Green appreciate and value the impact that friendly and approachable volunteers can have on encouraging families to shape and develop provision. There is huge added-value for families to come on board as volunteers, which then provides stepping stones into employment and economic well-being.

As a team we are always looking for more ways to be creative to ensure the families of our town receive a diverse range of accessible services.

Challenges

A major challenge has been the reassurance to other agencies within the town that Home-Start Corby, while working within the remit of a service level agreement, is not Pen Green. Both organisations still work very much within their own ethos and have their own identities. Home-Start Corby collects its own data using its own systems, and works across the town and not within defined catchment areas. Volunteers are recruited using a range of media and funding is sourced by service level agreements with partnership agencies. On Home-Start Corby's Board of Trustees and Advisors there is a cross-section of agencies who all contribute to the effective running of the scheme, in the light of the needs of children and their families. As this is the priority for all children and family agencies within the town, good relationships are vital and dialogue needs to be open so that professionals can share concerns freely.

Home-Start Corby has a small but very effective number of male volunteers – in total we have five. The challenge is to retain these and to recruit more. We work hard to identify the barriers to men volunteering for home-visiting services. The males who home-visit at present are working creatively to provide support to families. The families who are receiving their support are positive about male volunteers.

A challenge as practitioners is to learn about the experiences of males as parents from their own accounts. It would be interesting to learn of their challenges and how they view their role with their children and their development.

Volunteering provides opportunities for males and females equally. Home-Start Corby continues to look at improving this gap in our service by carefully advertising and actively encouraging males to express an interest and get involved.

Working within an integrated children's centre such as Pen Green has proved useful to male volunteers. By being visible and by getting to know families in a fun way barriers are broken down.

Funding continues to remain a challenge for Home-Start Corby.

Information-sharing can be a cause of tension in integrated teams. Each organisation has its own ethics and policies around confidentiality and information-sharing. Siraj-Blatchford and colleagues (2008: 98) explore this in their chapter entitled 'Negotiating the moral maze'. They state that complex ethical dilemmas require more than a 'one-size-fits-all ethical code', particularly in multi-agency practice. They report that inquiries into issues concerning the safety of a child 'have never asked why information was shared but have always asked why it was not'.

Points for discussion

- Share any experiences you have of volunteering (e.g. work experience, school governance).
- How have you approached the recruitment and retention of volunteers?
- Think about the systems you have in place to support volunteering in your setting.

References

Anning, A., Cottrel, D., Frost, N., Green, J. and Robinson, M. (2006) *Developing Multiprofessional Teamwork for Integrated Children's Services*, Maidstone: Open University Press.

Frost, N., Johnson, L., Stein, M. and Wallis, L. (1996) *Negotiated Friendship: Home-Start and the delivery of family support*, Leicester: Home-Start UK.

Gill, O. and Jack, G. (2007) *The Child and Family in Context Developing Ecological Practice in Disadvantaged Communities*, Dorset: Russell House.

Hardiker, P., Exton, K. and Barker, M. (1991) *Policies and Practices in Preventative Childcare*, Aldershot: Avebury.

Harrison, M. (2003) *Hooray! Here Comes Tuesday: The Home-Start story*, Dorset: Bamaha.

Hughes, A. M. and Read, V. (2008) *Building Positive Relationships with Parents of Young Children. A Guide to Effective Communication*, London: Routledge.

Lord Laming (2009) *The Protection of Children in England: A progress report*, London: HMSO.

Quinton, D. (2004) *Supporting Parents: Messages from research*, London: Jessica Kingsley.

Shakespeare, R. W. and Lewis, J. (1989) *Corby Works: A town in action*, Manchester: Brook Associates.

Siraj-Blatchford, I., Clarke, K. and Needham, M. (2008) *The Team Around the Child: Multi-agency working in the early years*, Staffordshire: Trentham Books.

Whalley, M. (1994) *Learning to Be Strong: Setting up a neighbourhood service for under-fives and their families*, London: Hodder & Stoughton.

Whalley, M. and the Pen Green Centre team (1997) *Working with Parents*, London: Hodder & Stoughton.

10

Growing Together for parents of children 0–3: so much more than stay and play

Felicity Norton, Judith Woodhead, Tracy Gallagher, Jo Benford and Cessie Cole

In this chapter we describe:
- using attachment theory and the concepts of holding and containment in groupwork with parents and infants, from birth to three years
- a recent example from practice.

Introduction

In this chapter, we describe the setting up of a weekly drop-in group for infants and their parents, which we call Growing Together. We spend most of the chapter explaining why we have set up Growing Together in this way and refer to the theories of attachment, holding and containment, in addition to the child development concepts used in the nursery and explained throughout this book. We consider the feelings of infants, parents and workers. Towards the end of the chapter we present an example from practice.

In early childhood services, there is often a gap in provision for parents with their infants from birth to three years. There is a need for children's centres to support infants and their parents during this period. One need has been researched by the Anna Freud Centre. The research stresses the importance of the development of the relationship between parent or significant other and child before the child is 14 months old. If the relationship is unsuccessful, then attachment issues can present themselves. The Growing Together groups at Pen Green aim to address this. Each group provides a time and an opportunity for each parent and child's relationship to develop. The idea grew out of the provision of groups for parents of children aged three and over, which facilitated the active involvement of parents in their children's learning: Parents' Involvement in Their Children's Learning groups (PICL). A group was then set up for parents with their children, from birth to three. Soon after the groups began it became clear that support was needed for all areas of the child's development. This included support for the relationship between parent and infant, and the emotions of both.

Attachment theory

Concepts derived from attachment and psychodynamic theory have added additional underpinning to the work. The concept of 'containment' (Bion, 1962) is particularly powerful to describe the emotional dimensions of development. Of course other similar concepts have been used to understand other aspects of development, for example the concept of 'scaffolding' (Wood *et al.*, 1976).

Key information

The three Growing Together groups that currently exist not only provide an opportunity for each relationship to develop, they also aim to:

- support parents in their own experience with their child/children
- facilitate parents supporting one another in their parenting
- give time to parents and support them to tune in to their child's development
- give time for sharing anecdotes about their child and new stages in development
- enable parents to see their child's issues and behaviour from other perspectives
- enable parents to experience other children at all ages and stages and interact with children other than their own
- provide opportunities for the child to experience different kinds of play and learning through play
- provide open permission that feelings can be spoken about and shared with others
- provide validation for a whole range of feelings within the experience of postnatal depression
- provide an opportunity for the child's feelings to be thought about by the parent, workers and other parents
- promote helpful attachment experiences
- provide a time and a space for the child and parent to socialise and develop relationships with others.

The Growing Together groups (including the kinds of toys and materials provided) are informed by the principles of other Pen Green services:

- the respectful and responsive way practitioners interact with children and families, bringing together and blending both parents' and professionals' knowledge in order to deepen the understanding we both have of their children (Easen *et al.*, 1992)
- sharing the child development concepts of involvement, illustrating what children look like when they are involved in the process of deep level learning (Laevers, 1997; see Appendix A)
- well-being: the signs children show when they are in states of emotional well-being (Laevers, 1997; see Appendix B)
- schemas: children's repeated patterns of action (Athey, 1990)
- pedagogic strategies: how adults facilitate and support children's learning and development (Whalley & Arnold, 1997)
- companionship: the manner in which a child and adult create a meaning out of a way of doing something (Trevarthern, 2002) that stimulates interaction between parents and professionals and supports a shared language.

What is new in the Growing Together groups is the conscious practical use of the concepts from attachment and psychodynamic theory. These concepts are applied in a practical way to the day-to-day relationships between mothers and children and staff. While psychotherapy may not be wished for, and is rarely available or affordable, the use of psychotherapeutic insights can bring an additional dimension to the work of children's centres such as Pen Green.

The most relevant concepts come from object relations theory (Klein, 1946). Central to this theory is the belief that human beings fundamentally wish to form relationships with others. But many obstacles exist in attempting to do this. We have found the concepts of containment, described by Wilfred Bion

(1962), and holding, described by Donald Winnicott (1965), to be invaluable (both were psychoanalysed by Klein). Attachment theory also provides concepts that are useful. We aim to support and promote helpful attachment patterns through focusing closely with parents on their infant, and on their patterns of relating with her or him, and through exploring alongside parents fruitful ways of tuning in to babies and young children.

Before outlining the concepts, it is important to stress that the ways we define and see the 'difficulties' parents experience with their children, that inform the development of specific services, are in no way used to pathologise people. We emphasise that, while we draw on concepts that seem to help, our intention is that the work is not in any sense expert-led.

Providing a kind of holding: the model of containment

Bion's concept of containment is based on the following: when an infant is very young (s)he is absolutely dependent on an adult for survival. The primary caregiver, if able to be attuned (Stern, 1985) to the baby, acts as a container for the baby's different emotional states. So when the baby cries, the caregiver is likely to notice, to hear, and hopefully to seek to understand why the baby is upset, and look to provide practical help and comfort. At this point the baby's cries have entered the parent's mind through 'projection', and are being thought about. Freud (Breuer and Freud, 1893) and Klein (1946) use the term 'projection' to explain how the infant, in this instance, attributes certain states of mind to the parent. The baby may be picked up, or cuddled or changed or fed and so on. If the baby cannot be settled, then the adult may carry or rock or talk or sing to her or him. The parent is serving as a container for the baby's discomfort and distress – receiving the distress, holding it in mind. In doing so they are communicating to the child that they can bear (just about) the baby's different emotional states – which to begin with are so raw and indigestible to the baby. By thinking about them, the parent accommodates the projected emotions in their mind and returns them in a modified way (through responses such as soothing, cooing, naming) to the infant. This may depend on the mother and father having experienced someone who was able to do that for him or her in their own childhoods. In Winnicott's words (1965) the parent(s) need to be able to be 'good enough', and able to experience a kind of 'reverie', a thoughtful state about the baby.

The child's experience of this kind of responsive thinking in the mother is of a container for their own early upsets, and emerging thoughts and feelings throughout early development. Slowly, over time, the infant can begin to develop an image within their mind of a caring parent who wishes to help rather than harm them. This then becomes like a developing model in the child's own mind; when the child experiences the containing process over and over again they are able to build a container in their own mind and develop a capacity to contain their own difficult feelings. But this is hard for a mother if she has a deep-down feeling that no one was ever able to be thoughtful about her and responsive to her own infant needs, particularly if poor economic, material and social circumstances are present in the parent's life.

Winnicott's work helps us to understand the difficulties that arise for all kinds of reasons, whether derived from acute deprivation, the baby's own problems, the parent's own difficulties, or a combination of them all. So, for instance, a mother experiencing depression may feel the opposite of attuned to her own baby, and may be unable to respond to her infant's cries or signals for affection. She herself may feel too vulnerable, for whatever reason, to be able to provide containment for her own baby. Winnicott calls the parental functioning 'holding'. When all goes well enough, a parent literally physically holds the baby, and also holds the baby in mind. When that is not able to happen it is as if the baby is 'dropped'. This in turn interrupts the development of helpful attachment patterns. And if the baby is particularly irritable or difficult, the problems can be exacerbated.

It needs to be stated that Winnicott's work was located in a particular time, and emphasised the role and experience of mothers as primary caregivers. We choose to use his theory and adapt it to inform our work also with fathers, adoptive and foster parents, and early years practitioners, within a context of diversity of current family structures, all of whom attend the Growing Together groups.

The provision of the Growing Together group for mothers and fathers and their infant is designed to provide space and time when both parent and baby can themselves experience containment. Mothers experiencing depression can benefit from finding a setting in which they can feel to some degree 'held', where they can be listened to or can listen to others or can just be. They require a setting in which their own anxieties can be voiced, if they wish, where they have permission to tell of their difficulties. Meanwhile, the infant also needs to feel 'held' with an adult or adults other than their mother who can think about them and try to make sense of what is happening. Simply naming the mother's feelings, and naming the baby's feelings, can serve as some form of containment that can be helpful for development.

Providing opportunities for developing helpful attachment experiences

In providing symbolic holding, we hope to provide opportunities for helpful attachment patterns. Attachment is about providing experiences in the parent–child relationship which enable the child to develop a feeling of security and well-being, which in turn is a sound foundation for active learning. When a caregiver is unable, through whatever personal difficulty, to meet the baby's early needs for holding and comfort, then it is possible the baby will show difficulties in attachment patterns through childhood and into adulthood. In the Growing Together groups we try to be sufficiently attentive to each baby present, and concerned for details in their development from week to week. We support positive relating between the parent and the child that can facilitate healthy attachment behaviour. By being supportive and showing interest, concern and care when a baby is distressed, we hope to help a mother internalise a 'feeling image' of how, if necessary, she may relate with her child in more varied ways. Much current work on attachment demonstrates how the way a mother or father experienced relationship in their own infancy can influence the way they relate with their own baby. So, if their own early infancy experiences were unsupported, and the odds were stacked against them forming helpful attachments, this may then occur in their own relationships with their children; the patterns may be repeated down the generations. We work with this possibility by providing opportunities, if parents wish, to talk about their own early childhood experiences and their memories of how they were parented. By becoming consciously aware of the difficulties they experienced, it is possible for them to become more aware of how they were parented. And with this, it is possible for them to become more aware of how they may be repeating the same patterns with their own baby. This provides for the possibility, through conscious awareness, to change their present patterns of relating. We also hope that the way we relate to parents, and try to be responsive to their emotional needs, even through nurturing them by offering a hot drink at the beginning of the session, we can help repair a little of their own feelings of having suffered emotional neglect in childhood.

Finally, attachment behaviour is about becoming more able to feel oneself as a separate individual, able also to feel related to others. To manage this is an achievement. Part of this achievement rests on having had successful, non-traumatic experience of many goodbyes and hellos in life, of the myriad everyday separations and reunions we experience. So all the arrivals and departures of the Growing Together group are important experiences for how to say goodbye and hello. They are things we may take for granted. In the group context they can help develop new experiences of safely separating and coming back. So for the children, as well as the adults, we pay attention to arrivals and departures. Within the session time, we support children who show clinging behaviours to be able to safely explore, knowing that their mother or father is still there and can be returned to immediately. Or it may be a case of supporting a parent who is anxious to let go of their child, to allow them to separate and go off and explore. In another instance it may be that an infant is overly independent and both parent and child need help to be more intimate with one another. In each case specific kinds of anxieties are being expressed around the theme of relating and separating, and naming the anxieties can help bring change.

In light of the above, we provide emotional support through tuning in to parent and child, taking in their state of mind at any particular time, giving appropriate responses which may include the naming of the kinds of feelings being experienced, so they can be talked about, and thus be more consciously recognised. We intend the group to function as a 'secure base' in which infants and children can safely explore, play and learn, while feeling their parent is safe with the child's own feelings contained.

The kinds of feelings experienced

Parents' feelings

For parents, relating to their baby arouses very strong feelings, mainly because of the weight of responsibility for understanding what an infant and child needs at any one time. Many mothers we work with are unsupported by a partner and often living away from their own family, so the mother herself may be in a vulnerable and isolated position. To then have a baby may increase those feelings. Also giving up work, with loss of independent income, can mean isolation from a former work community that may have provided support and routine. If we add in hormonal changes after birth, as well as any actual experience for the mother and/or baby of birth process trauma, then all the odds are stacked against feeling secure and well in relating to a new baby with what may seem like incessant controlling or even attacking demands. In the groups we try to allow all such feelings to be voiced, for once voiced they can feel less threatening. To hear that other parents also feel the same kinds of feelings at times can be a big relief. So we try to help all such feelings to be shared. One mother, for instance, may tell a new mother of how she too has been through really bad times. Loneliness, which can be a debilitating experience after the birth of a baby, can be relieved through mothers getting in contact with one another within and outside of the group times. Part of that loneliness can be due to birth evoking a feeling in a new mother of really missing her own mother, or a longing to be mothered herself at a time when she is having to do all the mothering. Unresolved feelings of grief from bereavements may also surface at this time. For fathers too the birth of their child may turn their world upside down, and the impact of the birth on their relationship with their partner may be great. There are also all the additional relationship pressures and possible further pressure on the partner to earn enough to support them all.

We would like to mention here that sexual abuse is an issue that seems often to come to light especially when a mother has a baby. The experience she has gone through in her body during intercourse, conception, pregnancy and birth may evoke feelings about physical, emotional and sexual abuse. These are experiences in which the boundaries and power relationships between people have not been respected, and inappropriate intrusions have occurred. It is important that a mother who feels she has experienced abuse finds support to deal with feelings that may threaten to overwhelm her, and is aided in finding expert help, although it may be very hard to access. At a different level, the boundaries around and within the group can help give a model of the need for boundaries, which protect developing relationships. So we pay special attention to trying to maintain boundaries, such as when the sessions begin and end.

Postnatal depression is a further frequent factor affecting many women after birth and often for a long time. We work with this as above, and feel that the groups are especially important for women who are very depressed.

The child's feelings

Infants themselves need to experience care that is reliable and secure. Particularly if home care is, for whatever reason, chaotic, they need to experience a pattern in the group time, and also the firm boundary at the beginning and ending. It simply helps them know where they are and what may be coming next, helping them to build a sense of consistency in some part of their day or week. They may also feel reassured to have their feelings named, so they can learn that their raw feelings can be understood, and made sense of. Then the feelings are not so frightening. This can help in building up some security in the imagery in their internal worlds.

The worker's feelings

The kind of work done in these groups can be very emotional for practitioners. One of the reasons for this is that babies have raw primitive feelings, which get inside those caring for them. They have to 'project' their feelings into those caring for them, as these are their only way of showing them what they may need or how they feel. Practitioners in the Growing Together groups absorb not only the feelings of the parents but also the feelings of the babies and children in the group. As this is pre-verbal experience, it may be subtle and unnoticed. It is essential for all those working with infants and mothers to have time and space to reflect on how the work is making them feel, how a particular experience has made them feel, so that the feelings can be shared and thought about rather than not dealt with. Feelings may also arise about one's own infancy and experience of being parented. It is not at all easy ever to find such time and space, and it all too readily gets eroded. This is partly for practical reasons, but may also be because it is easier to defend oneself through going on to the next thing and being busy, rather than having thinking space with others who can help reflect back their perceptions. Regular group supervision is built in for an hour a month to provide an allotted amount of time. It is prioritised so it does not get cancelled. In other words, workers need containing too.

Theory into practice

The idea is that in Growing Together, through the ways we structure the time and space of the sessions, we provide a symbolic kind of holding and containment.

Continuity of service and practitioner

Applying these concepts has many consequences for the development of parent and children's services. It requires that the provision is regular and reliable, so that both parents and infants can feel a security in the experience and know that it will not be cancelled or moved to a different place. The structure of the provision helps parents to feel emotionally contained, to feel that there is something there that is for them, and their needs are important enough for the provision to be made that meets those needs. It also gives the message that their child is important and has developmental and emotional requirements that are respected. It is vitally important that the parent's and the child's needs are nurtured and valued in order to support the development of emotional health in the infant and the parent. So the nature of the welcome that parents receive in the groups is important. The importance of continuity in the practitioners who work in the group cannot be over-emphasised. This means that the thinking in the work develops and builds up over time.

Structuring space

We are working in a room, which has to be set up for each session. We provide *treasure baskets* containing a wide variety of objects, such as wooden spoons, metal measuring spoons, sponges and so on (Goldschmied & Jackson, 1994). We have also put together small baskets for parents to use with their very young infants, containing for instance rattles, soft small toys, small safe objects that can be put in mouths and board books. We make full use of heuristic play objects. One of the problems in working with the varying play needs of a wide age range is how to provide sufficient for each child to find what they require for specific learning needs at any given moment, without providing so much that the floor quickly becomes a sea of objects, difficult for new little walkers to traverse. We also provide a sand tray and a water tray, both of which are much used by infants from the moment they can stand at them.

Figure 10.1 Children at the water tray

Spare clothes become a necessity so that children are not prohibited by the need to keep clean and dry. We make up play dough each week, and again find that it is much used from about one year upwards, with many children learning that it is too salty to be eaten.

We also include a cot and simple dollies not too big to handle, with blankets to wrap them in; a dolls' house with small world furniture and people; a wooden railway set which attracts children of all ages; some cars, large wooden lorries and wooden blocks. Paint could be a possibility but takes some managing with such an age range in a room with many other functions. Felt tips, crayons and paper have to be sufficient. The idea is that the play and craft materials provide for whatever any child is intrinsically motivated to explore. High-quality, supportive, safe bean-bags are really helpful for infants, so a mother can place the infant in the bean bag in front of her, to relate and communicate from a different position.

We aim to provide resources and play opportunities that can be used and recreated at home. In addition, we develop a culture in the group where workers and parents are very involved with the play going on, overcoming the tendency for adults to sit while the children are playing. We hope, in facilitating parents and children both playing, to support attachment processes, and to provide for moments of shared experience and enjoyment. Sometimes it feels as important for a parent to be able to play, for instance with play dough, as it is for the child.

Figure 10.2 A child deeply involved with dough and a worker responding

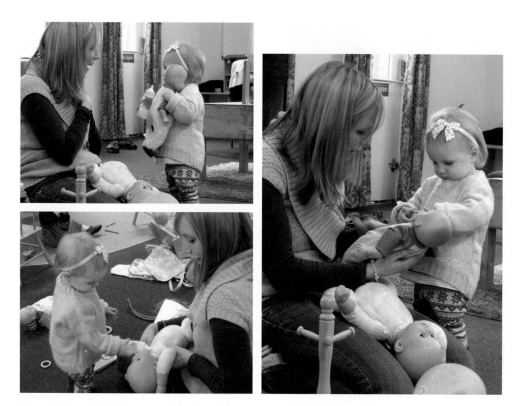

Figure 10.3 Parent and child interacting at Growing Together

Pre-session reflection time

We structure a thinking time before each session, for about 20 minutes after setting up the room. The Growing Together sessions last for an hour and a half. Having time to think beforehand is not easy to achieve, as there is always so much to be done, but it is important that we protect this time and space. We usually begin by thinking about the previous week's session, or a message from someone who has phoned in to say they can't come, or include thoughts about a mother and her situation or a particular child and their development. It means that the parents and children are already held in the minds of those working in the group.

We intend that the sessions should have a defined beginning and ending. Again this is hard, as sometimes parents arrive very early, and the thinking time beforehand does not happen. Knowing the importance of the pre-brief, we have created a comfy space external to the group room where parents and their children can sit and wait for the group to begin.

It makes a tangible difference to the work if parents and children likely to come to the session are held in the minds of practitioners, with reflections on what happened the previous week and especially any events that caused difficulty. For instance, on one occasion we thought of practical ways to help a two-year-old boy who would arrive in an unhappy mood and immediately kick everything over in the room. We thought about what he was communicating to us, and decided that one worker would give special attention to him and his mother as they arrived in the next session, which led to him beating the life out of some drums. Or in another example, when a mother seemed not to be relating to her baby, and unaware of the baby's needs for cuddling, we used the video to record her holding and talking to her baby, playing it back straight away showing how responsive her baby was to this, how much she wanted to 'talk' to her mum. We felt this seemed to amplify an experience that both found rewarding. This mother took away printouts of the images to show others and to take home.

Beginning the sessions

We have a defined beginning time, and provide a positive welcome, with hot drinks and adult-sized comfy chairs for parents. As much as anything, it is simply having clearly in mind that this is a specific session, with specific individual parents and children who have chosen to come, and is marked off from other work activities and responsibilities. We aim for the space and time to be protected from administrative intrusions and phone calls, which is practically difficult in busy workplaces, but the message to parents and infants, if the groups are intruded on as little as possible, is that they are respected. We do not have a concept of lateness; parents are welcomed whenever they can arrive, and can leave when they need to.

Video work

We use the video during the group and use equipment that enables us to play back the images through a computer. This allows us to do some very close focused work with an individual infant and parent. We then view this with the parent through the computer to strengthen and focus on the experience with their child. Sufficient time and members of staff have to be built in to allow this to happen, and it is something we struggle with.

We invite parents to be filmed at the beginning of a session. If a parent chooses not to be filmed they are able to say 'no'. When a parent chooses to say 'no' it is important that we, as practitioners, continue to offer the opportunity to be filmed at a later date. We would aim to video for approximately five minutes and provide feedback for one child per session. Some parents express to us that they do not wish to be in the film footage. We do try and encourage parents to be filmed alongside their child, even for a short period of the footage, so they can reflect on how they are together. However, we would never insist a parent or child do anything that they are uncomfortable with.

We invite the parent and child to be filmed together as close to the beginning of a session as possible in order to complete the process within the hour and a half, although it is important that parent and child are settled within the group before the filming begins. We usually talk to the parent about where they would like the filming to take place, for example they may prefer to be sat together on the sofa or on a bean bag. For a child who is more mobile we tend to discuss what the child may have an interest in and locate the filming around their interest and wait for the child to become involved in their play.

We currently use handicam video cameras to capture the video, however, we are experimenting with using iPads. It is important to make sure that when we are filming we are as unobtrusive as possible. Ethically, we believe we must stop filming if the child appears uncomfortable and will revisit the filming at a later session.

Each practitioner has a different way of prompting or starting the conversation about the video footage. Some workers ask the parent to watch the video through first and then ask them what they found interesting. Others ask how being filmed felt and whether there was any aspect they wanted to focus on.

During this reflection time relevant concepts such as 'involvement', 'well-being' (Laevers, 1997), 'schemas' (Athey, 1990), 'pedagogic strategies' (Whalley & Arnold, 1997) and 'companionship' (Trevarthern, 2002) are discussed with the parents. These concepts give us a shared language to enable us to talk with parents about their relationship with their child. Often the footage is slowed down in order to see children's expressions and the nuances of their behaviour. The parent chooses a set of images that they feel tells a story of what has been going on for that child during the video. The parent decides on relevant text to put on the page to go with the imagery they have chosen. For example, one parent while interacting with her eight-week-old baby recognised how when she moved her face closer towards him he became more animated and engaged with her. She chose a sequence of six stills showing his reaction when she was both close and then further away from him. To tell the story she wrote: 'Finley likes trying to focus on my face. Once we thought about the distance between us I realised he can see me better if I am closer to him. He looks at my mouth, eyes – focused.'

Sometimes children come with the parents to see the footage. At other times the parents ask their friends or one of the practitioners in the group to keep an eye on their child. The stills and narratives are then imported on to a page using PowerPoint and printed off on photo paper, enabling the parent to leave the session with a beautiful portfolio.

Figure 10.4 A parent, worker and child at the computer during Growing Together

Ending sessions

To mark off the ending of a session we have evolved a kind of symbol so that infants get to know that the end of the session is near. So about 15 minutes before the end of the session those working in the group begin to tidy the toys and equipment, usually helped by many others, so that the room is sufficiently clear and safe for 'bubbles time'. We hand out pots of bubbles and wands for anyone to blow bubbles, and children who are able to are helped to blow for themselves. Any kind of experience or activity could be used, provided it is regular and connected with the actual event of it being leaving time. Then it serves as a symbol that can help infants, and children, parents and workers too, with the ending.

Post-session reflection time

This is hard to achieve when workers have other tasks to go and do. Busy-ness is a powerful defence. But it feels essential to try and enable reflection time to happen. Rather as in the pre-session time, the aim is to think about all the experiences that have occurred during the session. Each individual worker will have experienced different relationships and interactions, and will have their own individual perceptions of events and people. This is a time for trying to make sense of the experiences, to take note of any practical action needed, and to have in mind something that may need to be borne in mind for the next week. But above all it is intended as a time in which workers in the group can process their own emotional responses, and the impact that a particular experience or child may have had on them. In naming and discussing these feelings, we mirror the work done in the groups, hoping that the worker is less likely to go away feeling too affected emotionally by their work. It requires the building up of a culture of valuing time for reflection and processing feelings, and has to be protected from disturbance. It is often easier to dash off to do other things than to stay with the pain of an episode that has just happened.

Confidentiality

A person's rights to confidentiality within the group have always to be respected. Difficulties may arise when liaising with members of staff in other parts of a children's centre, for instance with a Family Worker who may bring a parent and a baby to a group. Much care and thought has to be taken about what is said to whom, when, and how. A person's right to privacy is paramount.

Evaluation

Evaluation is ongoing through immediate parent feedback. In addition we have exit questionnaires, which we ask parents to complete when their time

Figure 10.5 Blowing bubbles to signify time to leave the Growing Together group

in the group is coming to an end. We are looking at ways, in addition to immediate intuitive measures, for improving how we know whether the groups are really effective in giving support and making a difference to families attending the group. We are looking at piloting the use of the 'Parents' Involvement in Their Children's Learning' (PICL) self-evaluation tool which the parents themselves devised. 'Parents rejected the measures commonly used in family support as they found the wording on them patronising and that the indicators did not reflect the outcomes that they had experienced through PICL' (C4EO, 2012).

The following case study illustrates how the Growing Together groups provided an opportunity for Rachael and her two children, Lucas and Jake, to be:

- thought about by workers and other parents
- provided with time and a space to socialise and develop relationships with others
- supported by other parents and how important this was in supporting Rachael's parenting
- enabled by parents and workers to see her child's issues and behaviour from other perspectives
- supported in her own experiences with her children
- provided with opportunities for Jake and Lucas to experience different kinds of play and learning through play.

Example from practice

Rachael, Lucas and Jake

When I found out I was pregnant a friend suggested that my friend and I should try the Pen Green groups because they were really good. We went to Baby Massage then Babycise then to Growing Together. Lucas was about eight months old. Tracy (my friend) and I started to come together as there is only four months between our children. We came together until Tracy started back at work about six months ago.

Parent-to-parent support

For the boys and me, Growing Together has been a really beneficial experience. I felt that if I had a problem I could speak to somebody, I could get advice from practitioners and other mums. Other mums being there helped enormously. Lucas didn't sleep and I was going through a lot of personal hassle – I felt like I was a bad mum because he wouldn't sleep and then had paddies and temper tantrums. Seeing and speaking to other mums who were honest with me, who said we used to do this and that, and having advice from practitioners was really helpful and made me feel normal and relaxed. Just the general conversation, having an adult conversation really helped. People asked how I was, not just how the boys were but how I was – it really helped. Even having a cup of tea felt like you were in a nice, relaxed environment and the kids were safe which was a really big help. If I hadn't have felt comfortable then I would have stopped coming.

For Rachael to feel able to share her feelings with other parents and to hear that other parents also have the same kinds of feelings at times came as a big relief. In Growing Together she had found a setting in which she could feel to some degree 'held', where she could be listened to and listen to others. Rachael's own anxieties about Lucas's lack of sleep and his temper tantrums were able to be voiced. Her feelings were 'contained'.

Example from practice

Example from practice

Workers' subtle support

I think Lucas noticed a difference in me because I was more relaxed. Because I was more relaxed, when he was having a paddy and being difficult, I was able to deal with it. I was less stressed; I was still a bit, but I was more able to deal with it. Plus people helped as well with him and me, which helped a lot. It helped him calm down and me calm down. There was a massive paddy once when I had just had Jake. Lucas wanted me to go and play with him, which was fine but Jake woke up in his car seat and he was screaming for his feed. I asked Lucas to wait until I had fed Jake. Lucas was having a paddy and screaming because he wanted my attention. One of the practitioners took him off to play in the water so I could feed Jake. Without one of the practitioners helping it would have been absolute chaos. It would have been manic without anyone stepping in. Lucas had really taken to this practitioner and was quite happy to be taken off to the water. He likes attention, he likes one-on-one attention which I think obviously when Jake came along, as much as I tried to really give him attention, obviously I had to be with Jake sometimes and he didn't like it. So when the practitioner came along he thought, oh I have someone to play with, and he felt fine, he was happy. It's that help when you need it that helps me to feel more relaxed. If it had happened in any other group then I probably would have got in my car and gone home. In Growing Together you feel it's okay, parents understand that's what happens and you can relax…

I wanted Growing Together to help with Lucas's independence because he was so clingy. I wanted him to be able to leave me, especially when I found out I was having Jake, as I knew there were times I needed to be with the baby. I wanted him to learn to go off. If I started off playing with him and he became happy he would then be happy with me leaving his side.

Within this excerpt you can clearly see how Rachael was able to contain Lucas's emotions because she was feeling contained herself. Because Rachael was relaxed she was more able to 'deal with' Lucas's paddies and temper tantrums – taking them on board, providing comfort and dealing with the distress. When the demands of both Rachael's children were made simultaneously, it is evident how a practitioner, who is familiar with the family, subtly steps in to support them. The worker, knowing that Lucas enjoys his time at the water tray, was able to receive his distress and support his interests. Rachael was then able to relax and focus on Jake's needs and feed him. In addition to this, Lucas was being 'held' by another adult, who was able to think about him and try to make sense of what was happening.

Rachael's ability to contain Lucas's 'paddies' supported his development and capacity to contain his own difficult feelings, resulting in him becoming more able to feel himself as a separate individual and also able to feel related to others. Attachment is about providing experiences in the parent–child relationship which enable the child to develop a feeling of security and well-being, which in turn is a sound foundation for active learning.

In order for the worker to contain Lucas's emotions, she also needed to feel contained. Regular group supervision, pre-brief and de-brief sessions all supported the worker to feel able to express her emotions and make sense of the experience for herself.

Example from practice
Example from practice

Understanding my child's learning and development

During one of the filming sessions I was introduced to the term 'transporting'. I can now see it every time Lucas does it. At the moment he is lining up all of the chairs between the sand tray and the drawing table. He stands there so proud of what he has done … I can remember when Lucas did his first drawing and he loves the trains … He remembers so many things. In the baby basket there is a scarf; Olivia [his friend] used to wear it as a skirt. When Olivia came back, after six months, Lucas picked it up and gave it to Olivia.

He plays lots in the dolls' house and he loves imaginative role-play, so we bought him a wooden kitchen to play with and a shopping trolley for Christmas. I never would have thought he would have loved that kind of thing, yet him and Jake love it, it's fab, one has the trolley and the other has the basket. They have a mop and a brush. If I hadn't been to Growing Together I wouldn't have known he would be interested in that. I would have got him more planes and trucks and things. He loves all of his role-play.

I like the fact you get a printout of the videoing process and I could show Stuart, my partner. Stuart's big concern when Lucas was having his paddies was that Lucas would be seen as a naughty kid. Lucas loves to show his daddy his pictures. Both of the printouts from the video filming are on our fridge. When Lucas asks what we are doing today and I say we are going to Growing Together, he walks to the kitchen and points to the fridge and says 'That one, mummy?' Jake has started to do this as well.

Lucas's ability to explore the environment shows how the group functions as a secure base in which Lucas and Jake are able to safely explore, play and learn, while feeling that Rachael is nearby. Lucas was free to explore the variety of play and craft materials provided for whatever intrinsically motivated him. Rachael was able to notice the resources and play opportunities the children enjoyed and recreate them at home for both Lucas and Jake.

Example from practice
Example from practice

Growing apart

Lucas will be leaving Growing Together soon as he turns three in February. I have just been told he has a place in the crèche which means I can continue to go to Growing Together with just Jake. It will be strange for Jake because at the moment all Jake does is follow Lucas around and I know he will be wondering where Lucas is. But then I think he will come out of himself more and I need to find out what Jake likes, so I want Jake to develop his interests and I am looking forward to spending some one-on-one time with him, as we don't get much of that at home.

One of the goals in the Growing Together groups is to help support parents and infants to grow apart, together.

Figure 10.6 Jake at Growing Together

Finally

We call these groups Growing Together but what do we mean by this? While much of the work concentrates on attachment relationships between parent and child, attachment is not just about bonding and being together. Healthy attachment relationships are also about developing capacities, as the child acquires a stronger internal working model, to become a separate person. So one of the goals in Growing Together groups is to help support parents and infants to grow apart, together.

Figure 10.7 Lucas at Growing Together

Points for discussion

- Discuss which kinds of groups you are working in.
- Consider the theories underpinning your practice with young children and families.
- How does the environment you create reflect your beliefs and values about working with families?

References

Athey, C. (1990) *Extending Thought in Young Children: A parent–teacher partnership*, London: Paul Chapman.

Bion, W. (1962) *Learning from Experience*, London: Heinemann.

Bowlby, J. (1988) *A Secure Base*, London: Routledge.

Breuer, J. and Freud, S. (1893) 'Case histories: (1) Fraulein Anna O. and (5) Fraulein Elisabeth von R', in *The Standard Edition of the Complete Psychological Works of Sigmund Freud*, Vol. II (1893–5), pp. 21–47 and 135–181, London: Vintage (2001).

C4EO (2012) *Validated Local Practice* [online]. Available from: http://c4eo.org.uk/themes/earlyyears/localpractice.aspx?themeid=1.

Easen, P., Kendal, P. and Shaw, J. (1992) 'Parents as educators: dialogue and developing through partnership', *children and Society*, vol. 6, no. 4, pp. 282–96.

Goldschmied, E. and Jackson, S. (1994) *People Under Three: Young children in day care*, London: Routledge.

Klein, M. (1946) 'Notes on some schizoid mechanisms', in *Envy and Gratitude and Other Works 1946–1963*, ch. 1, pp. 1–24, London: Vintage (1997).

Laevers, F. (1997) *A Process-oriented Child Follow-up System for Young Children*, Leuven: Centre for Experiential Education.

Steele, H. and Steele, M. (1994) 'Intergenerational patterns of attachment', *Advances in Personal Relationships*, vol. 5, London: Jessica Kingsley.

Stern, D. (1985) *The Interpersonal World of the Infant,* New York: Basic Books.

Trevarthern, C. (2002) 'Learning in companionship', *Education in the North: The journal of Scottish education*, new series No. 10, pp. 16–25.

Winnicott, D. W. (1965) 'The theory of the parent–infant relationship', *The Maturational Processes and the Facilitating Environment*, London: Hogarth Press.

Wood, D. J., Bruner, J. S. and Ross, G. (1976) 'The role of tutoring in problem-solving', *Journal of Child Psychology and Psychiatry*, vol. 17, pp. 89–100.

Whalley, M. and Arnold, C. (1997) *Effective Pedagogic Strategies,* TTA Summary of Research Findings.

11 Developing the use of video reflection with parents: thinking about feeling – facilitating reflection

Colette Tait

In this chapter, I present:

- some theory underpinning the process that occurs when parents reflect on their actions using video
- how a study was set up to take this idea further by working intensively with one parent and child over ten weeks
- the questions raised and the findings of the study.

Introduction

As you will have read in previous chapters, there has been a long tradition of sharing both video material and theoretical frameworks with parents at Pen Green. This chapter builds on this tradition, and considers whether it is possible to use video material and dialogue as a catalyst to facilitate reflection in others.

Reflection

The principle of 'reflection' at Pen Green is something that has been critical from the beginning. In her book, *Learning to Be Strong*, which documented the setting up of the Pen Green Centre, Margy Whalley states that staff in the nursery would be expected to 'read widely ... reflect on their own practice ... and to undertake practitioner research' (Whalley, 1994: 27). She states that Freire was one of the philosophical influences on the way in which services at Pen Green were conceptualised. Thirty years later, workers at Pen Green are still encouraged to be 'reflective practitioners', in the Freirian sense, thinking about their practice and drawing on theory to enhance their understandings. Freire states that, 'Revealing the theory embedded in practice undoubtedly helps the subject of practice to understand practice by reflecting and improving on it' (Freire, 1996: 108). Practitioners working effectively with parents also need to 'revisit the theory and review practice in the light of information proffered by the parents' (Whalley *et al.*, 2001: 138).

Through drawing on the 'specialist knowledge' parents have of their own children and sharing theories with parents, we know a shared language can develop (Easen *et al.*, 1992). This shared language can be the basis of an ongoing dialogue between practitioners and parents, which ultimately benefits the child. I had experienced this as both a parent whose children attended the Pen Green Nursery and then subsequently as a worker at Pen Green, co-leading both Parents' Involvement in Their Children's Learning (PICL) groups and Growing Together groups. I am a real advocate for working with parents in this way.

An earlier influence

In the early days of Growing Together I was also involved, to a small extent, in a project that had a profound impact on me. Natasha Charlwood was training to be a doctor. As part of her training she was undertaking a psychology degree, and an element of this degree involved carrying out a project at Pen Green. Her project was entitled, *Using Attachment Theory to Inform Practice in an Integrated Centre for Children and Families* (Charlwood & Steele, 2004: 59).

In this project Charlwood carried out Adult Attachment Interviews (AAIs) (George *et al.*, 1985) with parents attending the Pen Green Centre. Her hypothesis was that 'mothers' responses to the AAI would correlate with independent ratings of their children's social and emotional well-being' (Charlwood & Steele, 2004: 59). The AAI is a measure 'designed to elicit an adult's mental representations of their caregiver(s) and their relationship with their caregiver(s) retrospectively' (Schechtner *et al.*, 2006: 437).

The children's ratings of social and emotional well-being were carried out by two staff members at Pen Green, who knew the children well. The Pen Green staff used the Pre-School Rating Scales developed by Erickson *et al.* (1985).

Through Charlwood's study her hypothesis was confirmed and it was evident that 'ratings of mothers' probable past experiences and current states of mind regarding attachment were powerfully correlated with their children's well-being' (Charlwood & Steele, 2004: 59).

What struck me about the Adult Attachment Interview was the fact that it wasn't a judgement about the quality of experience of a person's early life, but a judgement about the coherence of their understanding of their early life, whatever the circumstances. Therefore, a person who demonstrates through the coherence of their narrative that 'malevolent relationship patterns are clearly relegated to the past' (Charlwood & Steele, 2004: 64) and who, through this narrative, is able to demonstrate that they understand how these 'patterns' have influenced their own development, may be classified as 'autonomous-secure'. A person with an autonomous-secure classification is likely to be 'capable of reflecting upon past relationship adversities' and therefore limiting 'consequent ill-effects [of their own upbringing] on children's well-being' (Charlwood & Steele, 2004: 70).

This idea brought together my thinking about reflection. It seemed to me that, through reflecting, feelings could be 'worked through' and changes for the better could be made.

These experiences all contributed towards my desire to find out whether it was possible to 'facilitate reflection' in others. Was one of the aims of Growing Together – 'to encourage reflective parenting' – something that could be done? And if so, how could it be done most effectively? On a personal note, I was becoming more and more interested in the idea of 'thinking about feeling'. Slade (2005: 271) refers to 'the capacity to think about feeling and to feel about thinking' as 'mentalization'. A parent's ability to 'reflectively function' – to 'mentalize' (Fonagy & Target, 1997: 679) – is likely to enable an infant to feel 'held in mind' (Winnicott, 1965).

This chapter tells the story of how I investigated whether it was possible to 'think about feeling' alongside another, and therefore to 'facilitate reflection'.

An example from practice

How my study was carried out

I wanted to draw on work already being carried out at the Pen Green Centre, and I was keen to use video in my research. We have found that 'video provides the technical means to observe, support and intervene in interactional processes' (Woodhead *et al.*, 2006: 139). I considered how the video filming and feedback sessions worked in the Growing Together groups where, because of the high numbers of families accessing the service, a parent and child might not be filmed more than once every few months. I felt it would be easier to develop a more in-depth dialogue with a parent if the filming sessions happened more often.

I decided that, for this piece of research, once I had found a family that was happy to be involved, I would set up a system of filming a parent and child, and viewing the film with them, over a ten-week period. I chose this period of time because:
- I thought it would be enough time to develop a dialogue with a parent.
- I felt it would generate enough video evidence to analyse, without being too overwhelming.
- I wanted to allow enough time for reflection. I knew that I would need time to think about what we had seen, what we had discussed, and to consider our developing thinking over time.

Once gathered, this video data would give me the 'crucial ability to replay a sequence of interaction repeatedly … and on multiple occasions' (Jordan & Henderson, 1995: 39). I hoped that by carrying out this type of qualitative research I would be able to 'obtain the intricate details about phenomena such as feelings, thought processes, and emotions' (Strauss & Corbin, 1998: 11).

Finding a family

I decided to approach Tina, a parent who attended Growing Together with her baby son, Michael.

Tina was 31 years old at the time, and lived with her partner, Richard, who was 32. They had been in a relationship for ten years and were planning to get married the following year. Tina and Richard had three children: Kimberley, five, Jayne, three, and Michael, five months old. Tina and Richard lived locally and used services at Pen Green. Tina had come to Growing Together since Kimberley was a baby. Richard worked full time, but had also come along to Growing Together when he had been off work.

I approached Tina one Friday afternoon when she was in Growing Together, explaining about the piece of research I wanted to undertake. After discussing it with Richard, Tina agreed. I wanted Tina to seriously consider the impact of becoming involved in this piece of research with me. I was aware that there was a possibility that the research, and I, could become a 'burden' to Tina. Stake advises, 'In discussing prospects of the study, burden on the host should be acknowledged. The researcher may be delightful company, but hosting delightful company is a burden' (Stake, 1995: 58).

We had some decisions to make about the practicalities of carrying out the research:
- where we would film
- when we would film
- when we would view the film.

I was very clear with Tina at the beginning about the ethical issues involved in carrying out a research project, and I thought carefully about what Tina could gain from the research. As Bell states, 'People will be doing you a favour if they agree to help, and they will need to know exactly what they will be asked to do, how much time they will be expected to give and what use will be made of the information they provide' (Bell, 1999: 37).

I shared with Tina the ethical guidelines that are used at Pen Green for carrying out participatory research. These guidelines are based, to some extent, on the BERA (British Educational Research Association) Ethical Guidelines (1992).

Key information

Research guidelines: ethical considerations

Research at Pen Green should always:

- Be positive for all the participants
- Provide data that are open to, accountable to and interpreted by all the participants
- Focus on questions that the participants themselves are asking
- Be based on a relationship of trust where people's answers are believed
- Produce results which are about improving practice at home and in the nursery [setting] or at least sustaining it.

(Whalley et al., 2001: 13)

In addition to these guidelines we negotiated some specific guidelines that we felt were important:
- Tina may choose to withdraw from this project at any time if she wanted to.
- All data gathered would be shared with Tina and a copy of all the video material would be put on to a DVD for Tina and Richard to keep.
- We would take video stills each week, and a copy would be printed out for Tina on a weekly basis.
- Names could be anonymised in the final report and this decision would be Tina and Richard's.
- If either of us was unable to keep to an agreed time for a meeting it was our responsibility to call the other and let them know.

Managing the filming schedule

I negotiated with Tina about where and when we would take the film and also where we would view it and discuss it. I was conscious that I did not want to overwhelm Tina, or take up too much of her time, although I was aware that 'educational case data gathering involves at least a small invasion of personal privacy' (Stake, 1995: 57).

With this in mind, we decided that it would be easiest to film Tina for five minutes each week in Growing Together, while Kimberley was at school, and Jayne was in the crèche at Pen Green. Tina was initially concerned about what the other parents might think if she was seen being filmed each week. I reassured Tina that I would speak to other group members about my study, and explain why she and

Michael were being filmed. I also assured her that the usual filming of parents and children in the session would still occur. Tina was happy with this.

We decided that it would be most convenient to view the film during a morning as Kimberley and Jayne were at school and nursery. We arranged for me to go to Tina's house on a Monday morning for one hour where we would view the film together.

I was nervous at this stage. I was worried in case we did not have enough to talk about when we were viewing the film together. Although I understood that in grounded theory 'the researcher begins with an area of study and allows the theory to emerge from the data' (Strauss & Corbin, 1998: 12), I was finding it hard to trust that this process would happen.

In order to alleviate some of this anxiety I wrote down some prompts I would share with Tina each time we were going to view a sequence of film:

Prompts

- What I want to do is learn about how looking at things together can be helpful to both of us.
- Thinking about the development of a mutual vocabulary – exploring words together so we have a shared meaning.
- What do we both see, what does each of us see?
- How did we get there – what process did we go through? How did it feel to talk about the video?
- Any other thoughts.

The process

Each week I would film as agreed and we would meet together to discuss the filmed sequence and Tina would select a sequence of stills. Of course there were some variations and deviations to our plan such as it taking longer than an hour to view the film with Tina, make a record of our conversation and select a sequence of stills. I realised that it would probably take longer than an hour each week, and this became a reality. As Bell points out, 'Interviews are very time consuming … Then there is the time needed to consider what has been said during the interview, to go through notes, to extend and clarify points' (Bell, 1999: 143). Of course, there were other variations to the initial plan, and how these variations were accommodated within the plan was thought about on a week-to-week basis as they arose. These variations included sickness, re-scheduling of appointments, and other people being present during the discussion.

We managed, however, to complete our filming and viewing sessions within the ten-week period. This was only possible as both Tina and I were willing and able to be flexible. Had this not been the case I wonder whether the discussions we had would have been as deep, or if we would both have felt a sense of power and control in the relationship. It was evident from the variations that occurred that both Tina and I felt able to make changes to the agreed arrangements.

During our viewing and discussion sessions I recorded what Tina said and asked, as well as my own responses. I then spent some time later in the day recording my reflections and my own questions as they occurred to me:

Questions

- How is the sharing of video material impacting on Tina? Can the shared viewing of video material change perspectives or behaviour?
- How does the naming or questioning of actions and behaviours bring them into a person's conscious awareness? Must this happen before change can occur?
- How does the sharing of theory aid the facilitation of reflection and does a person have to be at a particular stage to engage in reflection?
- Are comparisons a prelude to reflection? (Tina compares her own children and their behaviour. She compares herself to her father. Finally, she compares the childhood she is giving her children with her own childhood.)

Findings

How does the shared viewing of video material change perspectives and behaviour?

In the same way that the Anna Freud Centre uses digital video with parents, I was clear with Tina that the video 'is something that can be used collaboratively to help [both of us] understand more about [ourselves,] the baby and the ... process in which [we were] engaged – all three. It is not an expert- or assessment-led usage' (Woodhead *et al.*, 2006: 141). I wanted it to be transparent that the process was about both of us coming to a shared understanding about what was going on.

During the research process I felt that sharing the video material and our developing relationship was having a positive impact on Tina, and her behaviour. Tina began to consider where she would like to be filmed with Michael. One week Tina took him to the water tray as, 'Paul took him there once when he was younger, and he looked as though he was having a good time.' Tina said that she thought it would be nice to capture that on the video. On another occasion, Tina sat Michael on the floor near to the mirror as 'it looked like he wanted to interact with Charlie', who was also on the floor. Being the focus of the video filming seemed to help Tina to consider Michael's experience in the session in a way that perhaps she would not have done before.

She commented in the fieldwork on the impact of watching the video material. She said: 'It is something I wouldn't have thought about before – looking at expressions and thinking about what they mean – I would have done it automatically. Also, about where I sat – had to think about it – you just do what you think is right at the time.' She said that it was 'funny' seeing the film from a different angle (as she was in it). It was 'a totally different perspective'. Tina said that the video material and the questions I asked helped her to think differently, commenting, 'when you look back on stuff [view video material], you realise'. She also said that our viewing sessions had been 'eye-opening'. This has happened many times in Growing Together, particularly when we have slowed the video film down to look at the minutiae of an interaction. Parents are often surprised at what they are able to see and particularly at the amount of control the infant has in the interaction. This was undoubtedly the case in week two when Tina realised that, although she was able to move Michael physically, Michael actually had control of the eye contact between them. This was certainly the first time I had heard Tina consider that Michael was an active participant in their interactions, and could control when he took part and when he did not.

How does the naming or questioning of actions and behaviours bring them into a person's conscious awareness? Must this happen before change can occur?

I asked Tina questions about what we were seeing in the film right from the very first session. One of the first things I asked Tina was how she thought Michael might feel as she wiped his mouth from behind, giving him no warning. Tina's response was that she 'hadn't given it much thought'. On another occasion, Tina moved Michael without warning him, and commented about it, saying 'I will probably do it again … you know, going about my daily life'. This contrasted sharply with the way in which Tina, on other occasions, spoke to Michael about how he seemed to be feeling. On one occasion Tina patted Michael's back when he was crying and reassured him saying, 'You're not happy? You're not happy? Are you tired? … You're fighting … Shall we try you in your pram?' I commented on the way in which Tina was speaking to Michael and she responded by saying 'so I do it sometimes and not others'. In the fieldwork there were more and more occasions in which Tina responded to Michael in a very thoughtful way, sometimes warning him of events that were about to occur. Perhaps this process of seeing behaviours and responses and being asked about them did impact on Tina's behaviour.

I was interested to notice that by week five I had begun to comment on what was happening in the 'here and now' when viewing film, as well as what we were looking at on the film. This was not something I had thought about previously. I then remembered seeing a conference presentation in which a worker was reviewing a piece of video with a parent. Throughout their discussion the baby, sitting on the mother's knee, was ignored completely even though he was crying. I remember thinking, 'please stop talking, and see what is the matter with the baby'. I was surprised as I had begun to comment on the 'here and now' without thinking about it, and it was only after I read my weekly logs that I realised I was doing it.

I think that beginning to comment on the 'here and now' was probably a combination of feeling more comfortable and confident with Tina, alongside developing my skills as a facilitator/researcher.

I was also aware that, as time progressed, I noticed and was able to make reference to the way in which Tina was commenting on Michael's behaviour in relation to how he might be feeling, and the reason for that feeling. This 'capacity to link this awareness of her child's … own internal state to behaviour or to other internal states … is the hallmark of true reflective functioning' (Slade, 2005: 278).

How does the sharing of theory aid the facilitation of reflection?

Although theoretical concepts are shared with parents when viewing video material in the PICL and Growing Together groups, I did not specifically say that I intended to share theory with Tina when viewing the video material in this study. I think, in retrospect, this was because I was unsure which, if any, theory might be relevant to our discussions. Cohen and Manion make the point that 'Theory is emergent and must arise from particular situations … Theory should not precede research but follow it' (1994: 37). This was what happened during the course of my research with Tina. As Tina and I discussed the video material Tina asked questions. I then looked to the relevant theory to think about the questions Tina had asked, and shared this theory with her. This sharing of theory enhanced our shared understandings and enriched our discussions.

On the very first week Tina was sitting with Michael on her knee and we were watching the video footage together. Tina wondered whether Michael, while seeing the video footage, would remember the experience of playing with the items from the treasure basket. As a result of this I took *The Motherhood Constellation* (Stern, 1995) to our discussion the following week. We spoke about how babies, rather than remembering specific events, are building up a mental representation of 'being with' another. We returned to this idea on more than one occasion over the ten-week period. As my research progressed I became more and more convinced that the sharing of theory was key to the research. I also had a hunch that a person would have to be at a particular stage to engage with the theory, and to think about reflecting. Somehow, I felt that the timing had to be right.

In Tina's case, I felt that the time might be right for her to engage in the reflective process of watching video alongside somebody else. I thought this because of the way in which her relationship with Michael appeared to be a joyful one, yet at the same time Tina was able to articulate that she was struggling with Jayne. The ability to separate out both relationships and not just feel inadequate made me think that Tina would be at a point where she might like to reflect on one or more of her relationships with her children. Tina and I discussed this, and she said 'I like thinking about feelings'. We also spoke about somebody needing to be able to sit back, observe, feel and think in order to enter into this kind of reflective dialogue.

Bracketing theory

I had a revelatory experience about halfway through the research. Another member of one of the groups I co-lead, Kia, came to a session with an issue. Kia knew a student who was on a placement in a nursery. The student had seen a child be 'segregated from the others and made to eat lunch alone'. Both the student and Kia felt very strongly about this. Neither of them thought that this was good practice and both were worried about the impact this might have on the child. As Kia was relating this story to us in the group she was becoming very irate and saying, 'I mean, how will that child feel? … It can't be good for his well-being. If that happened to Evan [her son], I would go mad.' Kia then pointed to me and said, 'You know, all that schema and well-being stuff you used to say about.' Kia was referring to when we had talked about theory in relation to video material taken of her son in Growing Together some years previously.

Had I been asked to comment on why I thought Kia had come to Growing Together and what she had gained from her attendance I would probably have said that she came for some adult company, and for Evan to play with other children. I did not recall Kia engaging particularly with the theory. I had not imagined that the sharing of theory previously had impacted on her thinking. However, four years later I was sitting listening to Kia speak of this child's well-being and relate it to her experience in Growing Together. This was evidence of some impact for me.

This, in turn, made me think of something another student had said on a masters residential. She had talked of the idea of 'bracketing'. The idea that you could hear or experience something that you were not in a position to 'accommodate', and so you would 'bracket' it, file it away somehow. I wondered if this was what Kia had done? Perhaps Kia had had the experience of watching film of her son and been introduced to theoretical concepts such as schema (Athey, 1990) and well-being (Laevers, 1997) and then 'bracketed' those ideas until a situation arose in which she was in a position to draw on them.

If this were the case then it is another good argument for the sharing of theory with parents, at whatever stage of awareness they appear to be.

Perhaps the timing in relation to the sharing of theory is only relevant to the reciprocal aspect of the parent/worker relationship. If the timing is appropriate and the parent is able to enter into a reciprocal relationship then the relationship can progress and deepen with the aid of the theoretical knowledge being shared, which is what I believe happened in Tina's case.

I wonder if the theory that is 'bracketed' becomes drawn on as a result of an emotional trigger? Colwyn Trevarthen states that 'emotion is the motor of cognition' (2003). Kia was speaking irately, and was obviously feeling emotionally charged by the situation. Perhaps the way the situation made her feel enabled her to retrieve the bracketed theory that related to the instance in the nursery.

Tina shares theory

Tina also commented that she began to share theory with others, as a result of some of our conversations. She spoke with Richard about how a baby might feel being separated from their mum as soon as they are born, and put into a cot. She also communicated with some friends on a website where they share their concerns about parenting. On this occasion Tina shared theory that we had talked about in relation to separation anxiety. I was really pleased that Tina felt confident enough to talk with others about the discussions we had. As the theory we had discussed had usually been as a result of a question Tina had asked, it was very relevant for her. Perhaps this relevance to her own current situation was what enabled her to feel confident enough to share her knowledge of theory with others.

Are comparisons a prelude to reflection?

From the beginning of this process I noticed that Tina made comparisons between her children and their behaviour. This was never done in a detrimental way, but almost as if Tina were thinking out loud. On the very first week Tina commented about a swing she had in the living room, 'Kimberley loved it all the time, but Jayne didn't. Michael goes in it, but doesn't like it switched on.' Over time Tina continued to make comparisons between her children, and then she made comparisons between herself and Michael, both asthma sufferers, and herself and her father as both being interested in 'the behaviours of people'. Finally Tina began to make comparisons between the childhood she is giving her children, and the childhood she had had.

The making of comparisons throughout the project seemed significant, but I could not work out why. However, I now proffer the idea that these types of comparisons are a prelude to reflection. Zelenko and Benham argue that 'Videotape replay provides an accelerated access to early maternal memories and promotes enlightening awareness of the links between maternal past experience and present behaviours with her child, which can lead to insight and therapeutic change' (2000: 192). Are these comparisons, spoken out loud, Tina accessing memories from her childhood and thinking about them in relation to what is happening in the present?

The most amazing moment of the whole process for me was when on week eight Tina said, 'A few years ago I would have said I had a bad childhood – not bad as such, but I felt sad, but now since having children, very recently I think, well actually my mum and dad did lots for me, more than I thought they did … I understand why she was as strict as she was.'

I thought it was almost too good to be true. Tina had made comparisons, shown her reflective capacity by the way in which she referred to Michael's behaviour and thought about his emotional states, and now she appeared to be reflecting in a coherent manner about the way in which she herself was parented. I was able to talk with Tina about the Adult Attachment Interview and how the comment she had made would indicate that she has reflected on what happened in her childhood and that she has come to terms with it. If this is the case then it is very good news for both Tina and her family, as 'Coherence of mind implies a lively sense of self, organised and capable of reflecting upon past relationship adversities in such a way that limits the possibly malevolent influence of these experiences upon parenting, with consequent ill-effects on children's well-being' (Charlwood & Steele, 2004: 70).

A developmental partnership

I thought about the questions that arose over the course of the research, and began to think about the process that Tina and I had gone through. I feel we really did engage in a 'co-operative inquiry' (Schön, 1991: 352), which, in turn, became a 'developmental partnership' (Easen *et al.*, 1992: 287). The above questions prompted me to consider what constituted the 'developmental partnership' that I believe we built together.

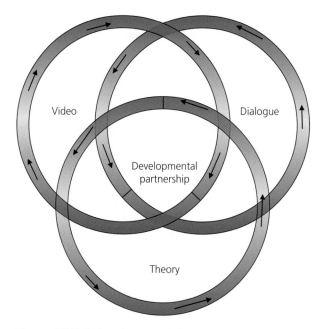

Figure 11.1 A developmental partnership

The developmental partnership was impacted upon by three things:
- video
- dialogue
- theory.

The video we watched acted as a catalyst for dialogue. It was a tool that allowed us to revisit, review and reflect on what had been filmed. Tina was able to see things from 'a totally different perspective'.

The dialogue we engaged in led us both to ask questions. The questions I asked Tina prompted her to think about her own actions in relation to Michael's behaviour. The questions Tina asked me led me to draw on theory to inform our dialogue. This theory was pertinent to Tina's interest in her relationship with Michael and led to her sharing this newly gained knowledge with others. In these instances our developmental partnership 'widened into a "developmental network" with all that implies for enriching the thinking of those involved' (Easen *et al.*, 1992: 294).

It was through the iterative nature of this developmental partnership that the facilitation of reflection occurred.

Finally

I think that the evidence presented in this chapter shows that 'facilitating reflection' is possible. There is certainly evidence of Tina showing capability to reflectively function. The video film seems, to me, to be a catalyst for the discussion, questions and theoretical input.

In this instance Tina then used this theory, in context, by sharing it with Richard and some friends. I believe that as the theory related to Tina's own experience she felt confident to share it with others.

I tentatively suggest that through viewing the video film Tina did access 'early maternal memories' (Zelenko & Benham, 2000), which may have led to therapeutic change. I suggest this as Tina compared her own childhood with that of her children, and then reflected on why her mother behaved towards her as she did. Taking part in this project may have speeded up this process and allowed Tina to move forward without the possibly malevolent forces of her own upbringing impacting detrimentally on her relationship with her own children (Charlwood & Steele, 2004: 70).

The use of digital video provides 'increased support for the development of reflective function and thereby enhance[s] the development of relational processes' (Woodhead et al., 2006: 140).

This whole process was very satisfying from my perspective. Woodhead comments on how the time given to parents to talk appears to be pleasing for the parent, 'the opportunity to talk at length about their baby, their emotions and their experiences of motherhood is a unique one and one they appear to relish' (Woodhead et al., 2006: 148).

I think that both Tina and I had 'relished' the sessions we had spent together. Both Tina and Richard commented on how much Tina would miss our weekly sessions. 'I'll miss it,' Tina said, and then whispered to Michael, 'there still won't be enough time ... we've got lots to say about you.'

Recent developments in professional development and practice

Following on from this and other small studies, Pen Green Nursery staff now have regular 'work discussion' sessions with Sebastian Kraemer in order to reflect on the emotional aspects of work with families. We have also set up a partnership with the Northern School of Psychotherapy, which is based in Leeds. For the third year running, staff from across the Pen Green Centre and a few workers from other settings are engaging in a course entitled The Emotional Roots of Learning. The course involves three aspects: reading and discussing papers from the psychoanalytic literature; engaging in the study of a young child, making weekly observations, and bringing the detailed written observations to discuss in the group sessions; and engaging in observation of and discussion of individuals' experiences in the workplace. An overall aim of the course is to 'extend and develop awareness and understanding of emotional development and interaction in the pre-school period' (Module Specification).

Points for discussion

- How comfortable are you filming and being in dialogue with a parent?
- How do you spend time reflecting on your practice with families?
- How could you use theory more effectively to inform your conversations with parents?

References

Athey, C. (1990) *Extending Thought in Young Children: A parent–teacher partnership*, London: Paul Chapman.

Bell, J. (1999) *Doing Your Research Project* (3rd edn), Maidenhead: Open University Press.

British Educational Research Association (BERA) (1992) *Ethical Guidelines for Educational Research*, Annual General Meeting.

Charlwood, N. and Steele, H. (2004) 'Using attachment theory to inform practice in an integrated centre for children and families', *European Early Childhood Education Research Journal*, vol. 12, no. 2, pp. 59–74.

Cohen, L. and Manion, L. (1994) *Research Methods in Education* (4th edn), London: Routledge.

Easen, P., Kendall, P. and Shaw, J. (1992) 'Parents and educators: dialogue and development through partnership', *Children and Society*, vol. 6, no. 4, pp. 282–96.

Erickson, M. F., Sroufe, L. A. and Egeland, B. (1985) 'The relationship between quality of attachment and behaviour problems in pre-school in a high risk sample', in Bretherton, I. and Waters, E. (eds), 'Growing points of attachment theory and research', *Monographs of the Society for Research in Child Development*, vol. 50, nos 1–2, Serial No. 209, 147–66.

Fonagy, P. and Target, M. (1997) 'Attachment and reflective function: their role in self organization', *Development and Psychopathology*, vol. 9, pp. 679–700.

Freire, P. (1996) *Letters to Christina*, London: Routledge.

George, C., Kaplan, N. and Main, M. (1985) *Adult Attachment Interview*, Berkeley: University of California Press.

Jordan, B. and Henderson, A. (1995) 'Interaction analysis: foundations and practice', *The Journal of the Learning Sciences*, vol. 4, no. 1, pp. 39–103.

Laevers, F. (1997) *A Process-oriented Child Follow-up System for Young Children*, Leuven: Centre for Experiential Education.

Schechtner, D. S., Myers, M. M., Brunelli, S. A., Coates, S. W., Zeanah Jnr, C. H., Davies, M., Grienenberger, J. F., Marshall, R. D., McCaw, J. E., Trabka, K. A. and Liebowitz, R. R. (2006) 'Traumatized mothers can change their minds about their toddlers: understanding how a novel use of video feedback supports positive change of maternal attributions', *Infant Mental Health Journal*, vol. 27, no. 5, pp. 429–527.

Schön, D. A. (1991) *The Reflective Practitioner*, Aldershot: Ashgate.

Slade, A. (2005) 'Parental reflective functioning: an introduction', *Attachment and Human Development*, vol. 7, no. 3, pp. 269–81.

Stake, R. E. (1995) *The Art of Case Study Research*, London: Sage.

Stern, D. N. (1995) *The Motherhood Constellation*, London: Karnac.

Strauss, A. and Corbin, J. (1998) *Basics of Qualitative Research, Techniques and Procedures for Developing Grounded Theory*, London: Sage.

Tait, C. (2007) *Thinking About Feeling: Facilitating reflection*, unpublished masters dissertation, MA in Integrated Provision for Children and Families, University of Leicester.

Trevarthen, C. (2003) 'Closely observing children in early childhood settings and in the home', Conference Presentation, Corby: Pen Green Research Base.

Whalley, M. (1994) *Learning to Be Strong: Setting up a neighbourhood service for under-fives and their families*, London: Hodder & Stoughton.

Whalley, M. and the Pen Green Centre team (2001) *Involving Parents in Their Children's Learning*, London: Paul Chapman.

Whalley, M. and the Pen Green Centre team (2007) *Involving Parents in Their Children's Learning* (2nd edn), London: Paul Chapman.

Winnicott, D. W. (1965) 'The theory of the parent–infant relationship', in *The Maturational Processes and the Facilitating Environment*, London: Hogarth Press.

Woodhead, J., Bland, K. and Baradon, T. (2006) 'Focusing the lens: the use of digital video in the practice and evaluation of parent–infant psychotherapy', *Infant Observation*, vol. 9, no. 2, pp. 139–50.

Zelenko, M. and Benham, A. (2000) 'Videotaping as a therapeutic tool in psychodynamic infant–parent therapy', *Infant Mental Health Journal*, vol. 21, no. 3, pp. 192–203.

12 Working with fathers

Flávia Ribeiro and Jackie Cole

In this chapter we discuss:
- why involving fathers in their children's learning is important
- studies carried out at the Pen Green Centre over the years that have helped us to improve our work with fathers
- where we are now with regard to involving fathers.

Introduction

As a dominantly female profession, we have to try extra hard to involve fathers as well as mothers to use our early childhood services. This chapter describes our commitment to engaging with fathers as well as mothers, and some of our efforts to involve fathers in different ways. The world has changed radically over the last 30 years and this is reflected in some of the legislation relating to fathers.

Why work with fathers?

One of our passions at Pen Green is and has always been working in partnership with parents. We truly believe in the idea of parents as their children's first educators and that their involvement in their children's nursery life and future academic life is paramount for their cognitive, emotional and social development. Whalley and Chandler furthermore state that: 'Parents and early years professionals need to work closely together if we are to provide the optimum opportunities for children to learn and develop' (2001: 74).

This links with Epstein's 'Theory of Overlapping Spheres of Influence' (2001), which takes into consideration the three key contexts that children are part of and where they learn and develop: 'school', 'family' and 'community'. Settings play a major role in bringing the three spheres together by promoting consistent and high-quality communication and interaction with families and communities. This will most certainly enhance children's learning and development.

Our belief and experience, which is supported by the literature, is that fathers play a very important role in their children's education. In a study by McBride and colleagues (2005), they report that fathers' involvement in their children's school life was linked to high attainment. They also found that the impact of fathers' involvement was greater in low-income families. This means that in general children from low-income families have, reportedly, a tendency for low attainment. However, when fathers become actively involved in their children's education, particularly by interacting with teachers and workers in schools, this tendency is less marked.

In another recent study, Sarkadi and colleagues also found that fathers' involvement has a significant impact in reducing 'the frequency of behavioral problems in boys and psychological problems in young women' (2008: 157). Moreover, they report that fathers' engagement promotes children's cognitive development and at the same time 'decreases criminality and economic disadvantage' in low-income families.

A small change

This decade has seen a shift in equal opportunities legislation in England, giving fathers the right to some paternity leave. Only recently, in the Queen's Speech, the government recognised that legislation marginalises fathers. In the UK, the Queen's Speech is read by the Queen at the State Opening of Parliament every year and outlines the government's agenda for the coming session. In May 2012, the Queen announced the government's intention to give fathers more paternity leave and even the right to share maternity leave with mothers. However, businesses do not welcome this new proposal, meaning that there is still a long way to go until fathers' involvement in their children's life right from the beginning is seen as important and essential, just like mothers' involvement.

Alongside some changes in legislation, within the last ten to 15 years numerous research studies on the importance of fathers' involvement in their children's learning have given us firm evidence about how fathers make a real difference, helping to fuel a surge of organisations dedicated to supporting fathers, for example the Fatherhood Institute and Fathers Direct.

Looking retrospectively at how we have been involving fathers at Pen Green

The context

Corby, where Pen Green Centre is based, was a steel town in the 1930s. Workers came from Scotland, other parts of the UK and from Eastern Europe to find work. The steelworks was open 24 hours a day and 365 days a year, so the majority of local families have grown up in a culture where shift-work is the norm, particularly for fathers. Although the works closed down in the early 1980s, resulting in 43 per cent of the male population being unemployed, a great deal of the factory work now runs on the same pattern.

The late 1980s

Involving fathers in their children's learning has always been a long-standing commitment and concern at Pen Green. In 1990 a research project on fathers' involvement in the early years, called 'Men as Carers', was launched in conjunction with the city of Reggio Emilia in the region of Emilia Romagna in Italy. The project highlighted some major points in terms of welcoming fathers into the centre, such as changes in the physical environment and changes in documentation, as well as the need to train and develop staff on gender issues and practitioner research.

Key information

As a result of this project, we made changes:
- Images of fathers with their children were put up in the nursery and other areas of the centre in an effort to make it more welcoming for fathers.
- A range of books and magazines for both men and women was provided, especially when parents were settling their children into the nursery and spending time in the nursery.
- Forms and letters were addressed to fathers specifically rather than 'parents' as it was recognised that quite often parents would mean mothers.
- When writing to parents both mother and father were named.
- Nursery application forms were also changed to include both parents' details, particularly working hours.
- The staff took part in training sessions around gender which meant looking at and sharing their own personal experiences, reflecting on how they had been parented by their own fathers and how it might affect their practice.

Currently there are several organisations, such as the Fatherhood Institute, that offer training on how to work with and to engage fathers in early years and school settings.

1992

In 1992 Angela Malcolm, then a Family Worker in the nursery at Pen Green, conducted a study on how parents' working hours and family life affected their involvement in their children's learning. She was particularly interested in fathers' involvement in the nursery. Angela found that fathers, at that time, felt extremely responsible for looking after their families financially, as well as for making time to be with their children. All of the fathers in the study mentioned the importance of having paternity leave and how they would have used it if it had been available. In 1992 paternity leave was not available in the UK.

This piece of research brought about benefits making fathers feel a bit more valued and acknowledged than previously. It helped staff to have a deeper understanding of fathers and family life as well as the importance of involving fathers in their children's learning in nursery. Small changes were also made to the practice in nursery, such as arranging groups and meetings at a time to best suit fathers' working hours and having a male staff member in meetings to encourage fathers' participation.

This particular example of a piece of action research underlines how important it is for settings to encourage and support their staff to continuously engage in practitioner research in order to improve practice.

1997

The Pen Green Research Base was set up in 1996. Our first big project was 'Involving Parents in Their Children's Learning'. By 'parents' we meant mothers and fathers, however opportunities to be involved were taken up much more often by mothers than by fathers. When we asked some fathers why this was the case, they said that they did not want to sit around drinking coffee and chatting but that, if they attended, they 'wanted to know they could make a difference to their child' (Tait, 2007: 46). We had to adapt our approach in order to attract the fathers.

When the PICL (Parents' Involvement in Their Children's Learning) study group was initially set up as part of the larger three-year research project, the staff really thought carefully about engaging the fathers. The PICL group is a weekly study group for parents led by nursery staff. In the group the parents can be a 'fly on the wall' and have the chance to look at short pieces of video of their children in nursery and have a shared discussion about their child's learning using different frameworks. (This group is explained in more detail in Chapter 3).

In order to attract fathers, this group ran and still runs in the morning, afternoon and evening each week. Obviously it is difficult for anyone working shifts to attend at the same time each week but any commitment to attending and discussing their child's learning is welcomed. We experimented with advertising the session as a 'meeting' rather than a group, which staff identified at the time to be more appealing to fathers. Staff also identified that wording posters and letters differently for mothers and fathers about groups and meetings worked better. For example, the same poster advertising a session for parents on 'schemas' for the fathers was worded as: 'Do you want to help your child excel? You *need* to know about schemas and how your child's brain develops.' For the mothers, there was a different approach to the same subject: 'How does your child play? Does he/she tie up your kitchen? Line toys up all the time?' (Tait, 2007: 47).

2003

In 2003, Annette Cummings focused her study of 'Working with Parents' on fathers. Annette interviewed four dads of nursery children and asked about their upbringing and their relationships with their own fathers. Annette was aware that strong feelings could be evoked during these sorts of interviews and arranged for one or more counselling sessions to be available for the dads if necessary as a follow-up. These four dads varied in age and one talked about a dad he rarely saw because of shift-work in the steelworks and a culture of going to the working men's club after work. Another dad recalled that his father left his family and he was never able to forgive him. He was determined that he would never let his family down in that way. Following the interviews, Annette encouraged their four nursery children to talk about their dads and, as they were all interested in painting, to express their ideas about their dads with paint. She displayed the paintings and what the children said in the nursery, thus making visible ideas about fathers.

2008

By 2008, things had moved on. Partly because of additional funding through Sure Start, Pen Green staff were now running groups for fathers on Saturdays and Sundays. What began as Baby Massage with dads on a Saturday morning developed into a group for dads and children that mothers occasionally attend. We continued to work with new groups of dads massaging their babies every Saturday. Independently of this group of fathers, a dads' group became well established, who met regularly on a Sunday to play with their children and to enjoy the provision at Pen Green.

Figure 12.1 A dad and his daughter enjoying Sunday Dads' Club

Eddie McKinnon, Principal Researcher at the Pen Green Research Base, led a piece of research looking at how weekend access to a setting enables fathers to engage in parent and child groups. The weekend provision at Pen Green offers *Dads' Baby Massage* on Saturday mornings, *Messy Play for Dads*, which overlaps with Baby Massage on a Saturday, and *Sunday Dads' Club* which runs in the mornings.

Some of the key findings in this research emphasised the importance of this kind of provision at the weekend. This was defined by the fathers as a 'special time' to be with their child, one-to-one; also a break for their partners to have some 'me-time'. One of the fathers described himself as the '50-Minute Dad' – 20 minutes in the morning and 30 minutes in the evening. He said: 'You can see why for me the weekends are really precious times.' The feedback given by the fathers was of their satisfaction with being able to access such high-quality provision and without 'competition from many other children and parents as it would be the case on weekdays'.

Although this research happened in 2008 it is still fairly recent and it does still show how fathers' working hours and patterns of work can make it difficult for them to access settings on weekdays, therefore it is important to cater for the fathers' needs, and settings should be able to do so.

Example from practice

Jackie, a co-leader of the Sunday Dads' Club writes:

'Pen Green has a strong ethos for the importance of engaging families in their children's learning and we have created many innovative ways of developing services in our local community. However, like many early years education settings, Pen Green recognised that fathers were considerably under-represented and since 2000 when research was carried out and training was given to staff, the Dads' and Kids' Club on a Sunday morning has grown and developed over the last 12 years with a database of 100 contacts. The group now spreads itself over the entire weekend, with Dads' Baby Massage and support for dads with court contact with their children. The dads who use the services are very diverse, with families from various socio-economic backgrounds and family units, but the group works: there is a wonderful atmosphere with a sense of teamwork, everyone respecting and supporting each other. There is a huge commitment from dads who have attended for many years.'

One feature Jackie also draws attention to is that the fathers using Pen Green at the weekend have a great deal of autonomy. She says, 'Over the years families have been actively involved in the decision-making, leading on activities and the development of the group. It has given everyone a vested interest in the future of the group.' What might seem a female-dominated environment Monday to Friday is now very different at the weekend.

Example from practice
Example from practice

One father's story

I left the family home seven months before T was born, leaving my eldest daughter in the care of her mother. Two weeks after T was born social services got in touch telling me my child had arrived and was in the special care unit and that she was very poorly due to being born chemically dependent. I felt very angry at this news and that I hadn't been told earlier, and also very worried and helpless that I couldn't do nothing to help my little girl. Both my girls were identified as being at [risk of] significant harm and neglect.

From that day I decided to fight for my children. That year and a half was very hard. I felt I had no support from social services and working with the law was very slow and one-sided towards mothers. All I could do was phone every day, talk to my children and hope my children were okay, that daily routines were happening and that my eldest was getting to school.

When T was given a place at Pen Green Nursery, that was the first time I felt I was being included in my child's life by an organisation. Family Workers would talk to me and tell me how T was getting on. They also told me about the Dads' and Kids' Club, which I started attending at the weekend when I had access. The group was a great support and it was fun and I didn't have to listen to mothers' conversations about everything, from birth stories to breastfeeding and dieting.

In November 2012 I was successfully granted custody of my daughter, which was the best thing ever.

My experience of being a full-time lone parent and being a father has been one big learning curve ... but apart from that it's been great fun. I enjoy spending time playing with my daughter, going to new places, doing new things, and I hope these experiences will help her to become a strong, independent, self-aware young woman with a good education and hopefully she will go on to university, but most of all I want her to lead a long and happy life.

This is an extremely sad case but one that gives hope to other parents, and importantly for workers, informs us about how it can feel, as a father, to be respected and included in a child's life.

Example from practice

Example from practice

Peter's story

Peter has been involved with Pen Green for the last 20 years as he was a 'looked after' child himself. He ended up being split from his siblings and fostered. He now has two daughters and is determined that their childhoods will be different to his: 'Although I had positive experiences in foster care and I had one stepfather that was a good role model for me, he read to me at night and played games with me, I still feel that I missed out on such a lot, and so to me it's very important that I'm always in my girls' lives to guide them and to make sure they grow up healthy and happy. Being a dad has been the best thing that ever happened to me and it has made me the person I am today.'

He, too, attends the Dads' and Kids' Club on a Sunday:

'My sister re-introduced me to Pen Green when I had my girls, and I enjoy spending time at the centre – it gives me the chance to bond with my girls, I get to spend quality time with them that I can't do during the week as I am at work. It's very important for me to be involved in my girls' learning so I can help them develop and I can bring out the best in them. My hopes for the future are that I keep building on my skills as a dad and I keep learning, as my girls get older.'

Peter sees himself as a lifelong learner and spending precious time with his daughters seems to contribute to what he is trying to achieve.

Figure 12.2 A dad and his son enjoying the Soft Room at Dads' Club

Figure 12.3 A dad and his baby in the Snoozelen at Dads' Club

Figure 12.4 A dad and his child playing with water at Dads' Club

2011

As part of my masters degree studies, I have conducted a piece of research on 'Getting to Know Fathers and Their Perspectives on Parental Involvement' (Ribeiro, 2011). The study consisted of case studies of three fathers: Peter, John and Steve. All three had children in nursery, in my family group. In the nursery we operate a key worker system: Elfer (2001) describes the key worker as someone who creates a close connection with the child and family, someone who is consistent for both. He believes that: 'nursery attachments may actually assist home attachments'. We call our staff Family Workers, as they work with the family and acknowledge that each child is part of a family context.

The case studies focused on understanding fathers from different perspectives in order to more effectively involve them when engaging fathers in their children's learning and development in nursery.

I chose to focus on fathers for personal reasons and because of a strong belief that they make a great difference to their children's learning and development when involved (Lamb & Tamis-Lemonda, 2004; Kahn, 2006; Fatherhood Institute, 2010).

Whalley (2001) discusses the importance of evidence-based practice. This was my starting point – I understood how important it was to understand fathers first, before putting any ideas into practice.

When I mention understanding fathers, my idea of it was always in a multi-dimensional way (Thomas, 2011). I really intended to know about their personal experiences of being fathers, going back to before they became fathers and how they felt. I think in general, parenting is always so much more about the role of the mother because of the obvious biological process and not so much consideration is given to the role of the father. Draper (2002) studied how 'rituals' are so strong in the transition into motherhood, mothers take centre stage, fathers not so much. She mentions how 'rituals' are also important in terms of supporting and easing the transition into parenthood. For fathers the transition is so much more difficult: 'despite the changing nature of men's involvement in pregnancy, birth and early fatherhood, men remain on the periphery of this process' (Draper, 2002: 90). Perhaps, for fathers, this 'remaining on the periphery' is extending to when children start nursery as well. As practitioners it is important to be aware of this and for all staff to make a conscious effort to make fathers feel involved and valued right from the start, but firstly to understand how they feel.

Main findings from the case studies

Transition into fatherhood

All three fathers commented on the anxiety of becoming a father and then how instinctively they embraced this role. Peter expressed how he felt 'scared stiff'. But when it happened, the fear gave way to joy and he found it easy being in a new role as a father, effortless; he explained, 'it is because I think it's quite instinctive'.

Play companions

The fathers also mentioned how they perceived themselves as 'play companions'. They seem to actively engage in play with their children, more so than their partners. John explained with pride how within their family dynamics, he is the one who plays more with Keira: 'I definitely play with her more. Joanne also plays with her, but I play with her a lot more, she wants to play with me a lot more as well.'

Hauari and Hollingworth refer to fathers having a special role when it comes to 'engaging directly in play and leisure activities with their children' (2009: 44).

Early years settings a daunting place for fathers?

For Peter and John coming into nursery felt a bit daunting, more so for John. For Peter, being part of the settling-in process was a big turning point in terms of feeling comfortable in the nursery environment. Peter described how he felt 'awkward in nursery scenarios'. He explained that the main reason was that it was a predominantly female environment, however, when describing the latter he mentioned mums rather than workers. He said: 'It's quite intimidating for a dad, just because more mums are there than dads. I went through that settling-in week with Laura and I got to speak to you and got to know some of the others [workers] that I felt a little more comfortable just turning up.'

Kahn (2006) identified in his study, 'Involving Fathers in Early Years Settings', that when fathers aren't familiar with the workers and routines in a setting they will feel less comfortable in it, which will affect their involvement.

In contrast, Steve feels really confident and at ease in nursery, as he explains: 'I have done it quite a lot in the past, it's mainly Sandra that comes in now. But I'm so used to it. It's quite familiar. I enjoy it.'

Perhaps this has something to do with the number of years he has been using the nursery and the centre, because as he described it, 'it's quite familiar'.

Also in some way or another all three fathers commented on how they would prefer to be doing something with their children if attending events or groups in the nursery or centre. John mentioned: 'Fathers would much prefer to be "doing something" with their children rather than talking to each other or talking to workers.' Horn *et al.* (1999) also mention that fathers prefer to focus on doing 'practical educational things' rather than talking about doing things.

Where we are now

The findings from Pen Green staff's practitioner-led research is supported by findings from much bigger studies (Goldman, 2005) and suggests that fathers generally tend to enjoy being involved in more active pursuits with their children. Pen Green staff organise an annual trip to the Science Museum in London for the children who will be moving on to school (and their families), and, although it involves a long, tiring day, a high proportion of fathers attend and enjoy the day out with their children.

Another important point Goldman makes is that 'once a father becomes involved, then they are more likely to stay involved throughout childhood' (2005: 83). So, involving fathers in baby massage, discussing their child's development and learning at Growing Together, and watching their child engage with Messy Play can all contribute to a longer term involvement and better outcomes for children and families.

Involving fathers in children's centres and early years settings is not easy. Most staff are female and, however hard we try to understand life from a male perspective, we can never completely manage that. Goldman (2005: 17) points out that: 'Recruitment of fathers is often challenging and time-consuming. It requires persistence, creativity, patience, sensitivity and sufficient practitioner resource.'

Although it is obvious, she adds that 'a good recruitment message is to explicitly tell fathers how their involvement will help their children' (Goldman, 2005: 17). So, each and every one of us, as workers in centres and settings, needs to be persistent, creative and sensitive, and needs to share messages from research with fathers about how their involvement will benefit their child in the long term.

Points for discussion

- A great deal of emphasis in the Pen Green context is on discussing development and learning with parents – think about the last conversation you had with a father – what did you talk about?
- How would you go about finding out what fathers already enjoy doing with their children at home?
- How are fathers represented in your setting?
- How could fathers be more visible in your setting?

References

Draper, J. (2002) 'Individual and family life transitions: a proposal for a new definition', in *Narrative, Memory and Life Transitions*, Huddersfield: University of Huddersfield.

Elfer, P. (2001) 'Firmly attached', *Nursery World* [online]. Available from: http://www.nurseryworld.co.uk/news/login/726847/key-person-approach-firmly-attached (accessed 2 Jan. 2011).

Epstein, J. L. (2001) *Schools, Family and Community Partnerships: Preparing educators and improving schools*, Boulder: Westview Press.

Fatherhood Institute (2010) *Fathers' Impact on their Children's Learning and Achievement* [online]. Available from: http://www.fatherhoodinstitute.org (accessed 20 Oct. 2011).

Goldman, R. (2005) *Fathers' Involvement in their Children's Education*, London: National Family and Parenting Institute.

Hauari, H. and Hollingworth, K. (2009) *Understanding Fathering, Masculinity, Diversity and Change*, York: Joseph Rowntree Foundation. Available from: http://www.jrf.org.uk (accessed 15 Nov. 2011).

Horn, W. F., Blankenhorn, D. and Pearlstein, M. (1999) *The Fatherhood Movement: A call to action*, Plymouth: Lexington Books.

Kahn, T. (2006) *Involving Fathers in Early Years Settings: Evaluating four models for effective practice development* (executive summary), report prepared for the Department of Education and Skills. Available from: http://www.pre-school.org.uk/document/750 (accessed 15 Nov. 2011).

Lamb, M. E. and Tamis-Lemonda, C. S. (2004) 'The role of the father', in Lamb, M. E. (ed.) *The Role of the Father in Child Development* (4th edn), Hoboken: John Wiley & Sons.

Malcolm, A. (1992) *Fathers' Involvement with their Children and Outside Commitments*, unpublished paper for Advanced Diploma in Child Care and Education, Corby: Pen Green Centre.

McBride, B. A. and Rane, T. R. (1997) 'Father/male involvement in early childhood programmes: issues and challenges', *Early Childhood Education Journal* vol. 25, no. 1, pp. 11–15.

McBride, B. A., Schoppe-Sullivan, S. J. and Ho, M. (2005) 'The mediating role of fathers' school involvement on student achievement', *Journal of Applied Developmental Psychology*, vol. 26, pp. 201–16.

Ribeiro, F. (2011), 'Getting to know fathers and their perspectives on parental involvement', unpublished assignment, MA in Integrated Provision for Children and Families in the Early Years, University of Leicester.

Sarkadi, A., Kristiansson, R., Oberklaid, F. and Bremberg, S. (2008) 'Fathers' involvement and children's developmental outcomes: a systematic review of longitudinal studies', *Acta Pediatrica*, vol. 97, no. 2, pp. 153–8.

Tait, C. (2007) 'Getting to know the families', in Whalley, M. and the Pen Green Centre team (2007) *Involving Parents in Their Children's Learning* (2nd edn), London: Paul Chapman.

Thomas, G. (2011) *How to Do Your Case Study*, Thousand Oaks: Sage.

Whalley, M. (2001) 'Developing evidence-based practice', in Whalley, M. and the Pen Green Centre team, *Involving Parents in Their Children's Learning*, London: Sage.

Whalley, M. and Chandler, T. (2001) 'Parents and staff as co-educators: "parents" means fathers too', in Whalley, M. and the Pen Green Centre team, *Involving Parents in Their Children's Learning*, London: Sage.

13 Routes through Community Education

Anne Gladstone and Heather Donoyou

> I had this drive to get as many qualifications as I could – because my middle daughter, she's excelling at school, she's nine – I thought, I'm going to do something myself – I'm going to keep up with her.

This chapter considers:

- adult education at Pen Green
- theories underpinning our approach to adult learning
- barriers to adults engaging in learning
- what needs to be in place to support adults returning to learning.

Introduction

This chapter looks at the nature of adult and Community Education at Pen Green, and the values and principles that underpin the commitment to adult learning as an integral part of working with children and families. We make reference to the work of some of the theorists who have explored the nature of adult learning. Through analysis of interviews with parents who have engaged in their own learning at Pen Green, we consider the barriers they have encountered as they return to learning, what motivates them despite these barriers and the impact on them and on their children of them becoming learners. Finally, we hope to identify what it is that needs to be in place if adults are to be able to embark on new learning journeys. This means identifying how we can:

- effectively listen to what they tell us
- create environments, relationships and opportunities that respond to what we hear, and
- best support adults to build the courage and confidence needed to overcome barriers, take risks and reach their aspirations.

The challenges around adult learning for us as an organisation, as well as for parents, are huge – funding has always been hard sought and fought for, and in the present climate this is as true as ever. Every bid has to be made against ever more stringent criteria, with restrictions to access, timescales, previous qualifications and so on – few of which have any bearing on the real needs and circumstances of many learners. Creative opportunities have to be recognised and taken; rather than a small team of workers dedicated to adult learning, all workers must share the responsibility for encouraging and developing parents as adult learners. Commitment to adult education at Pen Green has been an underpinning principle since its earliest days, in the belief that 'education is a major determinant of lifelong opportunities' (Flynn *et al.*, 1986).

Why are learning opportunities for parents so important?

Our commitment to adult learning has been based further on the knowledge that if parents are engaged in their own learning and see themselves as learners, the greater will be their involvement in their children's learning and the greater their aspirations for them will be. The converse is similarly true, as parents become involved in their children's learning, so they are motivated to return to learning themselves, thus creating a mutually beneficial cycle. Arleen Leibowitz notes that 'parental education, occupation, and income have been shown to be related to children's ability and educational attainment' (1977: 242).

Aldridge and Lavender (2000), when investigating the benefits of learning for adults, noted that respondents identified benefits to their children as a result of their own return to learning; these included improvement in their children's achievements in maths and reading, children appreciating the need for learning, and increased self-confidence and self-esteem. In addition, children's emotional well-being can be positively affected through their relationship with a parent who is involved with the child's learning (Aldridge & Lavender, 2000; Arnold, 2001; Horne & Haggart, 2004; Whalley, 2001). Parents have also reported that as a result of their involvement in Family Learning programmes their children were not only doing better at school but also that their behaviour had improved. Parents noticed increased confidence in their children, with them becoming less shy and more able to talk to other children and adults.

In addition, research has demonstrated that one of the positive benefits for adults when they return to learning is improved physical health and, importantly, emotional and mental health (Aldridge & Lavender, 2000). The benefits to emotional and mental health include:

- relief from symptoms of depression and anxiety
- feeling happier and more relaxed
- being more able to cope with stressful situations
- developing feelings of self-worth.

Clearly a parent's emotional and mental health will also have a great effect on the well-being of the child or children in the family. The links between infants' mental health and the mental health of their parents are well known and documented, particularly in the area of attachment theory (Goldberg, 2000). The parent's own mental health profoundly affects the nature of attachment and thus the infant's mental health. If the parent enjoys good mental health, a healthy attachment relationship between the parent and the infant is much more likely to be developed. Aldridge and Lavender's research has additionally identified that parents' everyday relationships with their children are also positively affected through their involvement in learning, which 'contribute to positive family functioning and social cohesion' (Hammond, 2004: 566).

Thinking about adults as learners

'Andragogy' is a term, adopted in the past 30 years, which is to do with learning strategies focused on adults. Malcolm Knowles (1975) developed this notion as a humanistic conception of self-directed and autonomous learners, with teachers as the facilitators of learning. For Knowles, andragogy was premised on at least four assumptions about the characteristics of adult learners that are different from the assumptions about child learners on which traditional pedagogy is premised. A fifth was added later.

1. *Self-concept*: as a person matures the self-concept moves from one of being a dependent personality towards one of being a self-directed human being.
2. *Experience*: as people mature they accumulate a growing reservoir of experience that becomes an increasing resource for learning.
3. *Readiness to learn*: as a people mature their readiness to learn becomes oriented increasingly to the developmental tasks of their social role.
4. *Orientation to learning*: as people mature their time perspective changes from one of postponed application of knowledge to immediacy of application and accordingly their orientation towards learning shifts from one of subject centredness to one of problem centredness.
5. *Motivation to learn*: as a person matures the motivation to learn is internal.

(Knowles, 1984: 12)

Our experience of young children as learners is that these assumptions link intimately to the motivation of children as learners. Indeed, Knowles came to change his position on whether andragogy only really applied to adults and came to believe that 'pedagogy–andragogy represents a continuum ranging from teacher-directed to student-directed learning and that both approaches are appropriate with children and adults depending on the situation' (Merriam *et al.*, 2007: 87). Paulo Freire saw the way for people to move forward as a process of 'transforming action' in which both they and others are involved. In order for this process to happen people have to analyse and understand their situation through dialogue with themselves and with others and then develop strategies to move forwards. Freire tells us that through 'hopeful enquiry … with the world and with each other' (1993: 53), people will develop 'a deepened consciousness of their situation' which will lead them to 'apprehend that situation as a historical reality susceptible of transformation' (1993: 66).

Barbara Rogoff describes the learning process as one of apprenticeship where 'novices advance their skills and understanding through participation with more skilled partners in culturally organised activities' (1990: 39). Jack Mezirow (1991: 1), when discussing adult learning, talks about transformative learning or 'perspective transformation', the process of which emphasises 'contextual understanding, critical reflection on assumptions and validating meaning through discourse'. According to Mezirow (1977: 5) 'transformative learning develops autonomous thinking'. This theme is developed by Colwyn Trevarthen (2002: 1) writing about 'learning in companionship'. He asserts that 'a desire to know more and to gain skill in ways that other trusted people recognise and encourage is the defining feature of young human nature' (2002: 3). He goes on to say that education in a play group or in a university should be 'situated and valued for [these] natural origins' (2002: 5). Our ambition at Pen Green for both adults and children as learners is to build on strengths and interests and uncover and encourage aspirations through the natural power of social relationships.

At Pen Green the community development approach has been about:
- developing the individual's capacity to be self-directing
- helping individuals to gain more control over their lives
- raising self-esteem
- promoting learning as a lifelong experience
- working towards equal opportunities
- pushing boundaries
- encouraging constructive discontent and not having to put up with things the way they are
- encouraging people to feel they have the power to change things.

Successful routes through Community Education – learning from parents

It can be seen that if parents do return to learning, this has proven and far-reaching benefits both for the parents themselves and for their children. Offering adult learning alongside other provision is a key piece of the jigsaw to ensure successful outcomes for children and families. However, anyone who has experience of working with children and families will know that it is one thing to want to get parents involved in learning, but quite another to be successful at doing this. There are barriers which both parents and professionals face which need to be overcome to support parents to take up learning opportunities. At Pen Green there is a strong tradition of community involvement and a way of working which is based on co-operation between parents and workers in order that the services which are offered are relevant, responsive and acceptable to local people. This approach where workers and parents learn from each other is key to understanding the needs of the parents and children for everything which is offered, including participation in adult learning.

It is, of course, vital to remember that every parent accessing learning opportunities is an individual, each with unique experiences, abilities and attitudes about themselves as learners, which they have acquired through their life experiences. However, there are some extremely important key features of individuals' experiences of learning which either enable a return to learning or which form a barrier to it. An understanding of these issues can help us to work with parents in a way which is truly supportive, helping parents to articulate and achieve their learning aspirations for themselves and for their children. These key features are set out next and are illustrated with comments from a sample of parents who were asked about their experiences of returning to learning at the Pen Green Centre.

Ghosts from the classroom – the effects of childhood experiences

There are many parents who identify extremely negative experiences of education, often from an early age – sentiments such as feeling undervalued and worthless are often expressed. Unsurprisingly, when parents talk about these experiences, their recollections are extremely clear and the emotions associated with them are very powerful, as if those experiences had happened very recently.

Examples from practice

Parents' comments

'I wouldn't call it a positive experience at all … [it] started from primary school, I got sat in the corner with a book and I can remember sitting there crying, not being a confident child, wouldn't put my hand up …'

'I had a lot of trouble in school, they said I was thick and lazy.'

'I couldn't sit in the classroom at all … My teachers didn't have any respect for me.'

'Obviously I think, from having a bad experience in school, you carry that label … I think you do wear it … I still wear it … It does make an impact on you, it really does.'

These previous unhappy and wounding experiences have a very powerful effect and inevitably leave them, when they in turn become parents, with a legacy of feelings and attitudes about themselves as learners. This legacy has, more often than not, contributed in great part to almost insurmountable personal barriers for individuals when they think about the possibility of returning to learning.

Examples from practice

Examples from practice

Parents' comments

'I didn't think I'd achieve anything. I thought this would be it for me, I would just keep having baby after baby because there was nothing else for me to do.'

'I didn't think I could learn basically and I thought well, what's the point? Nobody's going to help me … you're not going to get anywhere, so why even bother?'

Little wonder, then, that when we approach some parents about returning to learning we are met with barriers which can manifest themselves as lack of interest, derision, fear or even aggression. There are many barriers which we, as workers, might identify and try to help parents overcome; barriers such as lack of childcare or money, or perhaps learning opportunities not being in the right place or at the right time. These are indeed real barriers which many parents have to overcome to be able to return to learning. However, those personal barriers which individuals erect within themselves, and which we as workers come up against and perhaps experience as negative and unhelpful attitudes, are actually identified by parents as being the most entrenched and the most difficult to overcome.

When asked, many parents can identify that their personal barriers originated when learning had been difficult for them because of their individual needs or their family circumstances at the time and which they strongly feel hadn't been acknowledged or taken into account.

Examples from practice

Examples from practice

Parents' comments

'*Your* barriers are bigger than the childcare barriers, they're bigger than the financial barriers … It's about dealing with your own barriers.'

'I was kind of off the rails. I'd moved down from Scotland when I just started secondary school and just lost my dad and I missed my family in Scotland.'

'It was scary that I couldn't do stuff. It would give me barriers, like mental blocks, but … that's what the dyslexia does to you.'

'It seemed if you came from a poor background, as I did, you didn't get as much input … They didn't really care about us basically.'

The sense of injustice which this experience created is still very real and can be extremely pervasive, reinforcing individuals' negative feelings about themselves as learners. It may make individuals feel that, however hard they try, their situation will remain the same and there is therefore little point in returning to learning and exposing themselves to painful memories for no good reason or indeed struggling on with learning when past experiences continue to have a negative effect.

Examples from practice

Examples from practice

Parents' comments

'Sometimes I just wonder if it's worth the effort.'

'I need my maths and my English to go further … It's almost like the schooling had stopped that … It did make me really angry. It's almost like, no matter what I do, my past is always going to catch me up … put a brick wall in front of me.'

Despite all these experiences, many parents overcome these personal barriers (as well as the many other barriers they encounter) and do go on to see themselves as learners again, to regain their confidence in their ability to learn and to develop their knowledge and understanding as well as to gain qualifications and to move into voluntary work or employment. Parents are very clear about the things which provoked or supported their return to learning and the things which sustain them on that journey, just as they are clear about how past experiences make moving forward difficult.

Wanting more for your children

Many parents decide to return to learning for the benefit of their child or children, despite the difficulties this presents them with. Parents express high aspirations for their children and want them to do better than they did at school. They want to return to learning themselves so that they will be able to actively help their children with their learning. This can often be the spur to action – a very strong motivation which enables parents to face their fears about themselves as learners.

Examples from practice

Examples from practice

What parents want for their children

'I didn't want her following in my steps, because teenage parents, their daughters tend to follow them and become teenage mums themselves. I wanted her to know how important an education was.'

'I wanted to help my child and I wanted to understand how he was learning in school because it is so different.'

'That was my motivation, the boys – it wasn't about me at the start, it was about, I need to be able to help them with their homework.'

'You have aspirations for your children, you don't want your children to hurt the way you hurt … Sometimes you just want better for your children.'

The physical and emotional environment – how you feel in response

A key factor, which parents identify, in not only providing motivation but also in making returning to learning possible for them, is the environment in which they find themselves and the stark contrast this provides to previous educational environments where they generally struggled and often failed or abandoned formal learning altogether. This environment includes the physical space and how it looks and feels, as well as the emotional environment created by the people parents come into contact with and how those people interact and how people feel as a result. The learning environment parents experience at Pen Green has not been created by chance. It has been thought about with the strong ethos of the centre in mind, which is based on sound theories and contemporary research, mentioned earlier, which identify the needs of adult learners and how adults learn. This approach acknowledges the social nature of learning as well as the human need to feel emotionally contained in order to open one's mind to learning – it is not possible to focus on learning anything, trivial or sophisticated, if our levels of anxiety are high and feelings of fear are overwhelming us.

The physical environment is not always something which first springs to mind when considering the needs of adults who are returning to learning. When organising learning opportunities, we often have to make do with spaces which are also used for other purposes, or which feel quite institutional, such as a school classroom (often the very environment which contributed to parents' negative attitudes around their own learning). However, how the environment looks and feels is seen by parents as being crucially important in contributing to successful engagement in learning opportunities.

Examples from practice

Parents' comments

'It's not harsh, it's soft chairs, you can have a coffee … it's not classroom formality – sometimes that's too structured for adults that have had a bad experience.'

'It's the way the room's laid out as well, it's a lot less formal, because I can remember sitting in rows at school. I've done learning here and it's all round a table.'

It is therefore vitally important to be very aware of how we organise the physical environment to ensure that, from the learner's viewpoint, it appears informal, homely and welcoming. Simple strategies, such as thinking about the way furniture is arranged, if lighting is harsh and could be more subtle, and if the 'way in' looks calm, uncluttered and welcoming, can transform the environment from being a barrier to engaging in learning to being a positive asset in encouraging participation and making parents feel at ease and safe.

Figure 13.1 Learning English as an additional language

Closely linked with the physical environment is the emotional environment, which is experienced through interaction with staff. The quality of the relationships which parents experience is identified as a vital factor in not only becoming involved with learning again, but also in sustaining parents on their learning journey. This quality is experienced by parents as a sense of caring and understanding about them as individuals, together with the feeling of not being judged because of their situation or previous experiences.

Examples from practice

Parents' comments

'The environment is kind of welcoming and you're allowed to be yourself.'

'It's really friendly and you're not judged at all, because my background says I shouldn't be where I am now. I should be one of the statistics that's down in the gutters.'

Parents identify that because they are made to feel at ease and are respected as individuals by staff members, this enables them to build up relationships of trust, which are seen as a very important part of the whole process of re-starting their learning journeys. Through these relationships parents experience a sense of emotional containment, which in turn provides time and space to focus on their learning needs.

These relationships, where parents feel that someone believes in their abilities and potential, also provide much needed reassurance and encouragement, which contribute to the individual's sense of well-being and build confidence in their ability as a learner – giving them the impetus to start or continue with learning, particularly when circumstances become difficult or when self-doubt creeps in.

Examples from practice

The importance of relationships: parents' comments

'Somebody's thinking of you and holding you in mind as well as your children.'

'[My tutor] was a constant source of support. She knew I could do it, even when I didn't know I could do it.'

'I've had support and people have picked me up when I've been a bit low, [and said] come on, you can do it.'

'I think it's really important, especially if you're struggling, you need that little bit of, go on, keep on, you can do it.'

'Somebody put their faith in me, they got me up when I was at the rock bottom of my life.'

As parents have the possibility to reflect on their previous experiences of learning through these relationships with staff, it is as if they are able to rationalise those experiences and re-draw more positive mental images of themselves as learners. Through these nurturing relationships, parents are able to recognise their strengths and abilities and build on them to achieve their aspirations, rather than focusing on their fears and failures and not feeling able to take the difficult step back to learning.

'I think it set me on the journey to actually evaluate myself … it kind of set the wheels in motion to maybe find myself … Giving the empowerment back to me about my learning, my journey and that it's my choice and taking ownership.'

In addition, parents identify that previous negative experiences have galvanised their natural resilience, which comes to the fore. Alongside supportive relationships, this turns into persistence and a determination to succeed, even when there are many other difficulties in their lives, such as a lack of money, housing issues, family breakdown, bereavement or the host of other difficulties some families have to face constantly.

'Life's not exactly been easy … I have a day where I think I'm just going to give up, it's not worth it, but then I sort of pick myself up and think, you know, I have to do this – got these three children, I have to do this.'

Starting points for learning

When parents come to a children's centre or other early childhood provision with their children, the idea of returning to learning is probably not uppermost in their minds. Parents access groups and services which are focused on their children, and even if learning is part of the process, they may not even think of it as such. It seems that parents most often come to access learning opportunities for themselves through the relationships they develop with workers and the social networks they build up as they use services with their children.

This is another aspect of the crucial part which respectful, supportive relationships play in encouraging parents to think about and access learning opportunities. As parents and workers get to know each other and mutual trust develops, parents start to feel more at ease and more open to ideas about the benefits and the possibilities of returning to learning. With information offered at the appropriate time, and often on several occasions, together with encouragement and support, parents often move on to short taster courses which are in line with their current interests. It seems that even though many parents start to re-discover their learning aspirations as they develop their social networks and their confidence, they still need to 'dip their toe in the water' before embarking on a learning journey which may ultimately lead them to qualifications or employment.

'It was tie-dying, learning new sewing techniques and that's always been a real interest of mine, that sparked my interest and that was just little bite-sized courses, so they weren't too long … Very hands on and very practical.'

It is often through these initial experiences of learning that parents start to re-discover not only their confidence but also their aspirations, which they may have put to the backs of their minds. This can be the time when parents start to access more formal learning opportunities and start working towards building qualifications for themselves.

As we recognise and understand the nature of the hurdles which parents face in returning to learning and the sensitive, sustained support many of them need to succeed, it would be easy for us to construct a deficit model in our minds. However, many parents (although not all) have had some positive experiences of learning as children, both in the home and at school, which have given them a sense of worth and competency even if this has become forgotten as more negative experiences prevail. Through creating trusting, supportive relationships we can enable parents to re-discover these positive feelings and attitudes and to tap into them and reinforce them, building up their personal reserves of self-esteem and confidence in their ability to learn and develop.

When considering our role, it might be useful to think of individuals as having emotional reservoirs which can be filled or depleted, over their lifetime, as they internalise positive or negative aspects of relationships with others, both within and outside the family (Gladstone, 2007). When people need the inner strength to overcome barriers to learning, it is as if they draw on current positive relationships with workers and others, such as friends and family, to top up their emotional reservoirs. People with high levels in their emotional reservoirs, acquired from early supportive relationships, may still need a small top-up at times of stress when levels are lowered. However, people whose emotional reservoirs are low, due to earlier experiences, may have a greater need to fill their reservoir in order to move towards their chosen goal with confidence and a sense of self-efficacy. This could mean that they will need more time, encouragement and support to begin their learning journey. It can be seen therefore, that time-limited interventions may well not be the best solution for those individuals who have benefited least from the educational system so far. They will need ongoing support that is sensitive to their individual circumstances at a pace at which they are happy to move forward.

'[It's] respecting you've got barriers, walls are up and that it's okay to have them walls up and then you'll let them down when you feel comfortable and in your own time, and I think it's about the respect for the time that it might take you.'

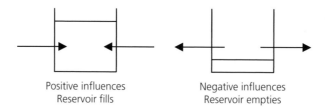

Positive influences
Reservoir fills

Negative influences
Reservoir empties

Figure 13.2 The concept of emotional reservoirs

Childcare provision

It is not surprising to discover that for many parents the availability of free childcare is a key factor in their decision to return to learning. It is not simply the fact that childcare is provided for their children, but the important feature for them is the quality of the childcare. If the childcare is seen as being high quality, where workers relate to their children as individuals and where children have opportunities to be nurtured and to learn and develop, then parents feel able to access their own learning opportunities while their children are being appropriately cared for.

Examples from practice

Parents' comments

'I couldn't have done it [without crèche], I don't have any other help – I don't have any help at all.'

'It's really important to know that your children are well cared for. If you're not sure where your children are then you're not going to be sat there and you're not going to learn.'

'If your children are settled and you're not having to worry, then they're not in your mind at that particular moment because you know that they're safe with their crèche worker and they're having a great time and they're learning something.'

Childcare being free was also seen as very important, as for many parents the cost of childcare, even for a short time, would be impossible or very difficult to meet.

Volunteering as part of the learning journey

Even though parents are usually motivated to return to learning for their children's benefit, they recognise that continuing their learning journey could lead not only to personal fulfilment, but also to an increased chance of employment and the possibility to working towards and following a career they may always have wanted to pursue, but were never able to.

'I always did want to work in childcare ever since I took my GCSEs.'

However, it can be a difficult prospect for anyone joining the employment market after having been out of it for a time, or to change direction to a new profession. The possibility of becoming a volunteer is something which parents see as a very positive thing, and which can be very helpful for them in terms of gaining employment, but which also, more importantly, gives them the opportunity to make a positive contribution to other families at the centre – to have the chance to give something back and to make use of their often very negative life experiences in a positive way. This again contributes to parents' growing self-esteem and confidence.

Examples from practice

Parents' comments

'For me it feels like I'm giving back in the only way I know how … It is so rewarding.'

'I totally relate to them [other parents], I know exactly where they're going.'

'It [volunteering] opens a lot of doors.'

What parents say about the benefits of returning to learning

It is truly amazing to hear from parents themselves about the benefits they and their children have gained as a result of their experiences of returning to learning in an environment which is in tune with their emotional and intellectual needs. For some of these parents this may have been the first time in their lives they have had this experience – little wonder then that it takes time to build the trust needed to move forward. However, as relationships develop and parents gain courage and confidence in their abilities, they recognise positive differences both in themselves and their children. The following comments are a very small snapshot of the benefits which parents identify, but they are completely in line with research, mentioned earlier in the chapter.

Examples from practice

Parents' comments

'[I'm] more confident – assured in my beliefs that I can do it.'

'I enjoy it [learning]. The self-satisfaction as well, the fact that you've done it, nobody can take that away from you, you've achieved it … I think the more you do, the more rewarding it is … It's a real joy.'

'I'm really confident now … because it [learning] was a real challenge, it was a real fear, I was petrified of it.'

'I never dreamed my children could be what they are … but they're excelling … and that's all three of them.'

From talking to parents at Pen Green, it is very clear that returning to learning has not only benefited them and their children as learners, but has also impacted positively on their parenting and thus on their children's early experiences.

Examples from practice

Examples from practice

Parents' comments

'It [learning] makes you more accessible for your children.'

'I'm a lot more patient, I'm just gentle with them and I listen.'

What happens next? Sustaining the learning journey

The beneficial effects of returning to learning identified by parents will undoubtedly make a real difference for them and their children not just in the present, but also in the future. However, despite the hopeful and positive stories which parents tell, there are still very real barriers to be faced by both parents and organisations with respect to the world of adult learning. A frequent issue for parents, initially, is the fear of having to move on from the centre at some point. While it is important and healthy for parents to move on as they become confident learners and achieve their goals, it is equally important for workers to be aware of this major concern and to be actively supporting parents to think about this part of their learning journey and to plan for the time when they will no longer be coming to the centre.

'I'm just in the situation where I'm absolutely terrified to leave here.'

Without support at this time of transition, there is a danger that successes will be swept away in the face of new barriers, and parents may well lose their renewed confidence and abandon their journey, which would very likely leave parents with feelings of anger, loss and frustration, which are classic outcomes of difficult transitions (Rogers & Tough, 1996; Bridges, 2003).

Becoming a volunteer, which some parents choose to do, could form part of the process of transition, but for each parent the solutions will be different and in the future parents will have to rely largely on the emotional and intellectual resources they have accrued on their learning journey so far. Workers can play a key part not only by acknowledging this time as potentially very difficult, but also by offering parents the time and space to think through their next steps. Many parents, when they reach this stage, may only need minimal support, while others may need much longer to reach a position where they feel confident to move on and to take up other opportunities and avenues of support.

'It's been so different here … I did think about going to a college and then I thought, well that's really scary, I don't know anybody … Basically it's a huge leap of faith in myself.'

Recent research indicates that there is often a mismatch between the needs of the individual learner, particularly those from working-class backgrounds, and the nature of educational organisations, which makes access difficult (Nesbit, 2006; McGivney, 2001; Reay, 2001). When the difficulty of crossing cultural and class boundaries is further compounded by notions of fear and risk, it is not surprising that this is an extremely demanding and emotional time for parents, which has been likened to the debilitating effects of bereavement (Marris, 1986).

Creating the possibility for parents to continue to access learning in an appropriate environment is therefore something which is vitally important to the overall success of Pen Green and other early years settings. However, this cannot be achieved in isolation and it seems there is work to be done by other learning and training providers to support adults with limited educational experience after school. Although there are some good examples of different sectors working well together to support adult learners, there is still much to be done. It is already well documented that many educational organisations are unprepared for the needs of adult learners who have not been able to take the conventional route into further and higher education (Nicholson, 1990; McGivney, 1990). There is much useful experience to be drawn on, from settings such as Pen Green, to enable more traditional learning providers to ensure the environments they create enable fair and equal access to the courses they provide as well as providing the support learners need to sustain and complete their journeys. It goes without saying that this would benefit the learning provider as much as the individual in these times of targets around participation and funding.

However, finding points of reference for communication and co-operation can often be as difficult for organisations supporting parents to return to learning as it is for individuals. In the current climate educational establishments often have reduced resources with respect to staffing levels and finances, while at the same time being under pressure to meet targets to ensure a continuation of funding. The fact still remains, though, that offering fair and equal access to adult education at all levels is vitally important not just for individual learners but for society as a whole, and this is an issue for everyone involved. The challenge, for those of us who work in children's centres and other early years settings, is to continue to make the learner's voice heard outside our own doors. This is not an easy task, but it is one which will hopefully enable strong bridges to be built – bridges which parents can confidently use to continue their learning journeys.

Lessons to be learned

It is easy to assume that we know what parents want when we think about encouraging a return to learning. However, no matter how much we as workers know about adult education, it is the prospective learners themselves who really know what their own learning needs are and when they are ready and able to embark on a new learning journey. It is therefore essential to create an avenue for ongoing dialogue with parents, to ensure we are clear about their current needs, before trying to organise adult learning opportunities for them. If we do not use first-hand information from parents to inform our strategies and our planning then we are in danger of having little or no take-up of services, which might lead us to the conclusion that parents are not really interested in accessing learning opportunities.

When we do speak to parents it is very clear that returning to learning (or even thinking about it) is about a great deal more than simply 'putting on courses'. What emerges very strongly is that the actual *process* of becoming a learner again is the vital key to success (both for individual learners and for the organisation) and also, crucially, it is key that this process is understood from the learner's viewpoint and is then supported in an authentic and meaningful way. It may seem a daunting prospect to organise consultation on such an individual and sustained basis but, in fact, it is the relationships that we build up day by day with individual parents which will act as the vehicle for dialogue about their needs in general (and those of their children) and about their learning needs in particular. These relationships and the emotional and physical environment which enables those relationships to flourish are the elements which parents identify as being absolutely fundamental to their decisions to return to learning and to continue on that journey. It is through these respectful and supportive relationships that we give parents the opportunity to build up their emotional resources and to gain the strength they need to break through the barriers which prevent them becoming learners again and, in the process, rejoining a part of society which may have been very inaccessible or entirely closed to them before.

What we also know from talking to parents is that they do not lack aspirations for themselves and their children or the motivation and the resilience to return to learning – they are indeed highly motivated, almost invariably by a desire to do the best for their children. It is crucially important for us to understand how to sustain motivation for parents and to provide access to learning in a way which is in tune with their needs and feelings. If parents continually experience barriers to participation, even the strongest motivation can be overwhelmed, leading to further feelings of failure and distress. What parents identify as an important part of the support they need is the time and space to articulate their learning needs, to recognise their personal barriers, to take risks and to have support to do this. This indeed forms a vital part of the learning journey, perhaps long before anything which might be traditionally thought of as learning takes place.

There is always a tension between our aspirations for the services we want to provide for parents and the resources we have available to us. It can often seem that our own barriers to achieve those aspirations are as insurmountable as those of the parents we work with. However, whatever political climate or financial landscape we find ourselves in, if we (and other learning providers) focus on supporting the process of returning to learning and the underpinning ethos, then parents will be much more likely to engage with available learning opportunities. The ethos and the process it informs can be applied in any context you are working in and on whatever scale, financial or otherwise. With an appropriate process in place, many parents you work with will have the possibility to achieve personal fulfilment through learning and, in all likelihood, will subsequently move on to become involved with volunteering, to gain qualifications or to move into employment. All this, clearly, has positive benefits for the parent but also, crucially, for the child. In other words, if we get the process right to enable parents to return to learning, the benefits this accrues for children and their families will naturally follow.

At Pen Green, supporting parents in this way is seen as a parallel process alongside supporting children's learning and development. The strong ethos which supports individual needs and encouragement of the learner makes thinking about the process of returning to learning for parents a natural part of the whole offer available to families, rather than an 'add-on' or an expensive luxury. The adult learning element is a key part of a truly integrated service which has benefits to children at its heart, but which recognises the vital importance of working alongside families to best support children.

Points for discussion

- What are the sorts of environments you create in your setting to encourage adults to return to learning?
- How can you and your team be more aware of parents' experiences of education?
- What are important first steps when trying to encourage parents to have the confidence to undertake courses?

References

Aldridge, F. and Lavender, P. (2000) *The Impact of Learning on Health*, Leicester: NIACE.

Arnold, C. (2001) 'Persistence pays off: working with 'hard to reach' parents', in Whalley, M. *Involving Parents in Their Children's Learning*, London: Paul Chapman.

Bridges, W. (2003) *Managing Transitions: Making the most of change*, London: Nicholas Brealey.

Flynn, P., Johnson, C., Lieberman, S. and Armstrong, H. (eds) (1986) *You're Learning All the Time: Women, Education and Community Work*, Nottingham: Spokesman Press.

Freire, P. (1993) *Pedagogy of the Oppressed*, London: Penguin.

Gladstone, A. (2007) *Learning to Return: What supports adults to return to learning?* unpublished masters dissertation, Corby: Pen Green.

Goldberg, S. (2000) *Attachment and Development*, London: Arnold.

Hammond, C. (2004) 'Impacts of lifelong learning upon emotional resilience, psychological and mental health: fieldwork evidence', *Oxford Review of Education*, vol. 30, no. 4, pp. 554–68.

Horne, J. and Haggart, J. (2004) *The Impact of Adults' Participation in Family Learning: A study based in Lancashire*, Leicester: NIACE.

Knowles, M. S. (1975) *Self-directed Learning: A guide for learners and teachers*, Chicago: Association Press.

Knowles, M. S. (1984) *Andragogy in Action: Applying modern principles of adult education*, San Francisco: Jossey Bass.

Leibowitz, A. (1977) 'Parental inputs and children's achievement', *The Journal of Human Resources*, vol. 12, no. 2, pp. 242–51.

McGivney, V. (1990) *Education's for Other People: Access to education for non-participant adults. A research report*, Leicester: NIACE.

McGivney, V. (2001) *Fixing or Changing the Pattern: Reflections on widening adult participation in learning*, Leicester: NIACE.

Marris, P. (1986) *Loss and Change*, London: Routledge and Kegan Paul.

Merriam, S. B., Caffarella, R. S. and Baumgartner, L. (2007) *Learning in Adulthood: A comprehensive guide* (3rd edn), New York: Wiley.

Mezirow, J. (1977) 'Perspective transformation', *Studies in Adult Education*, vol. 9, pp. 153–64.

Mezirow, J. (1991) *Transformative Dimensions of Adult Learning*, San Francisco: Jossey-Bass.

Nesbit, T. (2006) 'What's the matter with social class?' *Adult Education Quarterly*, vol. 56, no. 3, pp. 171–87.

Nicholson, N. (1990) 'The transition cycle: causes, outcomes, processes and forms', in Fisher, S. and Cooper, C. (eds) *On the Move: The psychology of change and transition*, Chichester: John Wiley.

Reay, D. (2001) 'Finding or losing yourself: working-class relationships to education', *Journal of Education Policy*, vol. 16, no. 4, pp. 333–46.

Rogers, M. and Tough, A. (1996) 'Facing the future is not for wimps', *Futures*, vol. 28, no. 5, pp. 491–6, Oxford: Pergamon.

Rogoff, B. (1990) *Apprenticeship in Thinking*, Oxford: University Press.

Trevarthen, C. (2002) 'Learning in companionship', *Education in the North: The Journal of Scottish Education*, New Series, No. 10, pp. 16–25, University of Aberdeen: Faculty of Education.

Whalley, M. (1994) *Learning to Be Strong: Setting up a neighbourhood service for under-fives and their families,* London: Hodder & Stoughton.

Whalley, M. (2001) 'New forms of provision, new ways of working – the Pen Green Centre', in Whalley, M., *Involving Parents in Their Children's Learning*, London: Paul Chapman.

14 Running a high-quality crèche in a children's centre

Jo Benford, Tracey Coull and Susan Fleming

This chapter describes:

- the history of offering a crèche to parents at Pen Green
- how the quality of care has improved
- the nature of professional development and practices that have helped facilitate offering a high-quality service to families.

Introduction

The crèche within the Pen Green Centre has become an integral part of the services we offer to children and their families. Crèche has developed over 25 years and the introduction of specific legislation has influenced the direction staff have taken. Training and staff development has had a positive impact on the quality of the service for children and their families.

The crèche in Pen Green was established in 1987 after parents began helping each other out while they attended groups or support within the centre. Initially the crèche was only used to support parents who were attending certain groups, however, it was soon established as a provision to support all of the groups within the centre. Today it is for all services within the centre. The *Collins Dictionary* defines the term crèche to mean, 'a supervised play area provided for young children for short periods' (Butterfield, 2004). We believe our crèche goes above and beyond this short-term provision for play. In this chapter we explore some of the reasons why we believe this, we draw on examples from families who have used the crèche, and staff perspectives on their journeys from parent to practitioner.

The history

In 1987, as the crèche was being conceptualised, the space available in the centre was in the old PE block of a disused secondary school. The room that was to become the crèche was converted from the changing rooms. Daylight came through high-level frosted windows. There were cupboards built to hide the large pipes running through the room, and the toilets were shared with the neighbouring playgroup, which later became a private playgroup provision. The kitchenette consisted of a sink and a cupboard, where staff made snacks for the children and prepared babies' feeds. The kitchen had a stable door so that staff could still see the children although the children were not able to see the staff unless staff leaned out.

There was no easy access to outdoor play. Children were all taken to the garden together when it was time to go outside, and this involved going through two doors and along a corridor. The children shared the garden space with children attending the playgroup.

The resources were sparse, often toys that had been donated, or were those not needed or wanted in other parts of the centre. However, parents report how important the crèche was: 'The crèche meant there was a way I could go to my group, and my child was being looked after by people that I knew, and that knew him' (parent evaluations, 2000).

Children were always booked into Crèche in advance; there was never an option for children to be left without notice. The decision as to which crèche workers cared for which child was based on who turned up first and if the parent knew them. A parent who used the crèche during this time describes how important it was that she trusted and knew who she was leaving her child with. Rather than this parent accepting her child could be left with whoever happened to be in the crèche each week, she negotiated with one of the crèche workers to ensure she was there each week to look after her child. This was the beginning of the now well-structured key worker system.

During these formative years, staff training and development had already started to be considered. The workers were often used to look after staff children while they attended training in relation to the nursery provision, and were always called upon to provide childcare for staff during team-building days. This meant the development worker had to find ways to ensure the crèche team were offered training and support that was appropriate for their needs, separate from what was being offered across the centre.

In 1998, a short ten-week course was developed that all of the crèche workers were expected to complete. Accreditation for this course was through the Open College Network. During the course, potential crèche workers were introduced to observation techniques, healthy eating, keeping children safe, and the idea that children explore schemas (Athey, 1990).

National Vocational Qualifications (NVQ) in Early Years were running in the centre, and some of the crèche workers had achieved Level 2, others were working towards Level 3. Today the qualifications of the crèche team are much higher: all of the team are qualified to Level 3, and just under half are graduates. Volunteers in the crèche are all in the process of, or have already completed, the now revised Crèche Workers Course. They are introduced to all of the key concepts used across the centre, such as well-being and involvement (Laevers, 1997), schema theory (Athey, 1990), pedagogic strategies (Whalley & Arnold, 1997), all of which you can read more about in other chapters. The course includes sessions on working with parents, safeguarding, attachment theory (Bowlby, 1977) and the role of the key worker (Elfer, 2011). A participant reflects: 'Completing the crèche course gave me the confidence I needed to carry on learning about children. The leaders were friendly, and helped me to understand what was happening in the crèche ... I have just completed my Level 3 (Children's Care, Learning & Development), which means I can apply for paid work now.'

Between 1999 and 2003 the centre became one of the first Sure Start Children's Centres in the UK, where the focus was on integrated care with education. The crèche continued to evolve through this time and funding from the Sure Start initiative meant that the building could be extended. The crèche had a new space which had been purpose-built, with resources and equipment appropriate for children aged between 12 weeks and five years. The new space was bigger than the previous room. It was light and spacious, and had direct access to a garden. The toilets had cubicles that children could access independently, with sinks and mirrors at children's height. Half of the room was fitted with carpet, the other half with hard washable flooring.

Figure 14.1 The crèche room as it is today

Experts in early years considered the design of the crèche room, and it included a mirror on the wall with a ballet barre, for young children to explore. This particular design was heavily influenced by staff in the centre having seen environments for young children in Reggio Emilia in the late 1980s and 1990s, during an exchange programme organised as part of a 'Men as Carers' project (see Chapter 12 for more information about that project).

The availability of funding to resource the space meant that all of the used, old equipment was replaced with new furniture, toys and equipment. On completion the space was registered for 20 children aged between birth and five years.

Legislation

Although the Department for Education and Skills (DfES) and the Department for Work and Pensions (DWP) had developed a set of guidelines for crèche provision, they defined crèches to be:

> Facilities that provide occasional care for children under eight and are provided on particular premises on more than five days a year. They need to be registered where they run for more than two hours a day, even where individual children attend for shorter periods. Some are in permanent premises and care for children while parents are engaged in particular activities, e.g. shopping or sport. Others are established on a temporary basis to care for children while their parents are involved in time-limited activities, e.g. a conference or exhibition.
>
> (DfES and DWP, 2001)

As each session was less than two hours long, there was no legal requirement for our crèche to comply with any of the standards set out in the guidelines and there was no requirement for us to be registered with OFSTED.

The introduction of the *Birth to Three Matters Framework* (DfES, 2002) was a turning point for our crèche. By this time, I was the lead practitioner within the crèche, I was responsible for the training and development of the staff team, and for improving the provision for children and families. I used the *Birth to Three Matters Framework* to help the crèche workers understand the importance of planning, documentation and working with parents.

Although there was still no requirement for us to document children's learning, or to show how we plan for children's learning and development needs, I felt this was crucial to our work. A parent who had used the crèche for many years offered her views on how it felt not to have their child's experiences documented: 'My child had been attending the crèche for nearly four years, she left when she started school. When I think back I have no record of this really special and important time in her life; she still remembers her crèche worker, but it would have been lovely to have had some photographs to remind her of some of the other things she enjoyed doing in the crèche.'

This particular feedback motivated me to plan very specific training days for the crèche staff. I planned days, where we explored the content of the *Birth to Three Matters Framework*, along with the 'key concepts' used by staff in the Nursery. (These are explored further in Chapter 3.)

It was during these sessions that the crèche workers began to understand the reason why we might want to consider each child individually. We discussed the possibility of children having a Record of Achievement file that would include photographic observations, narrative observations and information from home. I felt maybe we should start slowly and build up to all children having a file, however, one crèche worker was adamant we should offer all children the same service and should start to produce achievement files for every child who comes to Crèche. At that time it meant producing over 80 files. To do this we needed to begin thinking about setting up a key worker system. In 2005 each child was allocated a named crèche worker, who would be their key worker. The key person was responsible for the child's file, ensured each child was planned for and maintained dialogue with parents. The work of Peter Elfer and his colleagues (2003) on the role of the key worker and the idea of a key person influenced how we saw the role developing. Key workers would spend time with the child, would communicate with the child's parent or carer, and would write up any significant observations to be included in the child's file. Each key worker held a key group of up to 12 children.

We began by focusing on children's experiences in the crèche and considering what learning and development was taking place. I read every observation, made any amendments to spelling, grammar and punctuation, before they were put into the child's file. Parents were invited to contribute to the files, and were asked for their thoughts and ideas about how we could improve and develop them further. I was drawn to the work of Margaret Carr in New Zealand; she had been considering similar ideas although they were being referred to as 'Learning Stories' (Carr, 2001). We developed a format similar to this, the staff wrote a story to the child, considering what the child was doing, what they might be learning, and what the adults could plan to support the child to continue learning.

Lois is a child who attended the crèche during this period. Her file consisted of photographs that were taken on a digital camera – printed and glued on to a sheet of paper that had the written account of her experience on it.

Her key worker used the *Birth to Three Matters Framework* (DfES, 2002) to help plan experiences for Lois that were interesting and would provide opportunities for her to learn.

Each page of her file had a heading based on the four aspects of the framework: A Strong Child, A Skilful Communicator, A Competent Learner and A Healthy Child. Her key worker would identify which aspect was the most appropriate and would then use the components of the aspect to analyse the observations she made. A summary sheet was included in the front of each file for parents to see what we were using and why.

As we were working with some of the youngest children in the centre, we felt it was important to consider our child-to-adult ratios. Infants as young as 12 weeks could be left in the crèche. We thought it was essential to ensure these young children were being given the best possible care and attention. We increased the required ratio from one adult to three children, to one adult to one child. We then brought all of our other ratios up to ensure children had quality time with their key worker.

Age	EYFS ratio	Crèche ratio
0–1 year	1:3	1:1
1–2 years	1:3	1:2
2–4 years	1:8	1:4
4 years +	1:10	1:6

Table 14.1 Crèche adult-to-child ratios

Deepening our understanding

The introduction and implementation of the *Early Years Foundation Stage* (DCSF, 2007) brought together the three frameworks we had been using: *National Standards for Under-8s Day Care* (DfES and DWP, 2001), *Curriculum Guidance for the Foundation Stage* (DfES, 2000) and *Every Child Matters: Change for children* (DCSF, 2003). This supported the practitioners in the crèche to develop a provision that promotes the rights of the children, the families and the practitioners. Both frameworks support the notion of a 'key person' (Elfer *et al.*, 2011), however, in Crèche this has been challenging. Children sometimes only attend once; they may attend for a short period of time, then return months later for another short time. Other children start to use the crèche when they are 12 weeks old, and leave when they start attending school. The children may be using other settings, sometimes within the centre, sometimes elsewhere in the town.

One particular challenge was how to begin building relationships with the child's family, in particular their parents. We began to consider home-visiting in line with the rest of the centre, however, with so many children using the crèche this seemed an impossible task. Instead we introduced settling-in visits. This started with some research I carried out in 2005. When a child is allocated a place in Crèche they are also allocated a key person. My research demonstrated that parents needed time to settle their children into the crèche (Benford, 2005). This triggered a major shift in practice; parents started to visit with their child the week before they were due to start their group; the key person, the parent and the child could spend time getting to know each other. Elfer and colleagues describe this process as establishing the 'triangle of trust' (2011: 90). There were challenges to establishing this practice: group leaders in the centre were not used to allowing an extra week on to their course or group to ensure parents could focus on the settling-in visit. I arranged to present the findings of my research project to the whole staff team in the centre. This introduced the idea that staff in the crèche, the parents and children need to begin forming secure relationships with each other. It took over a year to establish but now it is considered normal practice.

The settling-in visit lasts for two hours, during which time all the appropriate forms are completed, permission sheets are explained and the child has the opportunity to explore the space with their parent. The key person and the parents engage in a dialogue about the child. We see this as the start of building their relationship with each other. This is a very different experience from that of a nursery parent and child attending our centre. They have the opportunity to spend two hours per day for ten days together with their key person.

The following case study shows how significant this process is for families using the crèche.

Example from practice

Example from practice

Jo has two children, Olivia and Alice. When they started to use the crèche, Olivia was 20 months and Alice was six months old. Jo had been referred to a group to support her with postnatal depression and the group leader had arranged for her to have Crèche places for both children. As the settling-in visit was arranged Jo recalls how important it was for her: 'You always think it is for the children, but it wasn't, I needed it as much as them, I needed to build my own relationships and attachments.' It was over the next six to eight weeks that this relationship became critical in sustaining Jo's use of her group. Through their conversations each week, Linda (Olivia's key person) was aware that Jo was feeling uncertain and anxious; she understood how difficult it was for her to leave her children. The group Jo was attending lasted for ten weeks, during weeks one to seven Jo spent much of her time coming back to settle Olivia. Jo describes how she was 'physically in the group but her mind was completely on Olivia in the crèche room'. By week seven Olivia was able to stay in the crèche for a full session, she and Linda had developed a good connection, and she was starting to trust her.

Without the time spent building the triangular relationship (key person, parent, child), this family would almost certainly have given up. It was very difficult for Jo, and she describes how easy it would have been to just stay in the house: 'The fact that the transport had been arranged for us, and the crèche team were waiting for us meant that I had to go, I had to find a way to get to where the bus would be waiting.' By Linda understanding how difficult it was for Jo, and by being there consistently to support her, it meant that Jo and her children were able to continue using the crèche for this and subsequent groups. The settling-in visit was the critical factor, as it is for many other families using the provision.

After the initial training sessions to conceptualise how to document children's learning while in the crèche, the team were excited and ready to move forward with the idea. Each of the children had a file within a month of the training. Since then it has become an integral part of what happens during the settling-in visit. Parents are asked for their permission for us to take photographs of their child so that we can begin building their file. Jo recalls her experience of having her children's files: 'The baby pictures of Alice are some of the only baby pictures I have … which is why they get pulled out all of the time, and they are cute!'

Staff training and development

Throughout all of these changes the opportunity for staff to have training and development sessions was paramount. Below you will see a table showing the main sessions that have taken place. Although these were the significant aspects of our work, alongside this the staff have regular meetings together, with time at the end of each session to reflect on the children, their activities, and the feelings of the staff. Supervision has become integral; staff have time each month to explore their work, their feelings and their expectations and hopes for the future.

Key information

Date	Area of training and development	Main areas of discussion	Outcome
2001	Supervision	During a team meeting the idea that each member of the team would be given supervision once a month was proposed and implemented	Staff were allocated a supervisor, and monthly supervisions began to take place
2002	Well-being and involvement	Discussing the work of Laevers (1997) and considering how we can use his ideas within the crèche	Documentation in children's files includes a section which considers their well-being and involvement
2002	Schema theory	Using video footage of children in the crèche, the team shared ideas about schematic play and subsequently considered how to use this to support planning	Schemas are used to help staff in the crèche understand what the children are interested in, and subsequently what activities the children might want to engage in
2003	Birth to Three Matters / Curriculum Guidance for the Foundation Stage	The team looked at both documents and considered how best to use them in the crèche	For the first time, the staff were able to track children's progress using guidance from both of these documents
2004	Attachment training	The team were able to think about what attachment was, and how it might be happening for them with their key children. It was a session that gave the team an opportunity to consider children's attachments to their parents	Staff began to understand their relationships with children in more depth. For some of the team it raised issues or concerns about their own relationships with their children at home or their experiences as children. Supervision was critical after this particular training day

(Continued)

(Continued)

Date	Area of training and development	Main areas of discussion	Outcome
2005	A review of how children are settled into the crèche	Staff realised that children needed to visit prior to being left, and that parents needed to be involved in the visit	Settling-in visits became the normal routine for children who were to attend crèche, groups were all advised to add an extra week on to the length of their group to accommodate this, and it was not negotiable
2006	Parents' Involvement in Their Children's Learning training for all staff	Each member of the team considered why we work with parents, how we work with parents, and what difference it makes	This deepened the team's understanding of involving parents, and encouraged them to ensure parents' voices were heard through the children's files
2008	Familiarisation of the Early Years Foundation Scheme (EYFS)	This is the first legally binding documentation the team have had to adhere to: the sessions consisted of the team exploring the framework and consideration as to how to use it within the crèche	Paperwork used in children's files was updated and amended to include aspects of the EYFS: staff familiarised themselves with the content of the framework, and began to use it to support their planning. Tracking of children's progress became embedded through summative sheets and focused child observations. Cameras were purchased to ensure images of children were used in files

(Continued)

(Continued)

Date	Area of training and development	Main areas of discussion	Outcome
2009	Psychoanalytical concepts of holding, containment and attachment	By considering these three concepts and theories, the team were able to begin to deepen their understanding of their role as key workers	This enabled staff to revisit the settling-in process, and understand the importance of it. It also helped to deepen thinking during the de-briefing sessions at the end of a crèche; the team had words to articulate what was happening, particularly in holding children in mind, and supporting their emotional well-being
2010	PICL training	The centre leadership team ensured any member of staff who had not attended PICL training previously was given the opportunity to attend a two-day workshop	Staff carried out studies on one of their key children, and worked alongside parents to consider children's experiences using video. Documentation in children's files changed and video reflection became a daily routine
2012	Using the Revised EYFS	Staff recently completed a day exploring the new EYFS and its implications for practice	New paperwork is being prepared to include the new elements of the framework
Future	Making Children's Learning Visible	As the requirement for settings to show impact, and demonstrate what difference we are making to children and families, staff in the crèche will need to be tracking and mapping children's progress with even more rigour	Training will be taking place over the next year, and any changes required will be implemented

Table 14.2 Areas of training and development for crèche staff

Figure 14.2 Crèche workers involved in training

The Crèche Workers Course in childcare is still a mechanism to support crèche workers as they start their journey towards being qualified early years practitioners. It is now a 20-week programme, during which time the group have the opportunity to discuss all aspects of working in early years. As it was reviewed and re-written, we took aspects of each of the training sessions staff in the team had taken part in, and planned to introduce the potential crèche volunteers to each idea and concept. In order to gain accreditation through the Open College Network, the learners are required to produce a study on a child, giving them the opportunity to practise observation techniques, planning for individual children and sharing their experiences with children alongside their parents. For many of the learners this is their first experience in a learning environment since school, and for many school had not been the best experience of their lives (see Chapter 13). Sensitivity to this, respect for their experiences as parents and their willingness to learn, makes this course successful. Over the past five years over 50 parents have attended the course, with just over half of them completing the accreditation. Almost all the learners who are successful in the accreditation move on to do a full Level 3 Qualification in Early Years, and this year saw two of those learners complete a BA (Hons) in Education with Early Years, and a further four complete their Foundation Degree in Early Years.

Having a deep understanding firstly of how children learn, secondly of the theory that influences our practice in the centre, and thirdly of each child's individual context means that the staff in the crèche are able to provide a space where children are able to feel safe, have fun and learn. Working closely with specialist group leaders means the staff are aware of the complex needs of many families who use our centre, and this supports them to ensure the children's needs are met in a thoughtful and respectful way. We work closely with our family visiting team, and when necessary we can offer some respite sessions for families who may be waiting for a place that will be funded through the government's two-year-old funded places grant. Staff in the crèche are being trained to carry out Common Assessment Framework (CAF) assessments and are currently working with our social worker and family visitors to ensure all children who attend the crèche and who may be eligible for a funded place are being supported to apply for the funding.

Example from practice

Supporting a child and family with a funded place in Crèche

Amy is a child who has been supported in this way. Her parents are registered deaf. She has full hearing. She attended the crèche twice a week for respite. Her key worker completed a CAF alongside her parents. At the first 'team around the child' meeting, a nursery place was arranged for Amy; the housing authority were able to arrange for a transfer to a larger home for the family and they were introduced to the hearing impaired service for their youngest child. The parents have stated that, in their opinion, none of this would have happened without the support of the centre, in particular the support of the crèche and their key worker.

This example shows how Crèche, when things work well, can be part of an important and effective support network for a family in need.

Points for discussion

- How have you approached offering short-term care for children in your setting?
- What would you see as the most important aspect when setting up a crèche?
- How could documenting children's learning enhance their and their family's experience of childcare?

The crèche is now known as The Nook in recognition of the fact that it is not merely a babysitting service, as the dictionary definition implies, but an additional space where children develop and learn, supported by their parents and key workers.

References

Athey, C. (1990) 'Extending thought in young children: a parent–teacher partnership', London: Paul Chapman.

Benford, J. (2005) *How Do We Support the Emotional Needs of Young Children as They Settle into a Crèche Setting?*, unpublished dissertation, BA in Early Childhood Studies, London Metropolitan University.

Bowlby, J. (1977) 'The making and breaking of affectional bonds: 1 Aetiology and psychopathology in the light of attachment theory, 11 Some principles of psychotherapy', *British Journal of Psychiatry*, vol. 130, pp. 201–10 and 421–31.

Bowlby, J. (1997) [1969] *Attachment and Loss. Vol. 1: Attachment*, Pimlico: London.

Butterfield, J. (ed.) (2004) *Collins Dictionary* [online]. Available from: http://www.collinsdictionary.com (accessed 26 Oct. 2011).

Carr, M. (2001) *Assessment in Early Childhood Settings: Learning stories*, London: Paul Chapman.

DCSF (Department for Children, Schools and Families) (2003) *Every Child Matters: Change for children*, Nottingham: DCSF.

DCSF (2007) *Early Years Foundation Stage*, Nottingham: DCSF.

DfES (Department for Education and Skills) (2000) *Curriculum Guidance for the Foundation Stage*, Nottingham: DfES.

DfES (2002) *Birth to Three Matters Framework*, Nottingham: DfES.

DfES and DWP (2001) *National Standards for Under-8s Day Care and Childminding: Crèches*, Nottingham: DfES.

Elfer, P., Goldschmeid, E. and Selleck, D. (2003) *Key Persons in the Nursery: Building relationships for quality provision*, London: David Fulton.

Elfer, P., Goldschmeid, E. and Selleck, D. (2011) *Key Persons in the Early Years: Building relationships for quality provision in Early Years settings and primary schools* (2nd edn; previously published as *Key Persons in the Nursery*), London: David Fulton.

Laevers, F. (1997) *A Process-oriented Child Monitoring System for Young Children*, Leuven: Centre for Experiential Education.

Whalley, M. and Arnold, C. (1997) *Effective Pedagogic Strategies,* TTA Summary of Research Findings.

15 Holding parents and their infants in mind during pregnancy and the first months

Judy Potts

- Pregnancy, birth and the first years of parenting can be wonderful experiences or overwhelmingly challenging.
- Parents who are preoccupied by historic or current adverse factors may be unable to form a consistent positive relationship with their unborn or newborn child, compromising the crucial secure attachment that all babies need for their healthy emotional development.
- Some parents may then develop postnatal depression, which can have further serious consequences for the baby's attachment and well-being.
- A range of universal and targeted multi-disciplinary perinatal services must be provided.
- These services are best provided in the community setting of children's centres where volunteer and peer support is also available.

Introduction

Pregnancy, birth and the first years of parenting can be physically, mentally and emotionally challenging for every parent, male or female. The quality of the attachment – the relationship between parent(s) and baby – is critical to the subsequent healthy development of the child, and services to support these relationships are essential. Adverse factors in parents' own childhoods and current lives can affect a parent's ability to form positive relationships with their unborn or young baby. This can lead to great distress for parent and baby, attachment difficulties, and postnatal depression, all of which can have serious consequences for the unborn or newborn baby. A coherent integrated range of perinatal services, universal and targeted, needs to be provided in partnership with health, mental health, psychotherapy, and family support services, with input from volunteers and other parents. This provides parents with a choice of which combination of services is most helpful and accessible to them. These services are best provided in the community setting of children's centres, where a wide range of further supportive services are also available. We describe the range of services provided at Pen Green Children's Centre and present case studies of parents' experiences of parenthood and the services they found helpful.

National perspective on early years, integrated working and children's centres

The government is clear about the importance of an infant's early years. The Department of Health states that:

> The start of life is especially important in laying the foundations of good health and well-being in later years. The period *from prenatal development to age 3* is associated with rapid cognitive, language, social, emotional and motor development. A child's early experience and environment influence their brain development during these early years, when warm, positive parenting helps create a strong foundation for the future. New evidence about neurological development and child development highlights *just how important prenatal development and the first months and years of life are for every child's future.*
>
> The Government wants to ensure that all parents and children have access to the support they need to get off to the best possible start, *with early intervention to ensure additional support for those who need it, including the most vulnerable families.*
>
> (DoH, 2011: 7)

To fulfill this statement of intent requires well-integrated primary care in:
- maternity services
- early years education services
- early intervention services, alongside national programmes such as the health visitor–delivered Healthy Child programme
- the Family Nurse Partnership
- the new Mental Health Strategy.

Children's centres have a key role as the preferred community location for the provision of these services in local communities. The innovators and providers of services need to be produced in partnership with parents and local statutory and voluntary sector organisations. Equally important is the understanding that all parents require perinatal services but that the most vulnerable require additional services.

The central role of children's centres is emphasised by the recent census of children's centres:

> Increasingly central to the continuation of:
>
> - health visiting reforms,
> - poverty reduction,
> - employment support,
> - relationship support, and
> - parenting and family support,
>
> children's centres are taking their place as important pillars in the welcome reconfiguration of local services towards early intervention and prevention. (DoH, 2011: 7; my italics)
>
> (4Children, 2012: 6)

The challenge, then, in our children's centre is how to deliver the best multi-agency, multi-professional perinatal services.

Pen Green has a long tradition of providing effective, multi-disciplinary services in partnership with local professionals and we continue to listen to and learn from our parents, and to develop our own services in response to their voices.

Providing high-quality infant–parent services is complex because the service must meet the needs of the unborn and newborn baby, while simultaneously meeting the needs of the mother and the father. Vulnerable parents' needs may be urgent and overwhelming, clamorous or hidden, and the well-being of the baby may get lost. The needs of vulnerable fathers-to-be and new fathers are relatively little known, understood or provided for.

Pregnancy

Pregnancy is a time of immense turmoil both physically and psychologically for every woman. Our society can promote idealistic notions of happiness in pregnancy and some women seem to sail through these huge changes and adjustments with comparative ease. But, for others, the physical and/or emotional demands are disturbing and sometimes overwhelming.

Pregnant women have to manage their ambivalence to their changing body, changing lives and changing place in the world. Most women experience misgivings after conception or as birth approaches.

Parker describes maternal ambivalence as 'a complex and contradictory state of mind, shared variously by all mothers, in which loving and hating feelings for children exist side by side' (Parker, 1997: 17).

In this state of mind, while engaged in the most creative of processes, pregnancy brings concerns about loss of identity, anxiety about loss of the baby, loss or change in important relationships, loss of confidence in being able to fulfil the maternal role.

Raphael-Leff (2000) describes the psychic turbulence of pregnancy and the permeability to archaic feelings in the perinatal period. She describes the heightened vulnerability to emotional distress during childbearing as 'a complex interplay between the unique constellation of each person's internal world and the circumstances of his/her external reality' (Raphael-Leff, 2000: 8). Thus emotional vulnerabilities from earlier life can combine with current adverse physical, emotional or social circumstances to cause great distress during pregnancy. Pregnancy offers time for a woman to make a relationship with the growing unborn, to start to prepare for the baby becoming a separate entity and to anticipate the maternal role of loving and caring for the baby when it is born. Women who are preoccupied and distressed may not have the psychic space to make these preparations and this can affect their preparedness for the baby and their ability to promote a secure attachment with their baby.

Distress in pregnancy also has physical effects on the unborn. A recent review of the latest research leads Dunkel Schetter and Tanner to state that 'pregnancy anxiety, pregnancy chronic stress and depression are among the most potent maternal risk factors for adverse maternal and child outcomes, leading to shorter gestation, with adverse effects on foetal neurodevelopment and child outcomes' (2012: 142).

The emotional and psychological states that pregnancy can arouse in vulnerable fathers-to-be can be very difficult for service providers to know about. Unintended, unwanted pregnancies can result in men feeling frustration and stress and deep uncertainty about their perceived role of provider. The care lavished on a pregnant partner can evoke furious jealousy, as can the thought of the baby monopolising her attention or becoming the most important person in the family. These vulnerabilities can lead to domestic abuse against the pregnant woman and her unborn (Humphreys & Houghton, 2008: 16). Sadly, 30 per cent of domestic abuse begins during pregnancy, and risks are even higher for teenage parents. This means that domestic abuse services must be integral parts of perinatal services. A recent survey found that only four out of 25 pregnant or parent teenagers who had suffered domestic abuse had been asked about this (Women's Health Matters, 2009). The feelings aroused by these attacks and the protection of the pregnant mother can preclude any thought for the disturbed father. But finding a way to know about these feelings and the distress of the fathers-to-be before abuse begins, and providing appropriate support, must be considered, as part of effective preventative services.

Adverse factors at conception, during pregnancy and at birth are now seen as highly predictive of low well-being for mother and baby after birth, difficulties with development of secure attachment, and the likelihood of postnatal distress developing.

My masters study (Potts, 2010) asked mothers who had difficulties with attachment with their babies to talk about these experiences. Many of their accounts placed emphasis on factors around conception or their pregnancy for these subsequent difficulties, thus corroborating the psychological frameworks described above. For many, pregnancy was unplanned and they felt unready or had a deep ambivalence about the continuation of their pregnancy or felt concern as to their suitability or capability as a parent. The enormous physical and psychological changes inherent in pregnancy seemed overwhelming for women who already had vulnerabilities from previous childhood abuse or neglect, or from current abuse, poverty or other difficult circumstances. These women strongly associated their postnatal failure to 'connect' with their newborn with adverse factors in their pregnancy, such as perceived threats to the continued viability of the baby, their own mental or physical health, substance misuse, trauma at birth, or difficulties with their partner. It was as if their own emotional and social preoccupations left no space for connecting with the coming baby. They did not encounter an antenatal service which provided the continuity of care or enough hope of a compassionate response to risk exposing their pain or shame to a professional. Often their only recourse was to the GP for anti-depressants.

Antenatal services

National policy and service delivery now acknowledges the need to provide both a universal service and an enhanced service for more vulnerable women, set out in the NICE Guidelines on Antenatal Care (2008), and Antenatal and Postnatal Mental Health (2007). NICE Guidelines for Pregnancy and Complex Social Factors (2010) provides specific guidelines for:
- women who misuse drugs and/or alcohol
- women who are recent migrants, asylum seekers, refugees, or who have difficulty speaking or reading English
- women who experience domestic abuse
- young women aged under 20.

The Family Nurse Partnership service for young first-time-pregnant women, and a Vulnerable Women's Midwife for pregnant woman with additional vulnerabilities provides enhanced support for limited numbers. Children's centres provide a location for all these midwifery services.

The philosophy of midwifery care is stated in *Midwifery 2020* (DoH, 2010) as 'The assistance of a woman around the time of childbirth in a way that recognises that the physical, emotional and spiritual aspects of pregnancy and birth are equally important' (p. 5).

Midwives aspire to provide such a service, but midwifery services are currently under great pressure with more women needing more complex obstetric care (DoH, 2010: 3) and birth rates rising. In Northamptonshire, actual births far exceed predicted rates and fertility rates are rising significantly. The prevalence of perinatal problems is high, with estimates of approximately 20 per cent experiencing antenatal anxiety and/or depression and even higher rates postnatally. As psychosocial factors are determinants in these conditions, areas of disadvantage, such as parts of Corby with high levels of poverty, underlying mental health problems and domestic violence, indicate much higher rates locally. The 'current need for appropriate services exceeds statutory sector capacity' (Barlow & Coe, 2012).

Thus midwives on their own do not have the capacity to provide this additional support, and at Pen Green we believe that services which include peer support and volunteer support provide appropriate, effective and accessible complementary antenatal services for vulnerable families.

Current universal antenatal services at Pen Green include:
- a midwifery clinic
- health visitor Parentcraft sessions for parents-to-be
- sessional health professional.

Current specialist services include:
- Vulnerable Women's Midwife clinics in partnership with outreach support from Family Visiting team and Home-Start Corby
- a range of services for young parents
- Great Expectations group – for any parent, including vulnerable parents.

Key information

Services for young parents

- Mothers and fathers may cope well with pregnancy and early parenthood, or they may find these experiences intolerably demanding and disturbing, especially if they already have emotional vulnerabilities.
- Young babies need good enough parenting, their attachment and emotional well-being can be seriously affected by parents unable to hold them consistently in mind.
- Children's centres need to provide a range of universal and specialist, professional and volunteer/peer, support and health services for all parents and their infants.
- Parents for whom pregnancy and early parenting are distressing are unlikely to reveal their feelings through profound shame and guilt.
- All workers and volunteers need to hold all parents-to-be and parents with young babies in mind and offer them the opportunity to share their distress and immediately offer a choice of professional and peer-support services.
- Workers and volunteers need excellent training, support and supervision to be able to bear to find out about parents and babies with emotional distress.

- In specialist groups, parents experience great relief to find others with similar difficulties and to share ways to cope.
- Services are mainly for mothers, better services for fathers-to-be and fathers need to be developed.

Services for young parents

Part of the newbuild for the Corby Sure Start Trailblazer Project, based at Pen Green, provided a dedicated space for the Centre for Young Parents, as young people had previously told us that they didn't feel comfortable using our mainstream services. They told us of the particular challenges they face, often with no housing of their own, struggling to become adults at the same time as making the transition to parenthood, trying to continue their education/training, often dependent on their own parents, yet wanting to be autonomous parents themselves. They told us they wanted services in the evenings and at weekends. Our Young Parent Midwife and assistant developed midwifery services and antenatal and postnatal groups that were flexible, attractive and accessible to young people, both young women and their partners, respectful and encouraging (see Chapter 16 on health professionals working at Pen Green).

Now, funding has changed and we no longer have a dedicated Young Parent Midwife. However, the community-based Vulnerable Women's Midwife looks after all vulnerable young pregnant women and co-leads young people's groups at Pen Green with a member of our staff. Pregnant young women and their partners can join at any time in their pregnancy, become a supportive network for each other, get professional support and advice, and prepare for parenthood. Groups are after school and college, with information sessions as well as time for a meal together. Members become familiar with the labour ward and make their birth plans. By the time they have their baby, these parents have formed social networks, are comfortable being in the centre, have been supported with employment, training and housing issues and are knowledgeable about the many services and groups they can attend. Our Young Parents worker also offers individual support and home-visiting in partnership with the Vulnerable Women's Midwife.

Great Expectations support group for pregnant women

In response to our understanding of perinatal distress the Great Expectations group was restarted.

This perinatal support group provides both a universal service and a specialist service for women for whom pregnancy/birth/motherhood is fraught and distressing. It sits alongside many other groups in the extensive groupwork programme (see Chapter 6). Pregnant women join at any time in their pregnancy by referral or self-referral. Most try to come each week but may have many other agency appointments to attend. Some mothers come very early in their pregnancies, some can only come regularly after they have gone on maternity leave. Some are expecting a 'normal' pregnancy, birth and establishing a place for their newborn in their family but value the time each week to reflect and travel alongside others on this most important journey. Other women are overwhelmed and despairing, feeling very isolated and thinking their anxieties or difficulties are unique, until they come and share them. They find relief in learning that others have endured similar distresses, they experience compassionate acceptance and suggestions based on other group members' experiences.

Figure 15.1 The Great Expectations group

Examples from practice
Examples from practice

Three recent group members and the situations that they had been facing when they joined the group:

- Teidi had just moved to the Women's Refuge in Corby from the North, escaping domestic violence. She knew nobody in Corby, and was seeking leave to remain in the UK. She was feeling very depressed, isolated and hopeless.
- Carla, a young parent, said, 'Life is hectic and difficult. I have trouble with my ex.'
- Helen said, 'I'm not coping at all well as the doctor told me to stop taking my anti-depressants and I was off them for nine weeks and I was a total mental and physical mess.'

The group provides consistent support from group leaders and group members while women move through pregnancy, birth and their new life with a small baby. This is in contrast to the fragmented service that they may experience in the community and hospital. Various group members said:

'The group was the only thing to keep me going. They felt like my support family.'

'It was something every week to look forward to, to feel part of a network of other mothers, all experiencing or understanding an individual's troubles or worries.'

'I enjoy the group time. I have made friends within the group and enjoy having *me* time for my pregnancy.'

'As we obviously got to know each other a bit better it went deeper and ... it started to make me feel that it was okay ... to be expecting this baby but still feel like s**t.'

Holding parents and their infants in mind during pregnancy and the first months

Groups at Pen Green always have two group leaders, but this particular group needs experienced group leaders with the skills to provide:

- emotional containment with the ability to encourage and support group members to voice their anxieties and distress
- specialist perinatal midwifery knowledge with detailed information in response to group members' particular needs and anxieties
- extensive knowledge of and connections with local maternity services, other relevant health services, services in the community and in Pen Green
- support to both pregnant women, new mothers and babies within the group and to promote their well-being together and separately, including skills to support very vulnerable mothers.

Recently, the group has been co-led by a local midwife and an experienced member of the Family Support team. The midwifery team was supportive of one of their colleagues co-leading this group. They refer in to the group and liaise with her to jointly provide the best care for the pregnant group members. The Vulnerable Woman's Midwife makes many referrals to the group and works particularly closely with the group leaders.

During group sessions, the midwife provides professional support on any topic concerning pregnancy, birth, the new baby's well-being and feeding. She arranges visits to see the labour ward, offers antenatal or postnatal checks after each group time. She will also see a baby if the mother is concerned and link with the baby's GP or health visitor. The Pen Green worker takes responsibility for the room, the register, evaluation, taking referrals, talking with potential new members, publicity and liaison with local health and welfare agencies and professionals. She will suggest and introduce other services to group members and arrange referral both within the centre and to agencies in the community.

Examples from practice

Group members have said:

'Our group leaders were very supportive and very well informed.'

'The best midwife I've ever had the good fortune to meet.'

'Answered midwifery concerns whenever we needed.'

The group leaders are consistently at the group before it starts, preparing both the group space and a space in their mind for each group member, their struggles and concerns. This preparation enables the group leaders to relate sensitively to each group member within their unique set of circumstances during the group. Mothers thus experience being held in mind, which can be sustaining in the maelstrom of pregnancy. It can also provide an experience for mothers to draw on and offer, in turn, to their babies when they arrive, so supporting their attachment with their babies.

As group leaders, we spend time after the group reflecting on what has occurred and deciding who will carry out which actions decided with group members during the group. We also think of the absent group members and arrange to contact them before the next group.

Key information

Co-leading this group, we need supervision to reflect on:

- co-leadership issues
- group dynamics
- emerging themes
- the impact of the group on us
- how we will carry out evaluation and record the difference the group makes.

This 'holding in mind' supported by supervision and training is systemically built in to all our infant–parent mental health work at the centre. Our supervision is provided by a psychotherapist who works sessionally in the centre and is a co-leader of the group for promoting attachment, Growing Together (see Chapter 10).

As group leaders we actively support the safeguarding of the unborn and newly born in the group by addressing risks with mothers either within the group or outside the group and offering additional services to support parents to manage and reduce risks. Attendance at the group can be part of the Pre-Birth Assessment recommendations or a named part of an Unborn Child Protection Plan.

A group member said, 'I had a session when my group leader asked me questions no-one else had about my situation with my ex and helped me to realise what my worries were. She then helped me to figure out a course of action to make sure I could ensure my baby is being born in to a safe environment.'

Examples from practice

Group members were asked what was best about the group during pregnancy:

'The other mothers' support, and the leaders' ability to find or source methods of support in the community.' (We were able to liaise with Home-Start Corby which arranged for this mother to have a volunteer during her pregnancy when she was very sick.)

'It was nice to have reassurance in my pregnancy with all my worries and meet other girls in similar situations.'

'The focus on pregnancy and it helped to get me out of the house to socialise.'

'Having a midwife there for appointments after the group. Knowing that other people were going through the same things.'

Group members still come after their baby is born. After birth, many women find it difficult to get out again. It seems that the group, with its unchanged, supportive group membership, provides the necessary incentive to return, to proudly introduce their new baby, tell their birth stories, share their wonder and love for their baby, or their exhaustion and despair. The group leaders and members draw on and share their various expertise and experiences as the mother and new baby try to settle in to their new relationship and way of life.

Examples from practice

Examples from practice

Group members were asked what was best about the group after the baby was born:

'To be able to go there after having A and to say pregnancy just turned into awfulness and now I have got this baby and I need to be helped … but they did help me … without it, I think coming out the other side after having A would have taken a lot longer than it has.'

'Support with experience of new motherhood. Support to lead on to other groups.'

'Release – being able to speak about things. Knowing that you are not alone – that things are normal.'

'Again, having the midwife there to check over the baby. Advice from other mums. A reason to get out of the house with the baby.'

Mothers become living role models in the group, for example through breastfeeding their babies each week in the group. This can lead to group members considering giving breastfeeding a try themselves. This wish can then be supported by the midwife group leader explaining what to do in hospital immediately after the birth and how to get the maximum support from ward staff, and later, community and centre-based breastfeeding support services.

The new babies too have an important role in the group. Pregnant members feeling ambivalent, negative, unprepared, anxious about the coming arrival of their own baby, can become enchanted by these little infants and this can awaken a hope for their own motherhood. More practically, mothers 'lend' their infants to others during the group to practise being with a baby, which again can increase confidence.

Mothers and their babies move on from the group when their baby is about 12 weeks old. Older babies are increasingly becoming more active and need a group which supports these needs, and they would, if they remained, become a distraction from the work of the group. Also, this group has a 'rolling' membership and so members must leave as new pregnant women join. This ending can be painful, especially for women for whom the group has been very important and who may have been attending the group for up to nine very significant months. We explain about the groups available to move on to, take mothers to visit the new groups, ensure that a group of mothers leave together and so provide a supportive network for each other so that they can then together try out other groups. Group members also support each other practically, passing on baby equipment and clothes to pregnant women joining the group.

'When I see somebody from Great Expectations you can remember what you felt and have seen (together) and it always makes you quite close.'

Being able to provide transport makes all the difference as to whether some mothers get to the group or not, especially towards the end of pregnancy when walking can be difficult and after birth when negotiating buses can seem too much.

Birth and postnatal parenting

Just as women's experiences of pregnancy vary so much, so too do their experiences of birth. For some, labour is manageable, for others, overwhelmingly traumatic. Some manage with relative ease to connect with their new baby, others are exhausted, preoccupied and unable to reach out physically or emotionally to their babies. Our society tends to idealise the baby's arrival and the first months of parenthood with expectations that mothers will naturally develop the ability to 'hold their baby in mind and develop highly attuned responses to them' (Underdown, 2012). For some parents, male or female, confidence and parenting skills increase in the ensuing weeks, others enter a downward cycle of exhaustion, anxiety and depression. Each baby is unique, some settle quickly into routines, others don't. Some feed well from the beginning, others don't; some babies cry a lot, some hardly ever. Each family's circumstances are different: some have lots of support, others have none. Parents who live together can share the burden of looking after the baby; some parents are separated and have some kind of shared-care arrangements, and some are managing single-handed. Again, relevant services need to be available to every parent and their family, wherever they are on this spectrum.

Pen Green offers a range of services for families with a new baby. For Young Parents and those in Great Expectations the same supportive group continues for them unchanged after their baby has been born. For those receiving one-to-one support from centre workers or volunteers in pregnancy, this can continue after birth. But most newborns are brought to our centre first to groups like Baby Clinic or Infant Massage.

The Healthy Child programme provides a universal perinatal health visiting service. The importance of continuity of care means this now starts in the 36th week of pregnancy. The health visitor Baby Clinic in Pen Green brings health visiting services into our local community. Locating the clinic in the children's centre provides an opportunity to let families know of our extensive range of services. Alongside the health visitor, we have a Pen Green worker who offers a warm welcome. She has extensive experience in Family Support, Pen Green groups and services, she enjoys meeting all families, she is an enthusiastic promoter of Infant Massage and she particularly enjoys meeting fathers and inviting them to the Dads' Baby Massage Group which she co-leads on a Saturday.

All group leaders need not only to provide a high-quality service in their group, but also to think with each family about their particular circumstances and to offer other groups, services in Pen Green, statutory services and in the community as appropriate. This responsibility extends to all Pen Green workers and volunteers, including those in the Family Rooms, the Nurseries, crèches – every family with a newborn might at some time need that extra support to get through particularly trying times.

Particularly important in the Baby Clinic is for parents to have time to meet others with babies of similar ages. Just as this model of Baby Clinic was developed in Pen Green's founding years, so too the Infant Massage groups have been long established. They offer parents the opportunity to learn how to massage their baby while becoming more aware of and responsive to their baby's cues, and thus more sensitively attuned to their baby. Every few years, interested parents, professionals and volunteers have been trained to deliver Infant Massage. We support male parents to train and become co-leaders in the Dads' Baby Massage group and young parents to become leaders in our Young Parents' Baby Massage group.

We support breastfeeding through our Peer Breastfeeding Supporters trained through a Primary Care Trust (PCT) initiative. They offer a 24-hour telephone service and a weekly group. Enhanced support is provided by our breastfeeding specialist from the PCT Trust and we lend breast pumps on request. Our centre health professional provides support and supervision.

There is a group for parents of birth to one year olds, Social Baby, run by Pen Green early years staff with input from our health professional. We also have birth to three Growing Together groups to support attachment between parent and baby (see Chapter 10).

We know that the networks that parents form in these groups are vitally important and, along with the friendships they have made in antenatal groups, and in the labour ward, these provide much-needed mutual support and information. So we encourage groups of parents with newborns to meet together informally, in the Family Room, the new Baby Drop-In or on the sofas in Reception and in the Community Café.

We now get, from the PCT, the name and address of newborns whose parents have consented to an introductory home visit from our Family Support team. Our social worker leads a team of volunteers seconded from Home-Start Corby to do this visiting and she works with them to provide support and supervision. Again, it is a great chance to ensure local parents know about our extensive range of services and to offer further support to those who are finding things difficult.

Health visitors and midwives, while providing enhanced support to struggling families, may refer on to Pen Green Family Visiting Team co-ordinated with Home-Start Corby for our home-visiting Family Support services. These workers and volunteers not only provide intensive support themselves, but have extensive knowledge of services, statutory and voluntary in the community, and support families to access these services.

Services also need to catch up with the increasingly influential role fathers play in their infants' lives and ensure they provide appropriate services for fathers. Fathers often want a more active role in preparation for the new baby, and in all the parenting tasks after the baby is born. Fathers' attitudes to breastfeeding influence mothers' decisions, fathers' smoking, drinking and drug use has the greatest influence on the mothers' habits, and a supportive father is a protective factor for postnatal depression (DoH, 2010). Conversely, fathers' postnatal depression is only recently being recognised with rates estimated at about 10 per cent, with correlation between paternal and maternal postnatal depression.

Postnatal depression

At Pen Green in 2000, women's and men's experiences of postnatal depression were recorded (Charlwood *et al.*, 2000) and factors associated with postnatal depression were found to be:

- a sickly baby
- exhaustion
- family history of mental health problems
- loss of previous identity/role
- disappointment about the reality of being a parent – burdens and responsibilities and impact on partner relationship.

Women also talked about their fear and reluctance to admit their distress.

Much has subsequently been written about postnatal distress and its bio-psycho-social determinants. A recent publication, *Suffering in Silence* (4Children, 2011), demonstrates the devastating effects of postnatal depression on families and children. Websites such as Netmums and NHS Direct provide other sources of information for families and workers (Netmums, 2012; NHS Direct, 2012).

Health visitors screen routinely for postnatal depression (PND). The Edinburgh Post-Natal Depression scale is no longer used locally, instead two nationally standardised questions on well-being are asked with a follow-up question where PND is indicated. Mothers still relate how unreliable their answers are to these questions, they can feel ashamed or anxious about the consequences of telling. However, postnatal depression rates are high, particularly in areas of poverty and social disadvantage, rates quoted vary from 10 per cent to over 30 per cent. Everyone working in the centre and in outreach services – workers, volunteers, parents – need to be ever-vigilant for parents who seem exhausted and depressed or who stop coming in to the centre. We need to consistently hold them in mind and check out very sensitively with them whether they are becoming increasingly overwhelmed, isolated and depressed.

Key information

We need to offer parents who are experiencing PND services to:

- alleviate their distress
- support the father or family to remain or become alternative caregivers so that the baby has consistent attuned relationships with the caregiver, for babies cannot wait on their own for their mothers to recover
- support the mother to connect or strengthen her connection with her baby when the time is right for her.

When, in 2000, the centre became the hub of a Sure Start Trailblazer Project it allocated resources for a training programme with local health visitors in the identification of postnatal depression and delivery of enhanced listening sessions. Simultaneously, a mental health worker was seconded from the local mental heath team to work alongside the health visitors, offering professional support and working particularly with the most seriously depressed women. Her successor and the local lead health visitor for PND started a new postnatal support group which is the forerunner of the group now running.

Postnatal depression group

The postnatal depression group was conceptualised as a group which provided peer support where group leaders offered information on postnatal depression and its psycho-social determinants and shared techniques for combating depression. In terms of a peer support group, members discover that they are not the only ones experiencing excruciating anxiety, shame and depression. This by itself can alleviate distress and reduce social isolation. Group members offer each other acceptance, wisdom from their own similar experiences and support each other to heal, make new choices and change and grow.

Examples from practice

'I'd always started groups and got halfway through and thought – I've got to that stage when I don't want to talk any more. I don't want to go any deeper than that 'cause that really irritates me, upsets me to think about stuff that I don't want to bring up or deal with anymore.'

'Listening to how deep we were gonna go and what we were gonna look at, I thought no matter how hard this gets I've got to do this, otherwise my son is gonna be here in so many years time because his mum was so depressed, she couldn't be bothered, she couldn't do this, or she started drinking and that isn't what I want for him. So I knew I had to do it, no matter how hard.'

This group continues to develop. Now, towards the end of the group, there is a focus on the parent–baby relationship and parents are supported to attend the attachment groups at Pen Green or take up specific attachment work with their health visitors. The ending of the group is a very significant event for members who would often like it to continue indefinitely. Then the task of the group leaders is to:

- keep reminding the members when it will end, and support them to grieve for the loss of such an important part of their lives
- introduce all the other services in the centre and the community, encouraging group members to try out new services together
- refer to specialist services when appropriate.

Currently, the co-leaders are a Family Support team group leader and a co-leader from the local mental health team. Not only does this provide a really effective skill mix but it enhances understanding and joint working between the centre and the local mental health team. These leaders ensure a safe, secure, consistent group experience where group members feel accepted and can trust that their feelings and personal situations will not be harshly judged. Group sessions can be very demanding for mothers and for co-leaders, who are exposed to each mother's distress and pain and may sometimes be concerned whether the baby is getting good enough parenting. Co-leaders need time to de-brief after each session, to decide if any mother needs further support and from whom. Safeguarding the babies in the group requires them to be consistently held in mind, concerns shared as soon as possible with parents who are supported to engage in necessary services. Supervision of these workers is vital, and currently that is given monthly by another member of the mental health team.

Recruitment is through referrals and self-referrals. The Pen Green leader contacts each woman and offers a home visit. The leader explains how the group works and the commitment required. The group runs for 20 weeks, often family sessions are run in the holidays to accommodate older children. Crèche is a vital part of this group. Participants have young babies; not all can arrange childcare during the group sessions and some choose Crèche, recognising the benefit for themselves and their baby.

'This was the first time I was leaving him with somebody and I knew that they all knew what to do, they know babies and it hasn't been 25 years since they had a baby in the house.'

'It was actually quite nice to have an hour that it wasn't me, when he was screaming, and he wanted something different and I didn't know what he wanted. It was actually someone else's turn, people who want to have him.'

The crèche team for this group are workers particularly interested in PND, and they receive enhanced training. Some of the babies will have insecure attachments, making separation from their mothers particularly painful, and will need skilled, sensitive support.

Crèche workers also tell group leaders if they have concerns about any baby's well-being or development. Group leaders will then work with the parent to provide appropriate services for that baby and family. Once babies are settled in the crèche, crèche workers, at the end of the group time, share with their mothers the babies' interests, enthusiasms and play while in Crèche. For mothers, this can alleviate anxiety that their PND has significantly damaged their baby's development, can kindle a new interest in their baby, and can provide suggestions for play which will support their interactions with their babies at home.

The difference these groups makes is illustrated by a mother who said: 'I think that if hadn't been for Great Expectations, if I'd never gone to the PND group, I would not have had the courage to do this whole mum thing.'

Summary

Each family has unique perinatal needs and chooses the services that are right for them. The following story illustrates this for a family for whom pregnancy and early parenthood were very challenging.

Zosime and Caleb's story

Zosime and Caleb had recently fled from their home country to escape serious harassment and intimidation from Zosime's birth family who had abused her throughout her childhood. They came to Corby, as Zosime's best friend already lived here. Zosime and Caleb got a very small flat – they were sleeping on an air mattress surrounded by packing cases and accepting any agency factory work. Zosime was extremely nervous about her family finding her. Almost immediately, she became pregnant, much sooner than she expected. She was very sick, some days she couldn't even stand up.

Her friend had told her how wonderful Pen Green was and her midwife explained about the Great Expectations group. The first time she came to the centre, she waited outside, looking in. She thought, 'I'm not English, probably they won't like me.'

However, she did join the group – 'a lovely group of ladies'. 'My friend thought I should be happy about my pregnancy, I found out in the group that it's okay to be sad when you're pregnant. It wasn't just me. I had just had so many changes; I'd had no time to settle before this big change of being pregnant. Being in the group was like a big weight off my shoulders. They suggested things for my sickness – they suggested travel bands, which worked.'

Zosime found it really helpful having the midwife in the group – to give her professional advice and do her antenatal checks so she didn't have to have more time off work. However, Zosime and Caleb were finding life very difficult and depressing. When Zosime stopped work, she was isolated: 'I just saw these walls.' They started quarrelling a lot and he told her she wouldn't be a fit mother. She said, 'In the group I felt safe, I wasn't being judged. I was living for each Wednesday.'

The midwife and group members gave her baby clothes. Zosime said: 'Babies were being born in the group – I was very sad but becoming excited too but although the midwife told me to get my bag packed, I was too depressed to manage that.'

Zosime became unwell at 37 weeks and was induced; labour was 'no problem', but after having Sophia she went into shock and was extremely ill.

Examples from practice

Zosime, Caleb and Sophia

Caleb said (when Zosime returned home): 'The midwife made such a short visit – not long enough. I was working so I never met her. I was afraid I may not do things right – I had nowhere to get this knowledge.

'Being a father – a huge sensation, [I felt] happy, sad, afraid. Happy – she's my daughter. Afraid – what happens if I die? I quit smoking for her. Now I must think of her first, then Zosime, then me.

'On Saturdays, I started going to Dads' Infant Massage. Zosime told me I could go when Sophia is six weeks. I wanted to try to get a link with her. I didn't have a link, [she was] a strange person to me. I loved her but didn't connect with her. The group helped us both – I learnt some tricks to help with the colic, and it gave a link, a relationship between Sophia and me.

'We were all together at the end of each day, and all night – I needed to take her out. It was very, very good to be alone with her. Pen Green helped us a lot with our [father and baby] relationship. And Zosime got some time alone.'

Later, Zosime struggled with the legacy of her childhood abuse and found nappy changing and breastfeeding almost impossible – she felt very ashamed of this. 'I forced myself to do these, but expressed my milk too so whenever Caleb was home, he did all that. I managed but it wasn't perfect. Many days I didn't want to get out of bed but I forced myself to go [to Pen Green]. It helped that other girls in Great Expectations felt the same.'

When she left Great Expectations, she moved on to Social Babies, Growing Together and the postnatal depression group. 'The staff were always friendly, I never met any discrimination from staff or volunteers, but I felt it sometimes from other parents; I wasn't English, I wasn't Scottish, I wasn't even Irish.'

Zosime told how she kept the environment very quiet at home, so she could hear if anyone was after her, 'it felt safer'. But she now thinks that Sophia was very bored: 'She slept whenever she got home yet she was so active at Pen Green and she would laugh all the time there! I got into a schedule – a different activity or group every day. It helped me bond with her, I was focusing on what I was doing not what I was feeling.'

'Once Zosime was at Pen Green with Sophia, she became a more sociable baby. She had other kids with her; she changed a little bit positively.'

'It started then – through watching other mothers with their babies. Their babies seemed more developed than Sophia. I thought, I'm not being a good mother, what am I not doing? What does she need? Another thing, I had a Home-Start volunteer. Her role was to get me out. She would say, "We'll just go out for a bit – it's good for you both." And we would talk and talk. She talked about what she did with her children; I wanted to know how I could do that. I didn't have a base from my childhood, only what I didn't want to remember, didn't want to repeat. She supported me to try Baby Massage, Sophia enjoyed it but it didn't feel right to me.'

'Then I got a respite childcare place in Crèche. Sophia always settled in Crèche. It was lovely knowing she was okay. I could shop or be at home, have a nap or have a coffee. It was meant to be for six weeks, but they extended it because I had postnatal depression. When I wasn't so bad, I gave the place up for someone else – as I knew there was a long waiting list.'

'Respite on Thursdays – it was very good. We could rest, have some silence, wonderful. We had two hours to discuss, both together, to start our life again. If it weren't for Pen Green, we would both be completely crazy.'

'(Through Crèche) I can leave Sophia with my neighbours and friends; I know she will be okay. Her experiences of life are not just her mum and dad.'

'The postnatal depression group – that was a big support. We talked a lot about PND, and I got a lot of information – how depression affects you. It helped writing down my feelings and thoughts, how it gets hold of you and what you can do to fight it. While I was in the group, I didn't need anti-depressants.'

'However, circumstances at home were very difficult. Sophia had had bad colic, been ill and in hospital several times. Caleb hated his work and we were both absolutely exhausted.'

'It's a little bit hard after a working day to come home tired and hear Sophia screaming all the time. After she was screaming day and night for two days, I screamed a lot with her. The screaming was like torture, [I thought] please let me sleep a few minutes.'

'Sophia's first five months were awful; she screamed non-stop. I don't know how it was possible, especially with all the problems Zosime had. Mix all these ingredients – it was explosive. Our relationship suffered a lot. We nearly split up.'

'I started feeling worse and went to the GP. He recognised our exhaustion and my need to work on my historic abuse. He referred me to the well-being team – they only offer short-term interventions and the specialist counselling service I was referred to – well, I'm still waiting (nine months later) for an appointment!'

'Our relationship was deteriorating, with verbal abuse and it was becoming physical. I went to the Freedom Programme at Pen Green. Being at that group both helped me see how abusive past relationships had been and allowed me to start talking about some of it. It opened a lot of doors in my mind.'

At this time, Zosime again found intimate care of Sophia impossible. She trusted the PND group enough to share her distress and shame. They were accepting and supportive and helped her to ask for and accept practical help from Crèche and her neighbour for aspects of Sophia's care.

'It was completely crazy. We have some friends, upstairs neighbours helped a lot – took the role of grandparents – but not the same as family. It was necessary to get some hope from the bottom of the hole we were in. In my country help like this is almost impossible. Zosime could get answers to some of her problems. Then if she is okay, then I am okay, and Sophia is okay.'

'At the end of the PND group, my group leader found out how vulnerable and suicidal I was feeling – she suggested I went to counselling at Pen Green. The work I am doing with my counsellor there is truly amazing.'

'As the PND group stopped, my Home-Start volunteer told me about the Relaxation group, so I started that instead. Now I do counselling, Relaxation, which helps with my anxiety, and supervised volunteering in Crèche. Sophia stays at home with her daddy and I'm learning a lot about how to be with young ones, how to connect with children in the proper way. I can now say 'no' to my daughter and can play games with her, letting her take the lead. I'm not comparing her development with other children, she's intelligent and I'm more confident about being a mum.'

'The only thing I don't like is fathers need more support. Times have changed in the last two decades, father is now the same as mother, feeding, bathing as well.'

Caleb described how he kept going to Dads' Baby Massage even when Sophia had long outgrown the group because he didn't think she was ready for the group for older children.

'When Sophia was born, everything was new. I needed a fathers' group – for fathers to share our doubts, manage our anxieties. It's good for fathers to be able to share the little things that work, to discover why Sophia is crying in the night, what else can I do? How can I make her more comfortable? We could benefit from sharing our experiences and perhaps meet with our partners there as well once a month. The PND group was meant to have a session for fathers but I was the only one who said they wanted to come so it didn't happen.'

Zosime's final comments: 'I'm one person with many layers to my problems and Pen Green helps me with all the layers. I still have a long way to go but I can now bathe Sophia and change her nappy. I cannot believe how far I have come in two years, I couldn't have dreamt it possible.'

Caleb said, 'Pen Green was the best thing we found in this adventure – something fantastic.'

This family's story illustrates how historic and current difficulties and vulnerabilities made becoming and being parents such a harsh experience for Zosime and Caleb and their baby. It also illustrates the range of universal and specialist multi-agency and multi-professional services they needed and were

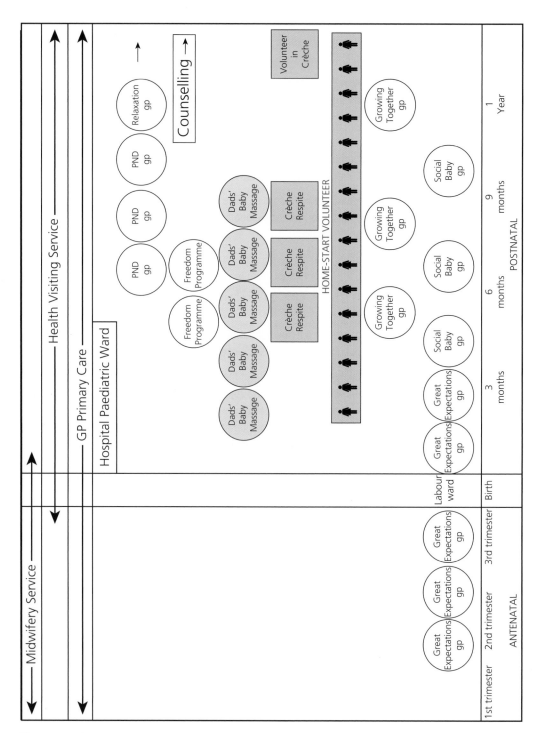

Figure 15.2 The services used by this family

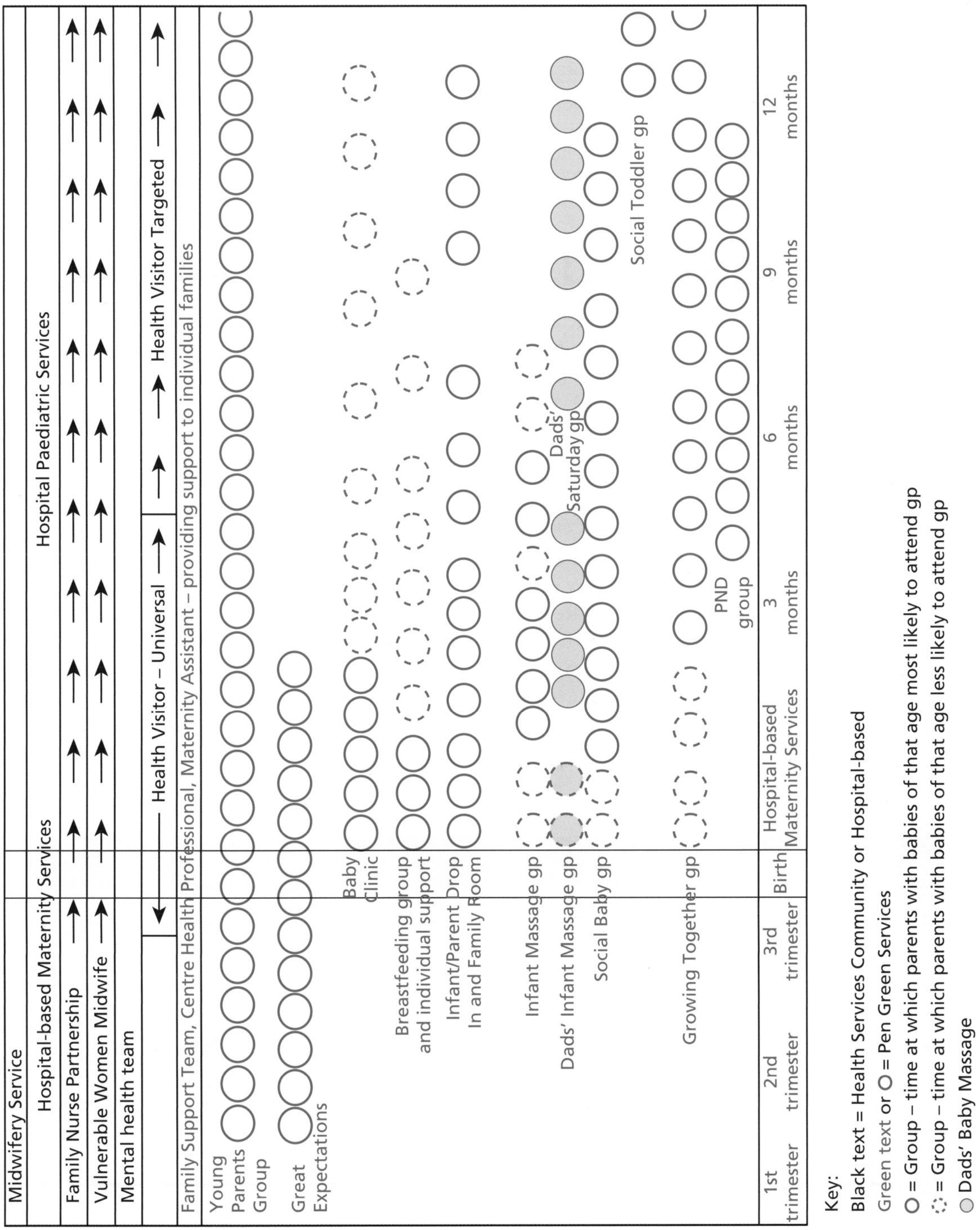
Midwifery Service
Hospital-based Maternity Services
Hospital Paediatric Services
Family Nurse Partnership
Vulnerable Women Midwife
Mental health team
Health Visitor – Universal
Health Visitor Targeted
Family Support Team, Centre Health Professional, Maternity Assistant – providing support to individual families
Young Parents Group
Great Expectations
Baby Clinic
Breastfeeding group and individual support
Infant/Parent Drop In and Family Room
Infant Massage gp
Dads' Infant Massage gp
Dads' Saturday gp
Social Baby gp
Social Toddler gp
Growing Together gp
PND group
1st trimester
2nd trimester
3rd trimester
Birth
Hospital-based Maternity Services
3 months
6 months
9 months
12 months
Key:
Black text = Health Services Community or Hospital-based
Green text or ○ = Pen Green Services
○ = Group – time at which parents with babies of that age most likely to attend gp
⁛ = Group – time at which parents with babies of that age less likely to attend gp
● Dads' Baby Massage

Figure 15.3 The perinatal services offered to families

able to access at Pen Green. It shows too how Zosime in particular was consistently held in mind and great care taken when she finished a group to ensure she moved on to further supportive services. It shows the importance of supporting the attachment that Caleb formed with Sophia and that we did not provide enough services for him. It also illustrates how vital the practical and emotional support from the community was – through their neighbours, their Home-Start volunteer and the parent members in the groups. It shows how Zosime recognised her need for good parenting experiences and chose our crèche as the place to learn.

Challenges and future developments

At Pen Green, we increase our knowledge as we gain experience in our work, and through reflection in our support and supervision, through the courses we attend for our professional development, and from the stories parents tell us of their experiences. We have heard many mothers' voices.

We need to hear more fathers' voices, both those for whom being a father-to-be and a father have been manageable and good experiences, and those who have encountered terrible distress and challenges. Mothers have many opportunities to learn and support each other in groups; fathers should have more opportunities too and we need to form partnerships with them to conceptualise and develop new services relevant to their experiences.

In the current economic climate, statutory services will not be expanding and we must make best use of the resources we have. Children's centres are informed of new births and need to be warm and welcoming to all families, the location for multi-professional, multi-agency working, the cradle where the inherent strengths, wisdom and support within families and communities and among parents are recognised and mobilised. Then all families can be supported and support each other on the turbulent learning journey of parenthood, each family can be consistently held in mind and those for whom pregnancy, birth and looking after a baby are difficult and distressing experiences can be offered easily accessible choices for timely additional support.

Points for discussion

- How can you get a meaningful discussion going with fathers, about developing services most relevant to them?
- How can you ensure all your workers and volunteers know about the prevalence of perinatal distress, have the capacity to recognise it in the parents they meet, and know how to respond appropriately?
- How can you develop the inherent strength, wisdom and skills within your community to support families where pregnancy and care of an infant is distressing and disturbing?

References

4Children (2011) *Suffering in Silence*, London: 4Children.

4Children (2012) *Sure Start Children's Centres Census* [online]. Available from: http://www.4children.org.uk (accessed 14 December 2012).

Barlow, J. and Coe, C. (2012) *Family Action Perinatal Support Project: Research findings report*, Warwick Medical School.

Charlwood, N., Tait, C. and Whalley, M. (2000) *Towards a Fuller Understanding of Postnatal Depression*, unpublished, Corby: Pen Green Centre Research, Development and Training Base.

DoH (Department of Health) (2010) *Midwifery 2020: Core role of the midwife work stream*, Final report, London: DoH.

DoH (2011) *Health Visitor Implementation Plan 2011–15: A call to action*, London: DoH.

Dunkel Schetter, C. and Tanner, L. (2012) 'Anxiety, depression and stress in pregnancy: implications for mothers, children, research and practice', *Current Opinion in Psychiatry,* vol. 25, pp. 141–8.

Humphreys, C. and Houghton, C. (2008) 'The research evidence on children and young people experiencing domestic abuse', ch. 2, in Humphreys, C., Houghton, C. and Ellis, J, *Literature Review: Better Outcomes for Children and Young People Experiencing Domestic Abuse – Directions for Good Practice*, Scottish Government. Available from: http://www.scotland.gov.uk/Resource/Doc/234221/0064112.pdf (accessed January 2013).

Netmums (2012) *Postnatal Depression* [online]. Available from: http://www.netmums.com/support/depression-and-anxiety/postnatal-depression (accessed January 2013).

NHS (2012) *Postnatal depression* [online]. Available from: http://www.nhs.uk/conditions/Postnataldepression (accessed January 2013).

NICE (2007) *Antenatal and Postnatal Health: Clinical Guidelines 45*, London: NICE.

NICE (2008) *Antenatal Care: Clinical Guidelines 62*, London: NICE.

NICE (2010) *Pregnancy and Complex Social Factors: A model for service provision for pregnant women with complex social factors: Clinical guidelines 110*, London: NICE.

Parker, R. (1997) 'The production and purposes of maternal ambivalence', in Holloway, W. and Featherstone, B. (eds) *Mothering and Ambivalence*, London: Routledge.

Potts, J. (2010) 'Mothers' experiences of difficulties with attachment to their babies: their views on services received and services they would have liked', unpublished masters dissertation.

Raphael-Leff, J. (ed.) (2000) *Spilt Milk: Perinatal loss and breakdown*, London: The Institute of Psychoanalysis.

Raphael-Leff, J. (2003) *Pregnancy: The inside story*, London: Karnac.

Underdown, A. (2012) 'Holding the baby in mind: the power of early relationships', paper given at *All Babies Count* NSPCC Conference, Royal Society of Medicine, University of Warwick, 7 Mar. 2012.

Women's Health Matters (2009) *Teenage Mothers' Experiences of Domestic Violence: Identifying good practice for support workers* [online]. Available from: www.ccrm.org.uk/images/docs/womens_health_matters.pdf.

16

Developing preventative health work with families in children's centres

Ann Crichton and Jo Ghani

In this chapter we will consider:

- how preventative health work at Pen Green is underpinned by values and principles
- why preventative health work matters
- the services Pen Green offers to support child and family health
- how health professionals work as part of the Pen Green team
- the implications for practice.

Introduction

The early years set the foundation for children's future development and have a profound influence on their life chances. From the start, health, social and educational inequalities are inextricably intertwined (Marmot, 2010). Children with better health have better socio-economic outcomes (Shonkoff *et al.*, 2011); people with higher educational outcomes live longer (Waldfogel, 2005). Put simply, improving health from the very start of life can help people live longer and have a better chance of enjoying their lives to the full.

Children's centres have a remit to improve child and family health and Pen Green has a long history of working closely with local health services to develop a community-based approach to improving health in our local community.

Values and principles

The importance of respecting parents as equal partners is discussed throughout this book, but it is important to stress that partnership matters just as much when it comes to health. As anyone who has ever tried to give up smoking, eat more healthily or take more exercise is painfully aware, good advice is seldom helpful and often counter-productive. Health promotion works best when people are active partners in designing and implementing programmes, 'given that people are most likely to take control of their health if they feel they are in control of other aspects of their lives' (Campbell, 2000: 186). Effective health promotion for families relies on the same principles as all other work with parents: it sets out to build on people's strengths and achievements, to provide knowledge and understanding to help them make informed choices, and to build their confidence in their ability to make choices and sustain change (British Psychological Society, 2008).

The core purpose of children's centres is to improve outcomes for children (DfE, 2011b), which should include providing parents with support to give their children a healthy start. However, we also need to remember that parents are people, with lives, concerns and needs of their own. Parents who are suffering from ill health or depression themselves will find it much harder to give their children all the attention and support they need to flourish and achieve their full potential (ChiMat, 2011). 'It is unrealistic to demand that women should be able to meet their children's physical and emotional needs when their own are not being met' (Katz et al., 2007: 9). This means children's centres should offer support to the whole family.

Preventative health work in children's centres depends on building and sustaining partnerships with health services. Health professionals bring specialist skills and knowledge but the Audit Commission (2010) found a common theme of parents feeling that health professionals would be judgemental. Children's centres can help to overcome parents' fears by offering accessible, welcoming venues and early years practitioners who already have regular contact and positive relationships with families. Later in this chapter I will describe how health and early years practitioners at Pen Green have worked together to provide services in a way that puts into practice the learning from research which tells us that:

- people want services that are:
  - receptive, non-stigmatising, flexible and focused on their concerns (Hill et al., 2007)
  - offer emotional support and practical help (Quinton, 2004; Browne et al., 2006)
  - provide long-term support rather than brief intervention (Bull et al., 2004)
- in order to make the best of partnership working, there needs to be:
  - a shared philosophy (Edgley, 2007)
  - a shared understanding of local needs (DoH, 2007a).

Children's centres are extremely well placed to work in this way and there has been an increasing tendency for midwives and health visitors to provide clinics in children's centres. In a submission to parliament, the Royal College of Midwives (2009) strongly supported this move, saying that children's centres 'are able to deliver improved quality of care, particularly for those less likely to access mainstream services'.

Example from practice

A young parent's story

Mandy was 16 when she found out she was pregnant. It was a 'surprise' and a bit of a 'shock' to discover at the first scan that she was 27 weeks pregnant. She was referred to Sure Start at Pen Green and to the midwife. Mandy recounts: 'She made me feel so welcome and relaxed about it. The midwife went through how lucky I was to have a supportive family and to have Sure Start and Pen Green's support and that I was with my baby's dad as well. I only had 13 weeks to do everything but after talking to her, I felt excited.' Mandy remembers that the midwife 'helped with resources – baby monitors, sterilisers and things like that.' Two years later Mandy had a second child and 'got her own place'. Again, the midwife from Pen Green supported her with practical things, 'like furniture that was lying around and baby clothes'. This time, Mandy chose to have a home birth. Her own mum was away working abroad and, although she had a different midwife, the Pen Green midwife 'offered to be the second person at the birth … she wasn't my midwife this time … She was just like 'my mum'. That's important when you're young and pregnant – you need someone you can trust … you need your mum, don't you?' Immediately after the birth, 'they cleared up and did the washing for me'. Mandy added: 'I'd need her again if I had another baby!' and also, 'She makes the dads feel welcome as well – she doesn't push them out, which is a big thing.'

Six years on, Mandy has recently become a single parent but she has big plans for the future. She has already completed the Home-Start course, has done some mental health training and is waiting to do a counselling course at the local FE college and also has two wonderful sons, who she hopes will be proud of her when they grow up.

Mandy's story is one example of how health workers can support parents by being:

- accepting of the circumstances (receptive)
- non-judgemental and non-stigmatising
- prepared to help in practical ways as well as providing emotional support (focused on the concerns of the parents)
- consistently available over time (long-term support).

Why preventative health work matters

The health service is currently undergoing radical reorganisation; funding will be very carefully scrutinised and commissioners will have difficult decisions to make about priorities. When funding is in short supply there is a danger of concentrating on short-term objectives and reducing investment into longer term, preventative work. This makes it even more important that children's centres should work with health practitioners to undertake preventative work that can make a real difference to children's health and well-being.

Before birth

More than four children per 1,000 die before their first birthday, with higher mortality rates in lower socio-economic groups; some of these tragic deaths are preventable (DoH, 2007b). Children's centres can help to engage with families early on and build a relationship before the baby is born. They can offer additional support around issues such as housing and domestic abuse, so that parents can start to deal with these pressures before the baby arrives. Group-based antenatal education can reduce anxiety and depression and help parents to cope better. Not surprisingly, parents find antenatal programmes more helpful if they involve fathers and if they encourage parents to participate and share their own thoughts and experiences. Parents also value programmes that have a wider focus than pregnancy and birth, covering topics such as relationships, parenting, bonding and attachment (Schrader McMillan et al., 2009).

Breastfeeding

Breastfeeding has significant, well-documented benefits for mothers and babies (UNICEF, 2012) and there is emerging evidence that breastfed babies may have better neurological and cognitive development (Iacovou & Sevilla-Sanz, 2010). Breastfeeding is an emotive subject and it is important to find a way of encouraging mothers to try breastfeeding and to offer support to continue, without making mothers feel guilty or inadequate if it is not for them (see Chapter 15 for more information on this).

Maternal depression

Maternal depression can seriously impede attachment and companionship but it often goes undiagnosed. All too often, friends, families and practitioners will be so engrossed with the child that they fail to ask how the mother is doing in a way that suggests they really want to hear the answer. It can be hard for mothers to admit they are struggling; for a new mother to tell someone that she does not feel she loves her baby would be an act of either immense courage or real desperation. Practitioners need to be sensitive to how new parents are feeling and to offer support through groups or home visits. There is also evidence that baby massage can reduce postnatal depression and promote attachment (O'Higgins et al., 2008).

Second-hand smoke

The Royal College of Physicians (2010) estimates that, every year, exposure of children to second-hand smoke causes around 40 sudden infant deaths, over 20,000 cases of lower respiratory tract infection, 120,000 cases of middle ear diseases, at least 22,000 new cases of wheeze and asthma, and 200 cases of bacterial meningitis. There is a misconception that tobacco smoke is only dangerous if children are present when people are smoking; dust from smoking, which clings to carpets, furniture and clothing, contains toxic chemicals. Young children have smaller airways, faster rates of breathing and immature immune systems, so they are much more vulnerable than adults (Bearer, 1995). Even minor illness, if it happens often enough, can reduce a child's well-being and affect their learning and development. Smoke-Free Homes schemes can help families reduce this risk without giving up smoking, although if an adult says they want to quit smoking, practitioners should know how to signpost them to support.

Domestic abuse

Domestic abuse often starts, or gets worse, during pregnancy (Mezey & Bewley, 2005). As well as the physical danger and emotional distress this causes adults, it can also affect infants' brain development and there is a real risk of ever-increasing harm to their physical, emotional and social development (UNICEF, 2006). The Freedom Programme (Craven, 2012) is offered by many centres, including Pen Green, to support women to keep themselves and their children safe, and many women have found this programme life-changing.

Healthy lifestyles

Overweight children are likely to stay overweight into adulthood, are more likely to develop diabetes and cardiovascular diseases at a younger age, and have an increased likelihood of musculoskeletal disorders and certain types of cancer (WHO, 2012). Obesity rates for ten-year-olds are rising. At age five, one in five children is overweight or obese (NOO, 2012) but this rate is falling, particularly for boys. There is no hard evidence to explain this but children's centres across the country have been promoting healthy eating and offering cook-and-eat courses. These may have made a direct contribution to reducing obesity rates, or it may be the case that, simply by paying attention to an issue, we can make a difference that could help people live longer, healthier lives.

Pen Green services

Because health, emotional well-being, freedom from stress and learning are so interlinked, it is hard to separate services into different categories. However, the ways in which child and family health are supported at Pen Green include:

- midwives and health visitors being accessible to parents coming into the centre
- the role of the maternity support worker, who works closely alongside the midwife
- the Young Parents group
- Baby Massage groups
- support with breastfeeding
- the Gap group, which offers support with postnatal depression
- groups to support attachment and attunement
- many of the Family Room activities
- many of the conversations which take place every day between practitioners and parents.

Figure 16.1 A father and child at Young Parents group

Figure 16.2 Having lunch at Young Parents group

Working with Families in Children's Centres and Early Years Settings

Health practitioners at Pen Green

It's about working in depth, not just skimming the surface.

(Practitioner)

For this chapter I interviewed two health visitors (one of whom is employed by Pen Green part-time and based at the centre), a midwife (who has now moved on) and a maternity support worker. Another health visitor also interviewed a family about their experience of accessing health services and Pen Green.

The following themes emerged from the interviews:
- engaging with families through:
  – adopting a community-led approach
  – building relationships
  – providing continuity of care
  – providing support that makes a difference
- learning and working in partnership across agency and professional boundaries through:
  – building a learning community
  – developing integrated working and a shared ethos
  – re-negotiating professional roles and identities
  – the commitment of the practitioners
  – the impact of leadership.

Engaging with families

A community-led approach

Consultation in 1999 showed that the community wanted more communication and better access to health services. Last year, the Pen Green health visitor asked parents for their views again and was told that expectant mothers want to meet others in a supportive atmosphere with warm and friendly staff; this is the approach practitioners strive to adopt.

All the practitioners talked about the importance of knowing the community; most live locally and take pride in their Corby heritage. Most talked about being seen as a mother figure; this was partly about being supportive and accepting but it was also about reliability and continuity – being there for the long haul, not the quick fix. A health visitor said: 'In many cases, I've been the mother's health visitor and now her daughter's – I've been around for a while.' The midwife agreed: 'The midwife knew all your history, and knew your boyfriend, knew your mum, knew your dad, knew your granny … knew the good things about them, knew the bad things that were going on for them … They weren't being judged because I knew who they were and they knew me.'

Corby is changing and this creates new pressures, with families moving into the area from Greater London, Eastern Europe and Africa. A health visitor explained the isolation that can ensue: 'They've all left, not just their families but their culture, behind them.' Understanding their context 'makes you a better practitioner because your eyes are opened to a lot more things that are going on'.

Practitioners talked about the generosity of the community and the way people who have received support want to give something back; the midwife was almost swamped by the quantity of clothes and equipment which people passed on to her for other parents.

Parents are more likely to access services which are responsive to their needs and respect their choices. The maternity support worker says: 'I'm willing to do whatever the parents want or need, so I might play with the child while the mum gets on with the ironing, or she might just want me to listen.' She understands that some parents, fathers in particular, can be reluctant to attend the centre, so home visits are an essential step in reaching all the families who might need support.

Sometimes there are practical barriers to accessing services. Pen Green will arrange transport when needed and provide a crèche place for older children so that parents can attend Baby Massage without feeling torn between their children's needs. Parents are encouraged to attend the Antenatal Group with their partner but they are also welcome to bring their mother or a friend.

Building relationships

Strange buildings and clinical atmospheres can be intimidating. Health practitioners and Family Workers at Pen Green often build relationships in the family home before accompanying parents into the centre and staying with them in groups until they feel confident. Fathers often get involved, even if they are not living with their partner and children. Practitioners have worked hard to generate a relaxed, informal and homely environment, with sofas, cushions from home and photographs of parents and children helping to create an environment that feels like a living room, not a clinic.

All the practitioners understood that families may worry about being judged. The parents who were interviewed said: 'You felt vulnerable, that people were talking about you.' At the same time, practitioners 'have to balance being accepting but needing to say what matters to support the child. It's the parent's need and the child's need.'

Practitioners emphasise the importance of time and perseverance in building trusting relationships – they will keep knocking on doors and accepting that 'you can have ten steps forward and 30 steps back and then you can have another ten steps forward'. The parents who were interviewed said it had taken them several years to feel confident about going to Pen Green. They explained what they think is needed: 'Get one of the services to go to that person and have a person next to them, who could speak for them and try and encourage that person ... to come to somewhere neutral where they can sit, feel comfortable, for however long the time is. Then, the next stage will be meeting a few different people ... then gradually, into a group, into a proper daily routine, where you go into the nursery and you can be there, around people, where you feel comfortable.'

Providing continuity

I'd be the one they came to for their pregnancy test ... I would look after them antenatally, then it just seemed natural to be there at the birth, then I'd see them at home ... Every time you pass the Family Room you see them later on ... they'd come along and talk to you about things and ... you supported them for much, much longer.

(Midwife)

The maternity support worker also offers long-term support: 'I still have parents who come in on occasion, just to show me their five-year-old, to show me how they are doing.' Handover from midwife to health visitor is a gradual process that ensures parents do not feel abandoned. When additional support is needed the practitioner will introduce the parent to the new practitioner, rather than just signposting. The health visitor would be at the nursery at pick-up and drop-off times to build a relationship with parents and staff. Practitioners value knowing the person they are referring to and families value the way practitioners work together to offer support: 'If you tell one person something, they will know who to put you on to.'

Support that makes a difference

The support of a known and trusted professional makes women feel safer during labour, and the maternity support worker feels privileged to have been a birthing partner for four women. The midwife believes that feeling safer reduces admissions to hospital with false alarms and reduces the need for analgesia during labour: 'They felt confident about what you've told them ... they weren't scared, they had the information.'

The practitioners and the parents all agreed that coming to one group makes it much more likely that parents will go on to attend other groups and will find it easier to ask for help when they need it. Groups were valued as a way for parents to make friends – as one practitioner said: 'I think the mother is the key person in the family. If she doesn't feel good, her partner isn't going to and certainly the children aren't.' Practitioners also noted that parents who have used services often become volunteers and some become paid workers.

The centre-based health visitor makes outreach visits to mothers with maternal depression and could accompany them to the support group, until they feel confident about attending. Baby massage has been shown to promote attachment and help alleviate maternal depression. A health visitor pointed out another possible benefit: 'Young girls who have been abused are often frightened of touch and this is a nice gentle way to encourage them not to be frightened of their babies, to touch their babies, and the power of touch as well, it's amazing.'

Health visitors were clear about the benefits of being easily accessible at the centre. Parents are able to ask questions and get support without having to make an appointment or feel that they are taking up professional time for what may be seen as trivial. Health visitors regularly give opportunistic advice on a range of health issues, including vaccinations, eczema, minor illness and sleep, and also advise and support parents with their own health concerns.

Less duplication and more communication can only enhance outcomes and working in a multi-disciplinary way helps professionals think beyond their own specialism. As the midwife said: 'I'm a lot more child-focused than I ever was before, to me it was always about the pregnant woman and the rest came in later, but now it's – hang in there ... if you can do something for the child then it's worth it ... You can't make everything correct for that woman's life at the time but you can start to make things better for the child.'

The parents felt they had received a lot of support over the years; they had gained a better understanding of their child's feelings and behaviour through attending Parents' Involvement in Their Children's Learning groups (PICL) but they also felt that having their child at nursery had given them vital breathing space to gain some perspective and they deeply valued being able to confide in practitioners at the centre. 'When we confided in you about what's going on at the moment with our health, that helped a lot – to actually tell somebody, instead of keeping it inside.'

Learning and working in partnership

I came out here and saw things differently, from a different perspective ... there are some very sad things that happen in life that we don't always like to think of and I was coming across that really for the first time.

(Practitioner)

Building a learning community

The practitioners all felt they had extended and enriched their knowledge and skills through integrated working. They participated in team training at the centre, including days where all the practitioners and agencies discussed their roles and values. They recognised the wide-ranging expertise of the centre practitioners and had shared their specialist knowledge of maternity care, child and public health with the Pen Green team: 'There is this wonderful two-way transfer of knowledge and skills.' They had also attended further training funded from the Pen Green budget.

Developing integrated working and a shared ethos

Working side by side has helped to build a shared ethos about 'prioritising the needs of the child, but also listening to the parental voice and empowering families'. It was very clear in the interviews that all the practitioners held similar beliefs about accepting people as they are, building on people's strengths and sticking with people through the hard times: 'I think sometimes with these young parents everyone wants a piece of them, whereas I don't want a piece of them, I just want to help and also there's that bit where I keep going back. They don't expect me to keep going back.'

Integrated working was seen as vital for gaining a deep understanding of families: 'You were meeting with the other workers in the centre, you'd meet with their nursery worker, you'd meet with their Family Worker if they had one as well … You got really involved with the whole family and you saw a much bigger picture of what goes on for people in life.'

A health visitor described how she had come to realise the importance of sharing her professional expertise in a way that allows parents to become the expert on their child. She had started out demonstrating baby massage by massaging a baby herself. She would then hand a calm, contented baby back, leaving the mother feeling completely de-skilled. She quickly changed her approach and now demonstrates on a doll: parents massage their own babies. She also talked about the importance of sharing the massage group with a practitioner from Poland, as this encourages Eastern European parents to attend and to feel welcome.

Renegotiating professional roles and identities

> I think to work across agencies is a great privilege … You get to know other people in their working environment and become familiar with their ways of working, their ethos and what complexities they have to manage to deliver quality services to families.

Moving outside mainstream health work and into a children's centre can be challenging. As one practitioner said, 'It was coming out of your comfort zone.' However, the midwife realised that 'It was all midwifery work I was doing; it was just in a different way', and recognised that her professional confidence and competence were what enabled her to try new approaches. Practitioners outside health need to understand nurses' professional accountability; they can lose their registration for behaving in an unprofessional manner and sometimes a child's life may depend on their judgement and skills. It takes courage and generosity to pass hard-won skills and job roles on to other people – there is a fear that they may not do the work well enough and a family will suffer and also a fear that they may do the work well, calling the professional's role into question. As a health visitor said: 'Maybe some people are a bit frightened professionally – that we might lose something', but she also explained how her professional accountability frees her to make decisions about how to carry out her work: 'I'm inclined to use my own professional judgement and do what I think is needed because, at the end of the day, I am responsible.'

The commitment of the practitioners

All the practitioners are deeply committed and highly motivated. They work long hours and are prepared to go the extra mile for families. They felt that this level of motivation was the norm across the teams working at Pen Green:

- 'I love the job, absolutely love it, but sometimes it's hard. It's emotionally demanding.'
- 'I was always very passionate about showing that you can do it, regardless of what your background is.'
- 'I thought it would be dead easy but I've learnt over the years it's not.'
- 'It was coming to do something totally different but that was the exciting bit about it.'
- 'They're all really normal people who are all dead passionate. You know, you think you're passionate about what you do and I'm passionate about midwifery, but they're all passionate about everything they do, so it was lovely being among people like that.'
- 'I believe in it.'

The impact of leadership

Integrated working needs committed practitioners but it also relies on effective leadership. Leaders, both in children's centres and in health services, need to understand new ways of working and be open to innovative practice. Children's centre leaders need to ensure that practitioners from other agencies are made to feel that they are a valued part of the centre team. Practitioners welcomed simple gestures, such as a centre leader making them a cup of tea or saying thank you, but they were even more appreciative of being included in team training, being funded to attend external training courses and, probably most importantly of all, the midwife talked about what it had meant to her to be given a small budget to enable her to buy equipment and resources.

Implications for practice

We are working in a difficult economic climate and all the health practitioners were conscious of constraints on their working practice. Their caseloads have risen and commissioning contracts can stipulate a list of individual tasks, rather than defining the outcomes to be achieved, which can limit the quality of their work. There is a risk of losing some of the creative, integrated practice that has been developed, not just at Pen Green, but at other children's centres across the country.

Despite this, the practitioners at Pen Green still believe there is scope for developing preventative health work further, perhaps through a community-led health promotion project. They would like to be more involved with groups and see a need to ensure that everyone in the local health teams knows Pen Green so that understanding of each other's ever-changing roles is strengthened.

The government has pledged to increase the number of health visitors by 4,200 by 2015 (DfE, 2011a). This is an opportunity to develop integrated working between health visitors and children's centres, to reduce duplication, improve information-sharing and communication, strengthen safeguarding, build the skills and capacity of the whole early years workforce by sharing knowledge and practice, and to reignite the creativity of overstretched practitioners. This will only happen if:

- there is a clear national steer from the Department for Education and the Department of Health
- commissioners of services identify shared targets and incentivise integrated working
- leaders are committed to getting the best possible services for families
- all practitioners work to build relationships across agency boundaries.

Effective integrated work helps families to access services under one roof without feeling that they are being passed from one agency to another – they only have to tell their story once and, most importantly of all, they are supported by people who understand their lives and the pressures they face and see the family as a whole, rather than as a series of issues or problems.

We owe it to the families and communities we serve to make the best possible use of this opportunity.

Key information

- Improving health from the very start of life can help people to live longer and have a better chance of enjoying their lives to the full.
- Effective health promotion for families builds on people's strengths and achievements, provides knowledge and understanding to help families make informed choices, and builds their confidence in their ability to make choices and sustain change.
- Families want health services to be welcoming, non-judgemental and easily accessible.
- Practitioners need to take time to build trusting, respectful relationships.
- For integrated working to be effective, practitioners need a shared understanding of each other's roles and a shared set of values about working with families.

Points for discussion

- What could be done in your setting to make health services more accessible for families?
- How could parents be involved in promoting health within your local community?
- How could you strengthen integrated working between health and early years practitioners?

References

Audit Commission (2010) *Giving Children a Healthy Start*, London: Audit Commission.

Bearer, C. (1995) 'Environmental health hazards: how children are different from adults', *Critical Issues for Children and Youths*, vol. 5, no. 2, pp. 11–26.

British Psychological Society (2008) *Improving Health, Changing Behaviour: NHS Health Trainer Handbook*, London: DoH.

Browne, K., Douglas, J., Hamilton-Giachritsis, C. and Hegarty, J. (2006) *A Community Health Approach to the Assessment of Infants and their Parents*, Chichester: John Wiley.

Bull, J., McCormick, G., Swann, C. and Mulvihill, C. (2004) *Ante- and Postnatal Home-visiting Programmes: A review of reviews*, London: Health Development Agency.

Campbell, C. (2000) 'Social capital and health: contextualizing health promotion within local community networks', in *Social Capital: Critical perspective*, Oxford: University Press.

ChiMat (Child and Maternal Health Observatory) (2011) *PreView Resources for Professionals* [online]. Available from: http://atlas.chimat.org.uk/IAS/resource/view?resourceId=54 (accessed 29 Oct. 2011).

Craven, P. (2012) *The Freedom Programme* [online]. Available from: http://www.freedomprogramme.co.uk/index.php (accessed 31 July 2012).

DfE (Department for Education) (2011a) *Supporting Families in the Foundation Years*, London: DfE.

DfE (2011b) *The Core Purpose of Sure Start Children's Centres* [online]. Available from: http://www.education.gov.uk/childrenandyoungpeople/earlylearningandchildcare/a00191780/core-purpose-of-sure-start-childrens-centres (accessed 19 May 2012).

DoH (Department of Health) (2007a) *Delivering Health Services Through Sure Start Children's Centres*, London: DoH.

DoH (2007b) *Implementation Plan for Reducing Health Inequalities in Infant Mortality: A good practice guide*, London: DoH.

Edgley, A. (2007) 'The perceptions of statutory service providers of a local Sure Start programme: a shared agenda?' *Health and Social Care in the Community*, vol. 15, no. 4, pp. 379–86.

Hill, M., Stafford, A., Seaman, P., Ross, N. and Daniel, B. (2007) *Parenting and Resilience*, York: Joseph Rowntree Foundation.

Iacovou, M. and Sevilla-Sanz, A. (2010) *The Effect of Breastfeeding on Children's Cognitive Development*, ISER Working Paper No.2010-40, Colchester: ISER. Available from: https://www.iser.essex.ac.uk/publications/working-papers/iser/2010-40.pdf (accessed 31 July 2012).

Katz, I., Corlyon, J., La Placa, V. and Hunter, S. (2007) *The Relationship between Parenting and Poverty*, York: Joseph Rowntree Foundation.

Marmot, M. (2010) *Fair Society, Healthy Lives: Strategic review of health inequalities in England post-2010* (the Marmot Review), London. Available from: http://www.marmotreview.org.

Mezey, G. and Bewley, S. (2005) 'Domestic violence and pregnancy', *International Journal of Obstetrics and Gynaecology*, vol. 104, no. 5, pp. 528–31.

NOO (National Obesity Observatory) (2012) *National Child Measurement Programme* [online]. Available from: http://www.noo.org.uk/uploads/doc/vid_15180_NCMP_Changes%20in%20children's%20BMI%20between%202006-07%20and%202010-11.pdf (accessed 31 July 2012).

O'Higgins, M., St James Roberts, I. and Glover, V. (2008) 'Postnatal depression and mother and infant outcomes after infant massage', *Journal of Affective Disorders*, vol. 109, nos 1–2, pp. 189–92.

Quinton, D. (2004) *Supporting Parents: Messages from research*, London: Jessica Kingsley.

Royal College of Midwives (2009) *Memorandum Submitted by the Royal College of Midwives to the Sure Start Children's Centres – Children, Schools and Families Committee* [online]. Available from: http://www.publications.parliament.uk/pa/cm200910/cmselect/cmchilsch/130/10011303.htm (accessed 16 July 2012).

Royal College of Physicians Tobacco Advisory Group (2010) *Passive Smoking and Children*, London: Royal College of Physicians.

Schrader McMillan, A., Barlow, J. and Redshaw, M. (2009) *Birth and Beyond: A review of the evidence about antenatal education*, London: DoH.

Shonkoff, J., Richter, L., van der Gaag, J. and Bhutta, Z. (2011) 'An integrated scientific framework for child survival and early childhood development', *Paediatrics*, vol. 129, no. 2, pp. 460–72.

UNICEF (2006) *Behind Closed Doors: The impact of domestic violence on children* [online]. Available from: http://www.unicef.org/protection/files/BehindClosedDoors.pdf (accessed 31 July 2012).

UNICEF (2012) *Health benefits of breastfeeding* [online]. Available from: http://www.unicef.org.uk/BabyFriendly/About-Baby-Friendly/Breastfeeding-in-the-UK/Health-benefits (accessed 31 July 2012).

Waldfogel, J. (2005) 'Social mobility, life chances and the early years', in *Maintaining Momentum: Promoting social mobility and life chances from early years to adulthood*, London: Institute for Public Policy Research.

WHO (World Health Organization) (2012) *Childhood Overweight and Obesity* [online]. Available from: http://www.who.int/dietphysicalactivity/childhood/en/ (accessed 31 July 2012).

Conclusion

Margy Whalley

In conclusion, children's centres must understand the 'fine grain' of their communities: they must be able to understand and interpret the data they collect on families and children. What such interpretation must be able to reveal is the complexity and variety of family needs within a community rather than a list of deficits. All single parents cannot be assumed to be vulnerable or struggling. The particular and detailed knowledge and understanding that can be assimilated by a skilled home visitor must be used to inform services that reflect this. Some teenage mothers may be coping well and wish to continue their education. Others may require comprehensive Family Support over an extended period.

The success of children's centres, and other integrated early years services, has been to show how disadvantaged families benefit from a comprehensive and accessible system, not a series of individual services. For example, a young parent who has had continuous and regular contact with one consistent midwife, who attended the birth, visits the home and co-ordinates a weekly group for teenage mothers, has experienced a seamless system in which she has exercised control and influence.

Children's centres are not simply *changing* communities in terms of the services they provide to families, they are also places where community is being *built*. Families are no longer passive recipients of services delivered by the state. There is still enormous potential to do more to support social networks, friendships and to create local communities of interest, and we are committed to developing this work in Corby alongside the children and their families.

Appendix A: the signs and scale of involvement

The signs of involvement

(adapted from Laevers, 1997: 20)

Concentration

The child's attention is focused on the one small area of his own activity. It is difficult to distract him.

Energy

The child puts a lot of effort and enthusiasm into his activity. This can be physically, for example by talking loudly, making grand movements or focusing in on a problem. It can also be psychologically, by being mentally very active.

Complexity and creativity

Children work to their full capacity, giving their undivided attention and a great deal of care to every aspect of what they are doing. Their play is not routine.

Facial expression and composure

By reading their facial expression and composure, we can see when a child is watching and listening intently, ready to move quickly and completely absorbed in what they are doing.

Persistence

Children who are actively involved in an activity do not give up easily. They want to dwell on the feeling of satisfaction that intense activity gives them and they are willing to work at keeping it going. They are not easily tempted away from what they are doing. Involved activity usually lasts a long time.

Precision

Children who are involved work meticulously. They show a remarkable amount of care for their work.

Reaction time

These children are alert and readily respond to new things that connect with what they are currently doing. They are motivated to act quickly to take up ideas that are of interest to them.

Verbal expression

Children make comments that indicate their enjoyment and enthusiasm. They put into words what they are experiencing or discovering.

Satisfaction

Children who are involved gain pleasure from what they are doing. They show their satisfaction in their body language and in how they treat what they create.

The involvement scale

Involvement scale	A description of the level
1	This child is completely uninvolved. Sometimes young children walk away, stare into space or do not interact with people or play materials. (A child can be involved by watching or thinking intently – the eyes show brightness and the body language is different.)
2	This child is only involved for brief periods. They may be wandering around aimlessly. Sometimes they do things that are too easy for them, so they are not learning anything new.
3	This child is involved some of the time but what they are doing is not very important to them. If you ask them to do something different, they will switch to a different activity without protesting.
4	This child is involved in something they have chosen, which is important to them. They are not easily distracted. Yet there are moments when they need a parent's or worker's interest to help keep them involved.
5	This child does not need you to get them going. They know what they want or need to do. They can choose to continue to be absorbed for long periods and show most of the signs of involvement.

Table A.1 The involvement scale (adapted from Laevers, 1997: 38–9)

Appendix B: the signs and scale of emotional well-being

The signs of well-being

(adapted from Laevers, 1997: 17)

Openness and receptivity

The child is receptive to his environment. His expression is alert, open and direct. He allows himself to be 'touched' by the stimuli presented to him. He is aware of the people around him and does not try to avoid them. He can accept both verbal and non-verbal attention from others, for example a cuddle, a compliment, a word of comfort, an encouragement, a spontaneous offer of help. He listens and often responds to suggestions made by others. The child does not cut himself off from new situations or people, but shows a willingness to explore them.

Flexibility

Children who are high on well-being readily adapt to their environment. This flexibility is especially noticeable in situations which are different or new to the children. They are not, or only briefly, confused or upset. These children can easily accept new situations and therefore experience them to the full. Flexibility also shows in the way children react to problems or frustrations. They do not dwell on them. They show a willingness to consider various alternatives or to make compromises.

Self-confidence and self-esteem

The child radiates a good deal of self-confidence. He is able to express himself and to let himself be seen or heard. He also shows a fair amount of self-esteem ('I am a nice person and worth knowing'). When this child is faced with new challenges, he will tackle them head on. He will try out new activities, risking the possibility of failure. When this child fails at something, he manages to get over it quite quickly. He does not dwell on failures or associate them with his own worth. This child will look for challenges at his level, neither too difficult nor too easy for him. He can admit that there are things he cannot do yet without feeling inadequate.

Being able to defend oneself, assertiveness

Children who are assertive will not be walked over. They will stand up for themselves, for their own wishes, needs and desires. They are strong enough to ask for the things they need, such as help, comfort or care. If they want something, they will ask for it in an appropriate manner. If something is said or done which does injustice to the child, he will object. Assertive children will not merely respond to the orders or suggestions of others if these will interfere with their own needs.

Vitality

This child radiates vitality and zest for life. He is full of life and energy. The vitality expresses itself in the child's facial expression and in his composure. His eyes are often glistening. This child is rarely hunched up with shoulders drooping. He tends to sit up straight and to move quickly and energetically.

Relaxation and inner peace

Relaxation shows in composure and movements. Facial expressions are natural and do not twitch. Most movements are flexible and smooth. These children usually keep up a 'normal' speech tempo and vocal volume. When you touch children who are relaxed, you feel their 'inner peace'. They do not bottle up tensions or jump when touched. They are often able to relax quickly after an exciting and active game. They are relaxed and active at the same time.

Enjoyment without restraints

Children who are in their element are enjoying themselves. They are happy and take pleasure in what they are doing and experiencing. The enjoyment is genuine. They are enjoying the right things in the right way (not, for example, hurting others). Some children express their enjoyment by beaming, singing spontaneously, smiling, humming or sitting quietly with eyes sparkling.

Being in touch with oneself

These children seem to know for themselves what they need, wish, feel and think. They do not turn away from these things but work through them. These children are at peace with themselves. They feel united with other people, animals and nature. They do not repress their needs, wishes, feelings or thoughts.

The well-being scale

Well-being scale	Appearance and behaviour
1	This child's well-being is very low. They show none of the signs of well-being. They show no interest in interacting with others or in playing. Their eyes are dull. They show little energy. This child looks withdrawn and becomes anxious quite easily.
2	About half of the time, this child displays signs of emotional discomfort. There is a lack of trust. This child may be watchful or cling to one person. This child cannot sustain enjoyment, worries about what other children have and may enjoy hurting others.
3	Most of the time this child is happy. Occasionally, this child may get anxious, seek reassurance or seem uncertain. This child may show distress at transition times, for example moving into group time from free-play time.
4	This child is generally happy and able to express their feelings. This child feels comfortable enough to ask for what they want and choose what they want to do confidently. This child rarely shows signs of discomfort.
5	This child has an extremely high level of well-being and behaves like 'a fish in water'. The nursery is 'their place' and they radiate vitality, relaxation and inner peace.

Table A.2 The well-being scale (adapted from Laevers, 1997: 36–7)

Index

absent parents, and home visits 56, 61
abuse 128–9
    domestic 219
    see also child protection
access, to setting 18
achondroplasia 46
action research 79
Adult Attachment Interviews (AAI) 142
adult education 166–80
    andragogy 167–8
    attitudes towards 169–71
    barriers to 169–71, 178–9
    benefits of 177–8
    childcare provision 176
    environments for 172–4
    and volunteering 176–8
advocacy
    for children with special rights 46–53
    and key person approach 23
    parental 5
    see also Home-Start
Aldridge, F. 167
Allen, G. 95–6
andragogy 167–8
antenatal services 198–204
    see also pregnancy
anti-bullying programme 26–7
Armstrong, D. 80
Aspergers 50
Athey, C. 17, 30, 33, 55, 60
attachment 32, 59, 64, 89, 99, 124–9
    Adult Attachment Interviews (AAI) 142
    autonomous secure classification 142
    and pregnancy 198
autism 48
autonomous secure classification 142

baby massage 75–6, 205
Bastiani, J. 30
bereavement 128

Bion, W. 52–3, 64, 124–5
birth 128, 204–5, 223
    trauma 128
    see also pregnancy
Birth to Three Matters Framework (2002) 186
Blanden, J. 63
boundaries, maintaining 128–9
Bowlby, J. 32, 59, 64
breastfeeding 205, 218
Bruce, T. 18, 30
bullying 26–7

Carr, M. 186
Celebration of Achievements folder 25
Chandler, T. 154
charities, Home-Start 111–22, 206
    see also volunteering
Charlwood, N. 142
child development, key concepts 35
child protection 3, 62, 103
    unborn child 203
children's centres
    as community centres 12–13
    role of 96, 196–7
    see also settings; Sure Start
children with special rights 46–53
Chrispeels, J. 30
Cohen, L. 147
Common Assessment Framework (CAF) 22, 63
community drop-in centre 83–93
community education 72–3
    see also adult education
community engagement 7–9, 12–13
confidentiality 135
containment 64, 124–6, 136–7
Cooper, A. 107
co-production 11–13
crèche services 183–93
    adult-to-child ratios 187
    key person system 187–8

legislation 185–7
  qualifications for 184, 192
  settling-in 187–8
  staff training 188–93
Csikszentmihalyi, M. 31
Cummings, A. 157
curriculum, enriched 26–7
Curriculum Guidance for the Foundation Stage
  (2000) 187

deep level learning 31
dependency, in group work 52
depression
  during pregnancy 197–8
  in mothers 126–7
  postnatal 129, 206–14, 218, 223
Devaney, C. 97
developmental partnership 150
diabetes 219
dialogue 33, 150
disability *see* children with special rights
domestic abuse 219
  during pregnancy 198
drug addiction 90–1, 100
Duchenne's muscular dystrophy 51
Dunkel Schetter, C. 197
dynamics, within groups 52–3

early intervention 95–6
Early Learning Partnership Parental Engagement
  group 55
Early Years Foundation Stage (EYFS) 15,
  54–5, 187
Easen, P. 33, 75
education
  adult 166–80
  attitudes towards 169–71
  pedagogy 167–8
Effective Early Learning Project 31
Eisenstadt, N. 92
Elfer, P. 162, 186
Elliott, M. 26
emotional involvement, of practitioner 67–8

emotional reservoirs 175–6
emotional well-being 32
  see also well-being
engagement
  of communities 7–9, 12–13
  of parents 2–10, 17–18
  see also involvement
English as an additional language 56
environment
  for adult learning 172–4
  home learning 15–20, 30, 41
  for meetings 35–6
  physical 18
  welcoming 18
Epstein, J.L. 154
Every Child Matters (2003) 62, 187

facilitating reflection 142–51
facilities 18
families
  access to services 71
  lone-parent 10–11
  see also family support; fathers; parents
Family Friends 109–111
Family Room 83–93
family support 95–108
  early intervention 95–6
  Home-Start 117
  marginalised families 98–100
  mediation 106–7
  in practice 98–106
  separated parents 104–7
  traveller families 100–2
farm visits 27
Fatherhood Institute 156
fathers
  groups for 157–61
  including 36
  influence of 15, 154–5
  involvement of 61, 92, 105–6, 154–64
  paternity leave 155
  as 'play companions' 162–3
  and pregnancy 197–8

Kirk, R. 86
Klein, M. 53, 125–6
knowledge-sharing approach 34–43
Knowles, M. 167–8
Kraemer, S. 151

Laevers, F. 31–2, 230–3
language barriers 56–7
leadership, in groupwork 52–3, 78–80
Learning to Be Strong programme 26–7
Liebowitz, A. 167
lone-parent families 10–11
low-income families 154–5
    see also poverty

Malcolm, A. 156
Manion, L. 147
massage groups 75–6, 205
maternal depression *see* postnatal depression
McBride, B. A. 154
McKinnon, E. 158
McMillan, Margaret 12
McMillan, Mary 84
mediation 106–7
meetings
    attending 22–3
    with parents 24, 35–6
mental health problems, parents with 98–100
messy play 77
Mezirow, J. 92, 168
midwife services 198–204, 222–3
muscular dystrophy 50–2

National Quality Improvement Network 97
National Standards for Under-8s Day Care (2001) 187
nursery, settling in 20–1, 32
Nurture Group 61–8
nurturing relationships 64

obesity 219
    see also health
object relations theory 125
off-site visits 27

Open College 38
Orr, R. 46–7

pairings, within groups 52
parent champions 9–10
Parent Forum 24
parental advocacy 5
parental engagement 2–10, 17–18
parents
    communicating with 60
    as experts 17, 21, 33, 55, 75, 97
    fear of being judged 55
    giving and receiving feedback 24, 33
    involving *see* Involving Parents in Their
        Children's Learning project
    lone 10–11
    meetings with 24, 35
    reflective parenting 74, 142–51
    separated 104–7
    training 4, 36–43
        see also adult education
    see also families; fathers
Parents' Involvement in Their Children's
        Learning (PICL) groups 124, 136,
        142, 157
Parker, R. 197
partnership, defining 54–5
paternity leave 155
patterns of action *see* schemas
pedagogy 34, 167–8
Pen Green, history of 1–12
Pen Green Loop 16–17
perinatal services 197–8, 205, 213
Phelan, J. 93
photographs, of home setting 19–20
play resources 130–1
Plowden Report 29, 33
political action 9
portfolio, of child's work 25, 38
postnatal
    depression 129, 206–14, 218, 223
    services 204–6
poverty 63, 96

practitioner
- emotional involvement of 67–8
- fears of 55
- feelings of 129
- professional development 27–8, 43, 77–80
- professionalism 61, 64–5
- reflective practice 80, 141–2
- safe working practices 61, 65
- and social networking sites 61

pregnancy 197–214
- antenatal services 198–204
- distress in 197
- and fathers-to-be 197–8
- Great Expectations group 200–4
- health services 222–3
- midwife services 198–204, 222–3
- perinatal services 197–8, 205, 213
- unplanned 198
- *see also* birth; postnatal services

preventative health work 216–26
professional development 27–8, 43, 77–80
professionalism 61, 64–5
projection 126
psychotherapeutic insights 125
Pugh, G. 97

Raphael-Leff, J. 197
Raven, J. 58
recession, effect on families 110–11
- *see also* poverty

reciprocity 75
record keeping 25
reflection, principle of 141–2
reflective parenting 74, 142–51
reflective practice 80, 141–2
Reggio Emilia 156, 185
research, ethical guidelines 144
residential trips 27
resilience 32
Rivero, E. 30
Rogoff, B. 168

safe working practices 61, 65
safeguarding 2
- *see also* child protection

Sarkadi, A. 155
scaffolding 125
schemas 30, 39–42
second-hand smoke 219
'sense of belonging' 20
separated parents 104–7
settings
- settling-in to 20–1, 32, 59, 187–8
- welcoming environment 18
- *see also* crèche services; environment

settling-in 20–1, 32, 59, 187–8
sexual abuse, memories of 128–9
shared conceptual framework 33, 35
Siraj-Blatchford, L. 115
smoking, second-hand smoke 219
social networking sites, and practitioners 61
special rights, children with 46–53
staff supervision support system 78–9
Suffering in Silence (2011) 206
Sure Start 1, 92, 96, 184
- Trailblazer Project 200, 207

symbolic holding 64, 125–7

targeted groups 71
task avoidance, in group work 52
'team around the child' 63
Think Family report (2008) 97
Three Cs of Early Childhood Curriculum 18
toddler groups 77
- *see also* groupwork

Total Place Corby 8–9
touch, importance of 75
Trailblazer Project 200, 207
training
- group workers 77–80
- parents 4, 36–43
- professional development 27–8, 43
- *see also* adult education

translation services 56–7
traveller families 100–2
treasure baskets 130
Trevarthen, C. 149, 168
Trevithick, P. 107
'triangle of trust' 187–8

U2 Can Be Messy 76–7
unborn child protection plan 203
unemployment 110–11
universal groups 71
unplanned pregnancy 198

video work 25, 133–4
   ethics of 34, 144
   in research 143–51

volunteering 4, 8, 83
   and adult education 176–8
   Home-Start 109–22, 206
Vulnerability Matrix 97
vulnerable children 61–8
   see also child protection
Vygotsky, L. 31

welcoming environment 18
well-being 32, 38, 142, 232–3
Whalley, M. 55, 88, 109, 141, 154, 162, 229
Winnicott, D. 52–3, 125–7
Wolfendale, S. 30
Woodhead, J. 75, 151

zone of proximal development 31

Notes

Use this space for your own notes.